The Superpowers and Nuclear Arms Control

The Superpowers and Nuclear Arms Control

Rhetoric and Reality

Dennis Menos

PRAEGER

New York
Westport, Connecticut
London

Library of Congress Cataloging-in-Publication Data

Menos, Dennis
    The superpowers and nuclear arms control: rhetoric and reality /
Dennis Menos.
        p. cm.
    Includes bibliographical references.
    ISBN 0–275–93458–6 (alk. paper)
    1. Nuclear arms control—United States.   2. Nuclear arms control—
Soviet Union.   I. Title.
JX1974.7.M452   1990
327.1'74—dc20   89–36700

Library of Congress Catalog Card Number: 89–36700
ISBN: 0–275–93458–6

First published in 1990

Praeger Publishers, One Madison Avenue, New York, NY 10010
An imprint of Greenwood Publishing Group, Inc.

Printed in the United States of America

The paper used in this book complies with the
Permanent Paper Standard issued by the National
Information Standards Organization (Z39.48-1984).

10 9 8 7 6 5 4 3 2 1

To Anne-Marie, Bert,
and their generation

Contents

Preface   ix

Abbreviations   xiii

1. Enough Is Never Enough   1

2. The Superpowers   25

3. The Impotent Opposition   49

4. Tearing Down the Few Past Accomplishments   71

5. The Politics of Arms Control   95

6. The Endless Negotiations   123

Appendixes: 145

    A. Technology Milestones   146

    B. Nuclear Testing, 1945–1988   146

    C. The Race for Better and More Powerful Strategic
Weapons, 1974–1988   147

    D. The Strategic Delivery Vehicles of the Superpowers, 1988   148

    E. Strategic Weapon Inventories, 1988   149

    F. Impact of START Agreement   149

    G. Strategic Weapon Levels, Mid to Late 1990s (Assuming
Conclusion of a START Agreement)   149

    H. Strategic Offensive Weapons During the Decade of the
1990s   150

I. Strategic Defenses During the Decade of the 1990s   151

J. INF and Shorter Range Weapons, 1988   152

K. Tactical and Battlefield Weapons, 1988   152

L. The Lesser Nuclear Powers: The PRC, France, and the
   United Kingdom   153

Selected Excerpts   155

Final Communiqués of Summits   155

Concluding Documents of U.N. Special Sessions on
Disarmament   159

Five Continent Peace Initiative   160

Selected Major Church Statements   162

Selected Bibliography   165

Index   173

Preface

As the undisputed superpowers of our day the United States and the Soviet Union shoulder many responsibilities; none, however, is more elemental than the need to arrest and reverse the nuclear arms race.

In this, their paramount role, the superpowers have failed beyond belief. Forty-four years after Hiroshima, not a single nuclear weapon, judged by them as necessary for their "national security," has been eliminated—the nuclear arsenals of the superpowers are larger, better equipped, and more deadly—mankind is at greater risk than at any prior time.

Recognizing that nuclear weapons can never really be abolished, is a nuclear age maxim that the superpowers are having great difficulty accepting. Their declared long-range goal of "total and complete disarmament," their search for defenses ultimately to make nuclear weapons "impotent and obsolete" are evidence of a pointless superpower search for easy solutions to the very difficult problem of controlling the nuclear arms race. They demonstrate also the superpowers' reluctance to accept the undisputed maxim of the nuclear age, that having invented the nuclear bomb, they must now assume responsibility for its future safekeeping. Any hope of mankind living again in a world free of nuclear weapons is not only unrealistic but plain foolish.

Their solemn declarations notwithstanding, the superpowers are also having great difficulty accepting the notion that a nuclear war should *never* be fought. This is not to suggest that the United States and the Soviet Union are eagerly anticipating nuclear war. Far from it; they both share an overriding desire to avoid a nuclear holocaust. Still, the superpowers are preparing for the eventuality of nuclear war with as high a degree of urgency as ever before, pursuing strategies that could lead to mutual suicide and acquiring nuclear weapons whose only justification is the execution of a successful nuclear first strike. Although neither superpower will openly admit it, both are longing secretly for the day when their scientists will make possible nuclear superiority over the other side, through a combination of first-strike capability and a nuclear defensive shield. Obviously, were the United States and the Soviet Union truly committed to a world free of the threat of nuclear war, none of these preparations would have been necessary.

Throughout the years the superpowers have applied enormous ingenuity in the area of arms development but only minimal effort toward the containment of arms. On the issue of managing the arms race, superpower behavior has been simply irresponsible. The enormous accumulation of arms on both sides, the missed opportunities for agreement especially in the areas of nuclear testing and strategic forces, and the bleak outlook for a practical arms control accord after some forty years of negotiations provide ample evidence of the prevailing apathy in Moscow and Washington to the consequences of the nuclear arms race.

Yet only the superpowers can reduce the likelihood of nuclear war (whether by accident, miscalculation, or crisis escalation), reduce and stabilize the strategic balance, or prevent the further proliferation of nuclear weapons. The world will remain in peril; there will be no stability until all these measures have been accomplished. The superpowers could make a start toward this goal by restructuring their weapons-acquisition programs, from threatening first-strike weapons to strategic forces that are invulnerable and nonthreatening to the other side.

My principal purpose in preparing this book was to evaluate how the United States and the Soviet Union are approaching the issue of the nuclear arms race, unquestionably their most elemental responsibility as superpowers. Evidence has convinced me that the two nations are not really interested in containing nuclear arms, unless such action can result in benefit to themselves, or alternatively, necessitate major sacrifices by the other side. The superpowers' irresponsible behavior is accompanied also by wholesale doses of irresponsible diplomacy, characterized by extended breaks in arms control negotiations, the consideration only of issues that advance superpower strategic interests, and the use of an entire array of negotiating tactics designed to stall the talks and to perpetuate the arms race. The need for effective arms control has never been greater; yet prospects for success have never been more bleak.

This book consists of six chapters of text and of certain reference materials for readers wishing to pursue the subject in greater detail. Chapter 1 is the story of the nuclear arms race and of the superpowers' continuing efforts to develop and accumulate nuclear weapons designed for war (not deterrence, which is the traditional justification for acquiring nuclear arms). Chapter 2 deals with the superpowers themselves, their lukewarm attempts at nuclear arms control, and their refusal to accept even the most minute risks to what they perceive to be their national security interests. Chapter 3 tells the story of the nuclear havenots, of their efforts at the United Nations and elsewhere, and of their struggles in the peace movement and the churches to guide the superpowers back to the road of nuclear sanity.

Chapter 4 examines the arms control "self-destruct" of the 1980s, evidenced by the unceremonious termination of the SALT regime and the not-so-secret plans of Moscow and Washington also to discard soon the ABM treaty. Chapter 5 reviews the growing congressional–executive split on numerous key arms control issues, most notably on strategic defenses (the Strategic Defense Initiative [SDI]) and nuclear testing. The split impacts adversely on this nation's capability to define and execute a coordinated and unified arms control policy. The book's final chapter is appropriately entitled "The Endless Negotiations." The United States and the Soviet Union have been negotiating major reductions in their strategic arsenals for twenty years and the cessation of their nuclear testing for even longer. Prospects for agreement on both areas are almost nil.

Abbreviations

ABM	Antiballistic missile
ACDA	U.S. Arms Control and Disarmament Agency
ACIS	Arms Control Impact Statement
ACM	Advanced cruise missile
ALCM	Air-launched cruise missile
ASAT	Antisatellite (system/weapon)
ASBM	Air-to-surface ballistic missile
ASW	Antisubmarine warfare
CFE	Conventional forces in Europe
CTBT	Comprehensive Test Ban Treaty
DOD	Department of Defense
GLCM	Ground-launched cruise missile
IAEA	International Atomic Energy Agency
ICBM	Intercontinental ballistic missile
INF	Intermediate-range nuclear forces
IRBM	Intermediate range ballistic missile
LTBT	Limited Test Ban Treaty
MAD	Mutual assured destruction
MBFR	Mutual and balanced force reductions
MIRV	Multiple, independently targeted reentry vehicle
MX	Missile experimental

NATO	North Atlantic Treaty Organization
NPT	Treaty on the Non-Proliferation of Nuclear Weapons
NST	Nuclear and Space Talks
NTM	National technical means (of verification)
OSI	On-site inspection
PNET	Peaceful Nuclear Explosions Treaty
SALT	Strategic Arms Limitation Talks
SCC	Standing Consultative Commission
SDI	Strategic Defense Initiative
SLBM	Submarine-launched ballistic missile
SLCM	Sea-launched cruise missile
SRAM	Short-range air missile
SSBN	Submarine, ballistic nuclear
START	Strategic Arms Reduction Talks
TTBT	Threshold Test Ban Treaty

The Superpowers and Nuclear Arms Control

Enough Is Never Enough

It threatens planet Earth with extinction and literally gives Man the power to undo Creation. It has been labeled *insane*, *obscene*, and a *crime against humanity*. The "it," of course, refers to the nuclear arms race— that endless, insatiable search by the world's nuclear powers for ever more powerful and capable nuclear weapons.

No event in history, no matter how horrendous, can even remotely compare to the folly of the nuclear arms race. Forty-four years after Hiroshima—four decades after acquiring knowledge of the bomb's dreadful potential for ending civilization—the two leading powers of the day are engaged in the process of accumulating weapons in numbers and lethality that defy rationalization. Not traditional weapons designed to defend freedom, independence, and territorial integrity but all-powerful first-strike monsters, whose use in an all-out nuclear conflict could well cause the superpowers' own destruction along with that of all of mankind.[1]

MANKIND'S GREATEST FOLLY

The obvious question is *why*? Why are the superpowers oblivious to mankind's most horrid threat? Why do they feel the need to add more weapons to their already bloated arsenals of more than 50,000 warheads? How could they possibly use additional explosive power, when weapons in their present inventory already contain 1 million times the explosive power of the Hiroshima bomb?[2]

Three explanations come to mind: The first reason for the spiraling weapons programs of the superpowers is probably also the most simplistic. It reflects the uncompromising commitment by both the United States and the

Soviet Union to a policy of never allowing the other an advantage in weapons development. The policy rests on the assumption that every new weapon built or technology perfected by one side ultimately must be duplicated by the other or else a fatal strategic disadvantage will ensue. As the superpowers pursue each other's weapons and technologies, allegedly to forestall the creation of a gap between them, actual need is seldom considered. The one and overriding purpose is to acquire at least as much as the other side has and in the process keep the opponent in check. Examples of such senseless superpower competition abound. In the United States, for instance, claims of a window of vulnerability and assertions that slowing down weapons acquisition will lock the United States in a "position of strategic inferiority" vis-à-vis the Soviet Union are serving as powerful stimuli for weapons development and procurement and are providing the basic rationale for the massive U.S. arms modernization program of the 1980s.

The second reason for the superpowers' undiminished appetite for nuclear weapons is the direct result of military strategy. Both nations subscribe to the strategy of nuclear deterrence, which in theory at least implies that the superpowers are acquiring nuclear weapons not for the purpose of using them but to discourage the other side from using theirs. But the strategy of nuclear deterrence also dictates that in the event deterrence fails a nation must be prepared to fight and "win" a nuclear war. It is to prepare for this contingency[3] that the superpowers are insatiably acquiring increasing numbers of more powerful and accurate weapons. No amount of sugar coating can conceal the fact that the superpowers' acquisition of nuclear weapons is designed, above all, to enhance their capability to fight and win a nuclear war; "deterrence" serves as the convenient cover. There is not a single U.S. or Soviet weapon that does not have a "war mission" assigned to it or that is not intended for use in the event of nuclear conflict.

The third and final explanation for the superpowers' unending accumulation of nuclear arms flows from their not-so-secret hopes for achieving a first-strike capability.[4] Neither nation will openly admit to such a goal, but the evidence is unmistakable. Achieving a successful first strike occupies a very warm spot in the minds and hearts of the military circles and scientific laboratories of both superpowers. Why, but for the purpose of delivering an overwhelming and devastating attack upon the other, are the superpowers deploying missiles of such awesome power and pinpoint accuracy while aggressively exploring the building of protective shields around their homelands? A first-strike capacity is the superpowers' most prized goal but one that, as we shall discuss later, keeps elluding them.

The Strategic Balance—An Irrelevant Issue

One would assume that, given the senseless accumulation of nuclear weapons by both sides and the enormity of the nuclear stockpiles on hand, some form of major opposition to the trend would surface at home. This has not happened, however. Odd as it may seem, the vast majority of persons here and in the Soviet Union are totally oblivious to their governments' continued acquisition of nuclear arms and to the threat to their own survival that the vast nuclear holdings entail. Except for an occasional voice of protest, there is no anger out there against the weapon policies of the superpowers, no clamor for reducing arms or for suspending further production and testing. Apathy toward the nuclear arms race runs so high as to suggest a public totally overwhelmed by the complexities of nuclear arms and incapable of formulating rational, well-reasoned judgments on the issue.

An exception concerns the issue of the strategic balance, that is, the degree to which one side or the other may be ahead in nuclear arms competition. In the United States there is a fairly active interest in this issue but not in its far more significant corollary, whether mankind can survive a nuclear war. When it comes to the consequences of nuclear war (the "unthinkable," as it is known in some circles), the only thinking that is being done is by military planners in Washington and Moscow. The public at large, the persons most directly threatened by nuclear annihilation, remain totally uninvolved.

With the superpowers controlling between them more than 50,000 nuclear warheads—less than 500 of them are sufficient to annihilate both nations and most of the Eurasian continent—is it not really absurd to ask: who is ahead in nuclear weaponry?

In the United States, hawks are forever painting a gloomy picture: the Soviets are striving for superiority in arms, they charge; they are fielding huge, accurate intercontinental ballistic missiles (ICBMs), which in one sudden swoop can wipe out most of our Minuteman force; they are taking a lead in missile *throw-weight* (the weight they can lift) and in *megatonnage* (the total explosive power of their warheads);[5] they could well be ahead of the United States in Star Wars (Strategic Defense Initiative [SDI]) technology. Comparable gloom of U.S. military superiority is being fostered also by the more hawkish elements of the Soviet military: the United States has an enormous lead in long-range cruise missiles, they warn; during the 1990s, every U.S. ship, submarine, or even barge could serve as a platform for launching sea-launched cruise missiles (SLCMs) against the Soviet heartland; the United States has in its new D-5 missile a weapon of unbelievable sophistication, reliability, and accuracy.

Every one of the above statements is absolutely true. Yes, the Soviets do have very powerful, accurate ICBMs that could in a perfectly synchronized and highly coordinated surprise attack destroy most of our Minuteman ICBMs in their silos. Yes, the United States' D-5 submarine-launched ballistic missile (SLBM) has unbelievable accuracy for a submarine-launched weapon.[6] But what these facts ignore is that the strategic balance is a composite of many factors, all of them germane to the equation. The balance cannot be expressed merely in terms of quantitative measures. Numbers, yields, and types of weapons are important but so are nonstatic measures, such as the readiness of forces, leadership, training, morale, and operational planning. Highlighting only two or three areas of imbalance, and claiming that this gives one side a significant lead in the strategic equation, is not only intellectually dishonest but also dangerous.

Submarines and their size are a good case in point. Of all submarines afloat, those of the Soviet Union are by far the largest. The Typhoon submarine, of which there are five,[7] has a displacement of 25,000 tons. Its U.S. counterpart, the Trident (Ohio Class), displaces 18,700 tons when submerged. But the Trident is a lot quieter than the Typhoon and will eventually carry more weapons than the Soviet model (twenty-four D-5 SLBMs versus twenty SS-N-20s on the Typhoon). As for the weapons that these submarines carry, those of the United States are more accurate than those of the Soviet Union, but the latter have greater explosive power. A larger submarine size, then, does not necessarily imply greater warfighting capability or a Soviet edge. If anything, it may demonstrate a vulnerability in Soviet technology, since obviously they are having difficulty designing smaller and more streamlined weapons.

Officially, at least, the United States refuses to provide an unequivocal answer to the "who is ahead" question or the related issue of who has superiority in arms. There is a better balance now, claims the Pentagon's basic reference on the Soviet threat, than had occurred during the 1970s.[8] Presumably, the imbalance prevailing a decade earlier was corrected by President Reagan's strategic modernization program. The official hedging notwithstanding, at present the two superpowers are about even in system-technology levels, with each side maintaining the upper hand in one or more areas of technology. Thus the United States is superior in ballistic nuclear submarine (SSBN), SLBM, and bomber technologies; the Soviet Union in ballistic missile defenses and antisatellite (ASAT) weapons. The two nations are about equal in technology levels for ICBMs and cruise missiles. In terms of specific weapon capabilities, the United States enjoys a lead over the Soviet Union in the number of strategic warheads[9] and the accuracy, reliability, and readiness of its ICBMs; it has a definite edge in antisubmarine warfare (ASW) and in the development of long-range cruise missiles. The Soviet Union leads the United States in the number of heavy ICBMs deployed and in the total throw-weight and megatonnage of missiles.

With the United States, then, and the Soviet Union holding their own on all areas of technology and weapons, it matters little which of the two nations is ahead or has superiority at any given time in the race for more nuclear arms. The superpower inventories of more than 50,000 nuclear weapons make the issue totally irrelevant. Except in the case of a nuclear war, initiated by means of a highly successful first strike, *both* nations assuredly will lay in ruins at the conclusion of the nuclear exchange, regardless of which party starts the fight or who was "ahead" in arms competition when the "gun" first went off. (It is this dilemma that makes a successful first strike such a tantalizing idea to the military planners of both nations—but more on this later.)

The Consequences of Nuclear War

The world received its first crash course on nuclear weapons' effects in August 1945, when two fairly small nuclear weapons (small, that is, in comparison to the weapons in existence today) practically blew the cities of Nagasaki and Hiroshima off the world map. Fortunately for mankind, the study of nuclear weapons' effects and the far more critical issue of the long-term consequences of a nuclear war have since moved to the laboratories and wargaming organizations of the superpowers.

So much has already been written about the world devastation that is likely to result from a nuclear war that there is little purpose in repeating the gruesome details here. What ravages are eventually inflicted on planet Earth will be the result of three conditions: how the war is started, the military strategy under which it is fought (countercity, counterforce, escalation dominance?), and the number and yields of the weapons actually detonated. A protracted, all-out nuclear exchange could well result in fatalities of 400 million and could be accompanied by unprecedented devastation of the earth's essential resources. Recent studies suggest that use of even a fraction of the world's nuclear arsenals could result in a state of "nuclear winter"[10] and place at risk life itself on planet Earth.

Since all forms of nuclear warfighting, except a successful first strike, promise mutual suicide for the combatants, is it any wonder that the superpowers in their never-ending search for "security" are seriously exploring the option of a first-strike capability? If deterrence had been their stated goal (which apparently in the 1980s no longer was), both nations should have stopped building nuclear weapons a long time ago—perhaps after reaching a level of 200 to 400 warheads. There is no military requirement for the tens of thousands of nuclear weapons that the superpowers now possess, except possibly as weapons of choice in a first strike. Gruesome as it might sound, a nuclear power contemplating the defense of its most vital interests may find a first strike to be an attractive alternative. Not only would it eliminate the opposition forever, but more significantly, it would spare one's territory from the ravages of nuclear war. (The basic idea of the nuclear first strike is to hit the opponent so hard in a surprise nuclear attack as to deny him the opportunity or will to retaliate.)

REACHING FOR FIRST STRIKE

Before reviewing in more detail the superpower efforts toward a first-strike capability, a comment on mutual assured destruction (MAD), the prevailing strategy of nuclear deterrence. The essence of MAD is that as long as neither power has a foolproof first-strike capability, aggression is deterred by the threat of retaliation. Any nuclear attack by one party will be met by a retaliatory strike severe enough to inflict unacceptable damage on the aggressor. MAD's supporters claim that the doctrine has been successful in deterring aggression during the past three decades. Critics, however, suggest that MAD can never be credible[11] as long as it is based on a threat to commit mutual suicide. A threat by one nation that it is prepared to kill its civilian population to prove a point cannot be taken seriously, and a threat that cannot be taken seriously will not deter. During the Cuban missile crisis, for instance, President Kennedy was deterred from considering the use of nuclear weapons against the Soviet Union because of fear of a Soviet retaliatory strike—this, despite an overwhelming U.S. superiority at the time of 5,000 weapons versus 300 for the other side.[12]

If merely 300 weapons were sufficient to deter the United States in the 1960s, why does the Soviet Union believe that today it needs 32,600 weapons for the same purpose? Similarly, if 300 weapons deterred us then, would not approximately the same number be sufficient to deter the Soviets today? Why does the U.S. need an arsenal of 23,400 warheads? The answer should be obvious: today's superpower arsenals have nothing to do with deterrence. Their role is to enhance the superpowers' ability to launch a successful first strike. Along with deterrence, interest in fighting a nuclear war is rapidly fading, since use of even a small number of weapons would be clearly suicidal.

Suicide or Surrender?

The gigantic superpower arsenals of the late 1980s have made totally irrelevant the issue of how much is enough.

Determining the optimum size of the U.S. nuclear forces (i.e., the number of nuclear weapons that the United States ought to have on hand) is an issue that was first addressed in earnest in 1961 by then Secretary of Defense Robert S. McNamara. The United States, he concluded, would not be secure unless each leg of its strategic triad was able to deliver 400 "equivalent megatons" on the Soviet Union.[13] Four hundred "equivalent megatons" in 1961 was what 1,000 missiles, or 300 bombers, or 41 nuclear submarines could each carry. But this was a long time ago, before the MIRVing of weapons (MIRV stands for multiple, independently targeted reentry vehicles) and before the Cuban missile crisis fueled the Soviet determination to catch up and even surpass the United States in strategic weaponry.

With the raison d'être for nuclear weapons shifting in the direction of a first strike, the relevant question is no longer how much is enough or how many additional weapons a superpower might need for purposes of deterrence or to fight a victorious war. The superpowers have enough weapons now on hand to destroy each other several hundred times. A single U.S. submarine, for instance, carries enough warheads to destroy every large and medium-sized city in the Soviet Union. With the warfighting role of nuclear weapons becoming less and less attractive (because of the enormous devastation inherent in any nuclear exchange), the nuclear weapons programs of the superpowers today address essentially one military requirement: how to plan and launch a successful first strike or, if the success of such a venture cannot be assured, how to checkmate the opponent into a position where he is left with only two options, surrender or commit suicide. Basic survival instincts suggest that the opponent would accept surrender.

A first-strike attempt by either the United States or the Soviet Union, as we will discuss later, would encounter truly insurmountable uncertainties. In fact, the nation attempting such an operation might be putting its own future survival on the line. In contrast, the "suicide or surrender" checkmate offers a superpower fewer uncertainties and a higher probability of success.

A "suicide or surrender" checkmate could result, for instance, from a sudden, massive, and unprovoked Soviet attack on the U.S. strategic triad,[14] resulting in the destruction of most U.S. missiles in their silos, submarines in port, and bombers not on alert status. With the attack leaving the United States minus its most accurate and reliable strategic weapons, how would the president respond? He might elect to strike at the residual Soviet strategic forces, but with the element of surprise gone, this would hardly be productive. The Soviet ICBM sites would be empty, their subs and bombers dispersed and very difficult to target. A far more potent option is available: the president could order a massive retaliatory attack on Soviet cities. That option would punish the Soviets, but it would also trigger an equally massive counterstrike against U.S. cities. Would any American president elect to pursue the countercity option when his decision would be synonymous with national suicide? As harsh as it sounds, "surrender" without firing a single shot would be the only viable alternative to the United States under such a scenario.[15]

It is this specter of either defeat or suicide that is leading the superpowers to shift part of their ICBM forces from land-fixed to mobile configuration (the Soviet Union has already begun deployment of significant numbers of mobile ICBMs; the U.S. plans for ICBM mobility are still being debated in the Congress) and to acquire accurate sea-based missiles. Possession of such weapons, it is argued, would limit the damage that the other side would be able to inflict on the friendly ICBMs and make a counterforce attack possible, without the need for resorting to a countercity strategy and risk retaliation.

A victim of the increased accumulation of counterforce weapons by both sides is the long-standing NATO strategy of blunting a Soviet invasion of Europe by means of selective nuclear strikes, escalating the attack up to and including strikes on the Soviet mainland itself. Given the tremendous devastation that the surviving Soviet strategic systems would inflict on the United States in retaliation, it is difficult to conceive of any American president initiating a strategic attack on Soviet territory just to stop an invasion of western Europe.[16] This again proves the folly of the superpowers' senseless accumulation of weapons, ostensibly designed to fight and win a nuclear war but whose only use can be in a first strike.

The Weapons of First Strike

Presently, neither superpower has the capability for launching a sudden and devastating attack on the other, the kind that would deprive the opponent of the ability or will to retaliate. This fact notwithstanding, both superpowers are troubled by the same uncertainty: they can never be sure that the other side will not at a future date attempt a first-strike attack on the strength of a major weapon breakthrough or scientific advantage. Acquiring, therefore, the capability to deliver a knockout blow before the other side does, and in the process to spare their nation the ravages of nuclear war, is very much a superpower goal and one that both are pursuing with zeal and determination.

A first-strike capability in the hands of only one of the superpowers would not necessarily lead to nuclear holocaust. The nation possessing the extra punch may elect to use it merely as a backdrop for political pressure and blackmail, not for military purposes. The United States certainly followed this course during the 1940s and 1950s, when it enjoyed a first-strike capability over the Soviet Union. A far more dangerous situation will confront mankind, however, when both superpowers gain a first-strike status. Suddenly, the likelihood that nuclear weapons will be used will become very real. Even in confrontations that both superpowers wish to contain, the potential will always be there, the pressure will be there, to strike first and thus preempt the other side from launching a disarming first strike of its own. A "use them or lose them" mentality will permeate superpower relations, with each nation determining that its survival requires that it strike first and ask questions later. In an era of first-strike capabilities, the nuclear threshold will be lower than at any prior time in history, and the world will be in greater danger than ever before.

Summarized below are characteristics of selected U.S. and Soviet weapons. Their mission is unmistakable. They are weapons of preemption, the kind required to launch a successful first strike with impunity.

On the U.S. side is the MX, a weapon of frightening size and lethal power, accurate enough to land its ten warheads within 300 feet of their targets. The mission of the MX in a first strike would be to destroy Soviet hardened missile silos and communication facilities and thus prevent retaliation. In theory, the MX could also be used in other missions, for example, in a counterforce role or to retaliate after a Soviet nuclear attack. It is the latter roles (not the first-strike role) that the U.S. government officially attributes to the weapon. The fact that the MX has an enormous hard-kill capacity, and thus is a powerful first-strike weapon, is not publicly acknowledged anymore than the Soviets advertise the first-strike advantages of their SS-18 and other heavy missiles.

The "other" MX—the United States has two MX systems—is the Navy's D-5 SLBM. Officially, this is also a second-strike weapon, designed to retaliate rather than preempt. The D-5 is needed, according to its sponsors, because it can survive a surprise attack on the continental United States, something that the MX in its silos probably cannot do. Hidden somewhere on the high seas onboard Trident II submarines,[17] the D-5 can then await the president's orders for launching retaliatory strikes. No one can honestly deny the D-5's capability for executing second-strike missions. But neither can its first-strike capability be denied, as evidenced by the missile's near-pinpoint accuracy (reported at about 400 feet), its enormous explosive power, and its hard-kill potential against Soviet nuclear-hardened targets.[18]

A multitude of other weapons (existing or under development) add to the U.S. first-strike potential. They include two new strategic bombers (the B-1B and B-2); hundreds of cruise missiles onboard ships and aircraft; a new class of submarine killers (the Seawolf), designed to intercept and destroy enemy SSBNs during the first moments of the preemptive strike; the all-powerful advanced cruise missile (ALC) now under development; and an entire array of satellite killers capable of destroying the Soviet Union's eyes and ears in space. The Stealth bomber or B-2 (officially unveiled in November 1988) is expected to have unique first-strike capabilities. Almost invisible on radar, the aircraft will be able to penetrate Soviet territory at will, attacking a multitude of targets critical to Soviet decision making.[19] The B-1B similarly is expected to have a first-strike mission, but since it would be visible on Soviet radar, its approach to targets would be low and underneath defenses.

As in the case of our first-strike force, land-based ICBMs are the predominant Soviet weapons with a first-strike potential. During the past decade, the Soviet Union has significantly increased the capacity of these weapons by introducing modern, accurate systems, with high-quality reentry vehicles. The centerpiece of the Soviet ICBM force is the SS-18, a monster of a weapon, designed to destroy hardened targets such as ICBM silos and command facilities. The SS-18s now in the Soviet inventory account for about 3,000 warheads; no more than 2,000 such warheads would suffice to destroy almost the entire U.S. ICBM force.[20] Not content with such awesome capability, the Soviets have already tested an SS-18 follow-on weapon. Reportedly, it is more accurate than its predecessor, and preparations for its deployment are underway. Two other land-based ICBMs add to the Soviet Union's first-strike potential. They include the SS-19 Mod 3, which is about the size of our MX and carries six warheads, and the less accurate SS-17 Mod 3, which is equipped with four warheads.

The Soviets are well ahead of the United States in the development and deployment of mobile ICBM systems. The SS-24, the most powerful of them, carries ten warheads and has the throw-weight and accuracy required of a first-strike weapon. The missile is being deployed in both a rail and silo configuration. A second missile, the SS-25, is road mobile, but it carries only a single warhead; the system's mobility makes it inherently survivable and capable of reload/refire. The SS-25 became operational in 1985.

The Soviets are also providing the other two legs of their strategic triad with first-strike weapons. They have already deployed five Typhoon submarines (roughly comparable in size to our Trident Ohio Class boats) and undoubtedly have plans for many more. Each Typhoon is equipped with twenty SS-N-20 missiles, each with six to nine reentry vehicles and with a range of approximately 4,500 nautical miles. The extended range makes it possible for the SS-N-20s to be fired from their home ports or from areas near the Soviet mainland where they would be under the protection of their land-based defense systems.[21] As in the case of their sea-based forces, the Soviets are continuing to improve and diversify their strategic bomber fleet. The Blackjack, a new intercontinental bomber now being readied for deployment, is similar in appearance and capability to the B-1B and would be a prime Soviet weapon in a first-strike attack against the continental United States.

Delivering a First Strike

The superpowers are aware that if a "calculated" nuclear conflict ever becomes necessary, as opposed to one initiated as a result of a nuclear accident, it would have to be waged in the form of a first strike. Any other scenario of nuclear warfighting is pure nonsense; and that includes NATO's plans for resisting a conventional invasion of western Europe by selective nuclear strikes on Soviet forces. With each superpower fearful of the other's preemptive first-strike weapons, a *slow* war, that is, one characterized by a *tit for tat* nuclear exchange, is totally improbable.

By definition, a first strike, to be successful, must be sudden and massive. It must hit the opponent with such force as to devastate his warfighting capabilities, even his will to resist. It would be the most cataclysmic event ever triggered by man.

With a first strike expected to cause such an unprecedented upheaval on planet Earth, why are the superpowers even considering this contingency? The answer was suggested earlier: from a military perspective, the massive accumulation of nuclear arms by both sides has made a successful first strike the only nuclear engagement that can any longer be justified. A first strike eliminates the opposition forever and, perhaps more important, spares one's homeland from the ravages of nuclear war. Only the loser lays in ruins at the conclusion of the cataclysm, not both nations as would be the case after any other nuclear conflict.

Delivering a disarming first strike, if it ever is attempted, would be one of the most complex military operations undertaken, replete with uncertainties and dangers, possibly even placing at risk the nation initiating the attack. (Only an SDI-type engagement against a swath of incoming ballistic missiles would rival a first strike in complexity and uncertainties.) A successful first strike would have to surprise and destroy on the ground the vast majority of an opponent's strategic forces—his ICBMs, intercontinental bombers, and submarines in port. Also, the attack would have to seek out and neutralize during the first moments of an operation the opponent's submarine forces patroling the high seas, before they received word of the catastrophe that had befallen their nation and when, presumably, they would be tempted to launch their weapons in retaliation. All of this would have to be accomplished with precision and be error free. No practice runs or rehearsals would be possible; all weapons would have to perform in perfect harmony and synchronization the first time out.[22]

For a first strike to be sudden and unexpected, its preparations would need to escape the satellites and other sensors of the opponent. In an age of high-technology intelligence collectors and instantaneous communications, this would be extremely difficult. Destroying the opponent's satellites at the outset of a first-strike operation could accomplish this end, but it would also give clear warning to the other side that something very big was in the works. Many other uncertainties and risks would confront the aggressor. Would launch reliability and accuracy of missiles be as expected? A miniscule error, for instance, in the firing of a booster rocket can send a missile several hundred feet off its target. Would fratricide, that is, the tendency of nuclear warheads to interfere with each other's detonation, be a factor?[23] Would the victim of a first strike accept defeat as a *fait accompli* and surrender, or would it likely sacrifice all in a savage counterattack with whatever nuclear arms had survived?[24] Would the first strike be free of nuclear winter effects, or would aggressor and victim likely be buried under a catastrophic cloud of dust and smoke? The nation attempting a first strike indeed would be placing its future survival on the line.

Under the circumstances, what are the chances that either nation will develop a first-strike capability in the not-too-distant future, one that is sufficiently risk free to venture a first strike? Neither side has this capability now, but the United States appears to be closer to the goal on the strength of its superior weapons technology and because of decisions made years ago that stressed weapons of preemption over weapons of deterrence.

The principal U.S. advantage, and, accordingly, Soviet vulnerability[25] to a first strike, results from the manner in which the superpowers have structured their strategic triads. The Soviet Union, for instance, has elected to deploy the majority of its strategic warheads (6,846 out of a total of 11,248) with its land-based ICBMs. In contrast, only 2,500 strategic warheads out of a total of 13,302 are deployed with the U.S. ICBM force. The numbers clearly favor the United States since land-based ICBMs are a lot more vulnerable than the other weapons in a nation's strategic triad. Comparable assymetries characterize the superpowers' sea-based leg. Despite the SLBMs' relative invulnerability to a first strike, the Soviets have deployed no more than 3,232 warheads on their nuclear submarines, against a U.S. total of 5,632. Other factors giving the United States an edge in the race for a credible first strike include the greater accuracy of its ICBMs, vis-à-vis those of the Soviet Union, and the fact that Soviet missiles are liquid fueled. (Liquid-fueled missiles require time to fuel—as such they are not suitable for mounting a surprise attack.) Sea-based missile and strategic air components similarly favor the United States, with the American forces being more invulnerable; and therefore more suitable for a first-strike role, than are their Soviet counterparts.

Shielding the Strategic Triads

The superpowers understand well that their prized goal of a first-strike capability cannot be achieved merely by adding more and more offensive weapons to their nuclear arsenals. As essential as this process is, equally important is the development of a "shield" behind which offensive forces can execute the intended mission. On the high seas, the "shield" is to be provided *offensively* by antisubmarine warfare (ASW) forces; in outer space and on land, by strategic ballistic *defenses* of the type contemplated under SDI. Needless to say, in line with the importance afforded the first-strike option by the superpowers, both U.S. and Soviet ASW and SDI programs are being pursued with a sense of major urgency.

The goal of ASW in a first-strike scenario would be to locate and destroy the opponent's missile-carrying submarines at precisely the same time that his land-based missiles and bombers are being attacked. This would be an enormously difficult undertaking because of the increasing number of warheads deployed on the high seas and advances in science and technology that make submarine detection and tracking progressively more difficult. (Presently, the United States has the upper hand in this area, its submarines being virtually invulnerable to detection because of their low noise levels. A major Soviet breakthrough in killer submarine technology, however, could change this overnight.) The challenge confronting the ASW programs of the superpowers is not how to track and destroy *some* or even *most* of the other side's submarines but how to detect and track *all* of them. Even one boat escaping detection could spell doom and destruction to millions of innocent civilians.

Unlike the function of ASW, which would seek out and destroy the opponent's sea-based nuclear forces as part of a first strike, the mission of the ground- and space-based "shield" would be to protect a nation during and after a first strike. Neither superpower can seriously consider the first-strike option without the benefit of an SDI-type shield to protect it against the possibility of retaliation by the victim of the strike. It is this role of SDI,— the mission to "shield" its national territory while its ICBMs, bombers, and SLBMs are carrying out their surgical and disarming first strikes—that leads critics to suggest that SDIs are "offensive" systems, not "defensive" systems, as their supporters in Washington and Moscow wish the world to believe.

Critics of SDI defenses have traditionally maintained that ballistic missile defenses, no matter how perfected and advanced, would never be able to cope with the thousands of nuclear warheads and decoys that would be directed against them in the event of a nuclear war. They believe that the incoming traffic would simply overwhelm them and that SDIs, therefore, are useless.

This assessment may be accurate in the event of an all-out nuclear war, in an exchange involving hundreds of weapons, but would not necessarily be true under conditions of a nuclear first strike. Even a partial or leaky SDI system could play a decisive role in a first-strike situation. ("A leaky umbrella," observed former Secretary of Defense Robert S. McNamara, "offers no protection in a downpour but is quite useful in a drizzle."[26]) The reason should be obvious. A nation possessing an SDI "shield" can launch a first strike, destroy most of the opponent's strategic forces on the ground and in the high seas, and then use the shield to absorb retaliation[27] and intercept what few missiles might have escaped the first strike. In the first-strike scenario, as a partner in offense, SDI has found its strongest booster and supporter.

EXTENDING THE ARMS RACE TO OUTER SPACE

Building an SDI shield will be an enormous undertaking. Even a partial one will explode the arms race into outer space and trigger the most massive ever buildup in offensive arms. In terms of cost, an SDI shield could set back the superpowers hundreds of billions of dollars, perhaps even a trillion dollars each according to some projections.

Yet this is precisely the route that the superpowers are pursuing. In the United States, the official goal is to build an impenetrable missile defense, one that will render nuclear weapons "impotent and obsolete." Everyone, except possibly a handful of diehard supporters, is aware that the goal does not square with reality[28] and that there can never be such a thing as a perfect defense against missiles.[29] Still, research on the program is under way in hundreds of laboratories across the United States to the tune of $4 billion annually, and plans are being readied for early deployment of a partial system. By continuing to pour billions of their scarce resources into ballistic missiles research, the superpowers are openly acknowledging the offensive role of their SDIs, especially their first-strike potential.

The development is troubling not only because it fuels the arms race in space, but equally, because of its impact on weapons programs on earth. It is an old axiom of warfare: acquisition of defensive weapons by one nation invariably leads its opponents to intensify the search for offensive weapons to overcome the defenses and also to develop defenses of its own. This in turn spurs greater weapons buildup on the part of the first nation, the process continuing on and on with the sky being the limit. The axiom was fully appreciated by the superpowers some twenty years ago, when they agreed to conclude the ABM treaty in an effort to halt the escalation of offensive arms that would result from the erection of ABM defenses. But that was before advances in microelectronics and artificial intelligence, the revolution in space travel brought on by the space shuttle, and the development of high-intensity lasers.[30] Every one of these scientific breakthroughs has important missile defense implications that the superpowers are eagerly attempting to exploit.

Before examining briefly the SDI programs of the superpowers (U.S. and Soviet), a reminder to the reader. SDIs, despite their official designation, are not, and can never be, purely defensive. The technologies being researched in U.S. and Soviet laboratories promise an astonishing array of new offensive weapons built on lasers and space-based kinetic kill vehicles.

The Soviet SDI

Despite its frequent and pointed criticism of the U.S. SDI, the Soviet Union has had a Star Wars program of its own for more than twenty years. Until recently, the Soviet SDI did not exist officially. But in November 1987, in a burst of *glasnost*, the Soviets acknowledged what the United States already knew: an aggressive research program for ballistic missiles defenses is under way in the Soviet Union, possibly of a scope and dimension exceeding that of the United States.[31]

Unlike the U.S. SDI program, which focuses primarily on the development of advanced technologies for ballistic missile defenses, the Soviet effort embraces six major categories of effort. Thus the Soviet Union maintains the world's only operational antiballistic missile (ABM) and antisatellite (ASAT) systems, an expanding network of ballistic missile detection and tracking radars, an active civil defense program, a massive strategic air defense posture against bombers and cruise missiles, and extensive research into advanced technologies for defense against ballistic missiles.

The ABM system is designed to defend Moscow and its immediate surrounding area against an ICBM attack. The system is entirely "legal," that is, it derives its authority from the ABM treaty, which allows each super-power to build and maintain an ABM defensive complex at a site of its choosing. Although the United States has elected to abandon its site, the Soviets have been steadily upgrading theirs. It now consists of a two-layer defense of one hundred launchers, able to intercept incoming warheads in space as well as within the earth's atmosphere after reentry.[32]

Concurrently with the modernization of its ABM complex, the Soviet Union has been vigorously pursuing expansion of its network for the detection and tracking of ballistic missiles. At the apex of this effort are nine large phased-array radars, currently in various stages of construction. The controversial Krasnoyarsk radar, which even the Soviet Union agrees that it violates the ABM treaty because of its location and inward orientation, is one of them. On completion, the nine radars will enormously enhance the Soviet capability for detecting and tracking incoming ballistic missiles and will provide a major input into the Soviet military's ABM battle management plan.

The Soviet research program into advanced technologies covers many of the same areas currently being explored by the U.S. SDI. According to the Pentagon, the effort exceeds that of the United States in terms of plant space, capital, and manpower.[33] Of the various advanced technologies being explored by Moscow, emphasis on high-energy lasers appears to be the greatest. This is one area in which the Soviets hope to gain an upper hand, especially as it would apply to strategic air defenses, ASAT missions, and, conceivably, defense against ballistic missiles. As of 1989, the Soviet Union had ground-based lasers with some capability to attack U.S. satellites; before too long it could also have a space-based ASAT laser capability. But a Soviet ground-based laser against ballistic missiles is not expected for a long time.

Soviet scientists are no more likely to succeed in building a perfect SDI defense than are their U.S. counterparts. Many of the same problems and uncertainties that trouble the U.S. program impact on that of the Soviet Union. Soviet science has made remarkable strides during the past three decades, but these successes, most notably its space exploration accomplishments, would be no match for the difficulties the construction of a leakproof SDI shield would entail. Inexpensive countermeasures in the form of additional MIRVed warheads, decoys, and chaff would easily confuse, overwhelm, and pierce any shield, with both superpowers being able to add more "offense" (by means of additional warheads) than the opponent's SDI defenses would be able to absorb. Given these uncertainties, why are the Soviets pursuing an SDI? The answer was suggested earlier: a perfect SDI is impossible to erect, but a partial one is not, and it is only a partial shield that the Soviets would require to protect their homeland from a weakened U.S. retaliation in the aftermath of a Soviet first strike.

The U.S. SDI

The American SDI was born with President Reagan's "Star Wars" speech of March 1983. Six years later, the nation's scientific community is still not convinced of the programs's overall feasibility or likelihood of success. This fact notwithstanding, the program's "research" phase enjoys unprecedented support nationwide and especially on Capitol Hill, where funds for it are authorized and appropriated annually with fairly light opposition.

Why the United States is pursuing an SDI should be no mystery by now. Throughout the years, a number of official yet contradictory explanations have been offered: to make nuclear weapons impotent and obsolete, to protect the U.S. population, to help defend NATO (Europe too?), and to enhance the survivability of the U.S. deterrent. The latest U.S. explanation, which includes none of the above, is contained in the Department of Defense's (DOD's) "Report to the Congress" dated April 1988. Note the language:

the goal is to conduct a vigorous research and technology program that would provide the basis for an informed decision regarding the feasibility of eliminating the threat posed by nuclear ballistic missiles of all ranges and increasing the contribution of defensive systems to U.S. allied security. Within this goal, the SDI Program is oriented to protect options for *near-term deployment of limited ballistic missile defenses* as a hedge against Soviet breakout of the ABM Treaty.[34]

The U.S. SDI program focuses essentially on three research and technology areas. The first, and probably the most critical, aims to develop the required sensors for detecting the launching of enemy missiles, tracking them during flight, discriminating nuclear warheads from nonthreatening objects (such as decoys), and providing intercept guidance to the managers of the various defensive weapons systems. Development of the actual weapons for use in the space battle is the goal of the other technology areas. Two kinds of weapons are being explored: kinetic energy and directed energy. Kinetic energy weapons would be ground- or space-based and would be launched by chemical rocket boosters or projected by hypervelocity electromagnetic or electrothermal guns. According to the Pentagon, this is the most "mature" SDI technology and one that will provide the basis for the system's Phase I deployment. Development of directed-energy weapons is far behind. The effort brings together four basic concepts identified as promising to the needs of a multitiered defense (which SDI would be): space-based lasers, ground-based lasers, space-based particle beams, and nuclear directed energy weapons.

THE INF TREATY: A MINIMUM OF SACRIFICES

You are probably wondering at this point: if the superpowers are indeed preoccupied with the process of augmenting their nuclear arsenals, and a first-strike capability is their prized goal, how do these policies track with the recently signed treaty on intermediate-range nuclear forces (INF)? Was not the treaty proof of the superpowers' genuine desire to put a lid on the nuclear genie and to reverse the direction of the past forty years?

Not really! Despite the oratory emanating from Washington and Moscow about the virtues of the INF treaty and of the resulting elimination of an "entire class of missiles," the treaty should be understood for what it really is: an extremely modest effort at limiting nuclear arms, surrounded by enormous superpower self-adulation and public relations hype.

The INF treaty, it will be recalled, will eliminate over a three-year period 846 U.S. and 1,846 Soviet intermediate and shorter range delivery vehicles currently deployed in Europe and elsewhere.[35] On the U.S. side this would involve the removal of 846 warheads from the European theater; in the case of the Soviets, 3,154 warheads worldwide. The term *removal* is being used here intentionally, for under the terms of the INF treaty, delivery vehicles only are to be destroyed, not their nuclear warheads. The superpowers are free to remove and reuse these warheads in other weapons. Despite, then, all of the clamor about the benefits of the treaty, none of the 56,000 or so nuclear warheads now in the U.S. and Soviet arsenals are being reduced or otherwise affected by it.

With the exception of the U.S. Pershing II missile, which because of its great accuracy could have been a weapon of choice in a U.S. first strike, none of the delivery vehicles called for elimination under the terms of the INF treaty were first-strike weapons. By agreeing to eliminate them, the superpowers lost nothing in terms of a first-strike capability. The United States and the Soviet Union managed also to retain intact their tactical or battlefield weapons now deployed in Europe. On the U.S. side this involves approximately 3,500 warheads; on the Soviet side, probably twice as many, deployed on short-range missiles, nuclear artillery, and nuclear capable aircraft. The INF treaty notwithstanding, 10,000 or so warheads remain in Europe, enough to destroy the continent one hundred times over. The total does not include the INF forces of France and of the United Kingdom, which are similarly not affected by the treaty.

The NATO Modernization Plans

If the INF treaty was intended to begin the process of controlling nuclear arms in Europe, the evidence is hard to ascertain. Both superpowers (the United States more than the Soviet Union) are already exploring options for recovering their INF losses by the introduction of new battlefield weapons into the European theater or the upgrading of weapons unaffected by the treaty. The continued interest in nuclear battlefield weapons is disconcerting. The low accuracies, high yields, and short ranges of these weapons make them unsuitable for use in the European environment and increase the risk of preemption by strategic weapons.

As usual, the true modernization plans of the two sides are veiled by heavy doses of propaganda. The Soviets, who are especially adept at this game, continue to deluge Europe with seductive offers of a nuclear-free continent, unilateral cuts in their own short-range forces, and conciliatory assurances that a military threat to Europe no longer exists. As far as it can be ascertained, however, the Soviet rhetoric has had no impact on Moscow's real modernization plans for battlefield weapons, which are proceeding unabated, especially for land-based aircraft and short-range nuclear forces, two areas in which the Soviets have traditionally held a significant numerical advantage over NATO. Improved nuclear capable guns and howitzers also are being introduced into the Soviet ground forces, along with the SS-21, a new short-range ballistic missile designed to replace the FROG-7.

The NATO modernization plans are still undecided, despite a summit in May 1989 that attempted to reconcile opposing views within the alliance. At issue are NATO plans for the development and deployment of an updated version of the Lance missile (its present range is 70 miles—the proposed upgrading would give it a range of 150 miles) and of a new air-to-surface missile with a range of between 200 and 300 miles. The Lance upgrading, and continued deployment of NATO short-range missiles, is opposed by the Federal Republic of Germany for fear that if used, these weapons will be detonated over German territory. (The U.S. view is that NATO battlefield weapons are essential to European security and that NATO must be able to respond to a Soviet invasion of the continent with nuclear weapons.[36])

At the NATO summit in May 1989 the Lance modernization decision was put off until 1991–1992. A negotiating formula, agreed to, assigns first priority to the reduction of conventional forces in Europe, with talks for nuclear forces reductions to follow. The nuclear talks, however, would aim only at a *partial* reduction of missiles (not all, as Moscow allegedly favors), allowing the United States to maintain a nuclear deterrent in Europe. Depending on the direction of the nuclear talks, the Lance modernization may or may not be implemented. If it is, the Pentagon will be prepared: $150 million has already been programmed for FY 1990 research and development on the Lance follow-on.

THE ISSUE OF NUCLEAR NONPROLIFERATION

Nuclear proliferation ranks with the world's greatest threats. The reason should be obvious: with five nations already holding nuclear weapons status and four others standing on the sidelines, who needs more? This is also the official view of the superpowers but, as usual, a wide gap separates U.S. and Soviet arms theory from practice.

The fact that the superpowers support the traditional concept of nuclear nonproliferation should not come as a surprise. As the leading nuclear powers of our day, their national interests dictate that membership in the exclusive nuclear weapons club be kept to a minimum. The fewer the nations with access to nuclear weapons, the smaller the possibility of a nuclear war starting by accident or design. The superpowers' opposition to nuclear non-proliferation is not new. They were opposed to it in 1968 when the Non-Proliferation Treaty (NPT) was concluded and have continued to oppose it ever since.[37]

In the real world, where a dozen or so nations appear determined to cross the nuclear Ribicon regardless of consequences, the superpowers are show-ing little inclination of keeping their policy pristine and unadulterated. Their reluctance to lead is especially troublesome when friends and allies are involved, and they appear to be openly acquiescing those nations' nuclear aspirations. In the case of three nations, for instance, with strong ties to one or the other superpower (India, Pakistan, and Israel), the barn doors of nuclear proliferation are wide open, the horses have left, and the super-powers are merely standing by as casual observers. Even nominal enforce-ment of the international nonproliferation regime[38] would have sufficed to bring the nuclear weapons programs of these nations to a halt.

Examples of the superpowers looking the other way while friends and allies violate the international nonproliferation cause abound. India, Paki-stan, and Israel especially come to mind.

India and Pakistan

India, despite its neutral status, has traditionally maintained close rela-tions with the Soviet Union. These relations became especially cordial during the 1980s, when Pakistan, India's adversary, began drawing closer to the United States because of common interests in the Afghanistan war. Pakistan ranks today among the principal U.S. allies in Asia and is the recipient of substantial amounts of military and economic assistance.

Nuclear proliferation made its first appearance in South Asia in 1974 when India tested a small nuclear device. Since that date, no additional tests have been held although undoubtedly India has the capability of conducting further tests at will.[39] Production of plutonium for weapons use remains substantial, with India judged now as being capable of assembling more than one hundred nuclear devices by 1991.[40] Indian leaders have disclaimed interest in their nation becoming a nuclear power but warn that they will not hesitate to build nuclear weapons at the first indication of a Pakistani nuclear test. India has consistently rebuffed Pakistani suggestions that both nations sign a test-ban treaty as a first step toward a nuclear weapon-free zone in Southeast Asia. The nuclear question, said India, is global, not regional or bilateral.

As for Pakistan, despite repeated denials by its leaders ("Pakistan does not possess or intend to make a nuclear device," said Pakistani Prime Minister Benazir Bhutto on June 7, 1989, to a joint session of the Congress), no doubt exists that it has already joined the ranks of the nuclear nations. It has sufficient plutonium on hand to build a handful of weapons and is aggressively pursuing capabilities, often illegally, that will allow it to match India's superior nuclear potential.

None of the Indian or Pakistani facilities used for the production of plutonium or other nuclear materials are under International Atomic Energy Agency (IAEA) safeguards. Under the terms of the NPT, which both nations refuse to sign, they should be. In India these facilities include two nuclear power reactors, a research reactor, and two reprocessing plants. In Pakistan, a large uranium enrichment plant forms the cornerstone of that nation's nuclear program; until recently its purpose was shrouded in secrecy, but there is no longer any doubt as to the purpose of the plant at Kahuta.[41]

How are the superpowers responding to these developments? With kid gloves and by being highly protective of their national interests. Naturally, neither side wishes to lose the friendship of India or Pakistan by actively pursuing the sensitive nonproliferation issue, so the convenient way out of the predicament is to counsel moderation and otherwise do little. On the few occasions when the superpowers did attempt to put some muscle into their message, the attempts turned sour. In 1979, for instance, the United States enacted legislation that cut off aid to Pakistan because of its efforts, illegally, to import nuclear technology and its refusal to place its nuclear facilities under IAEA safeguards. Two years later, prompted by the war in Afghanistan, U.S. military and economic aid to Pakistan was resumed without Pakistan meeting any of the earlier U.S. demands. Also in 1986, at the urging of India, the Soviet Union warned Pakistan in a strong statement against nuclear arming. But despite the authenticity of the Soviet charges, the United States came to the immediate defense of its ally, pointedly reminding Moscow of its strong commitment to Pakistan's security. The United States really outdid its nuclear appeasement of Pakistan in October 1989, when the president, despite irrefutable evidence on the purpose of the Kahuta facility, certified to the Congress that Pakistan did not technically "possess a nuclear explosive device"[42] and that, therefore, it should continue to be the recipient of U.S. aid.

Israel

Israel's status as the world's sixth nuclear weapon state (after the United States, the Soviet Union, China, France, and the United Kingdom) can hardly be disputed. Its scientists, engineers, and intelligence operatives have been pursuing this goal with fanatical dedication for more than twenty years.[43] Presently, Israel is estimated to hold a stockpile of one hundred nuclear weapons, sufficient to destroy every one of its Arab neighbors and more.

Israel's nuclear program, especially the reactor at Dimona, which serves as its lead installation, has not gone unnoticed here or abroad. But the United States, traditionally a champion of Israeli interests, has refused to take action that might be regarded as inimical to Israel or as challenging its nuclear advances. At most, the United States has urged "restraint,"[44] suggesting also that the Israeli weapons not be tested. It has done this despite a national policy that proclaims nonproliferation as a priority objective and the obvious fact that American national interests dictate that the Middle East, of all areas in the world, remain free of nuclear weapons.

In summary, forty-four years after Hiroshima and four decades after the knowledge of the bomb's dreadful potential for ending civilization, the two leading powers of the day are engaged in the process of accumulating weapons as never before in history. There is no rational purpose for these weapons. The superpowers already have enough on hand to deter each other a thousand times over.

The weapons currently being acquired by the superpowers are clearly designed for first-strike purposes. Their mission is to execute with impunity a disarming first strike and to deny the other side the capability and will to retaliate. Success in a first strike, however, cannot be assured without the availability of a defensive shield (i.e., SDI) to protect the friendly forces against the possibility of retaliation. This is the area the superpowers are focusing on next, to the detriment of their own security and the future of all civilization.

NOTES

1. The total number of fatalities resulting from a nuclear war would depend on how and by whom the war was initiated and how it is fought. In his book *1999: Victory without War* (New York: Simon and Schuster, 1988), former President Nixon estimated that more than 400 million people in the United States and the Soviet Union would be killed in an all-out nuclear exchange.

2. United Nations General Assembly, *Study on the Economic and Social Consequences of the Arms Race and Military Expenditures* (New York: United Nations, May 19, 1988), p. 20.

3. The basic military strategy of the United States, notes the FY 1989 Military Posture statement by the chairman of the Joint Chiefs of Staff, is to "deter war ... and if necessary defeat aggression across the entire spectrum of military conflict."

4. A "first strike" is a nuclear attack carried out at such devastatingly high levels of violence as to destroy an opponent's capability to launch a major counterstrike or to even continue in the conflict.

5. Michio Kaku and Daniel Axelrod, *To Win a Nuclear War: The Pentagon's Secret War Plans* (Boston: South End Press, 1987), pp. 273–78.

6. Ibid., p. 202.

7. U.S. Department of Defense, *Soviet Military Power: An Assessment of the Threat, 1988* (Washington, DC: U.S. Government Printing Office, 1988), p. 48.

8. Ibid., p. 101.

9. Although the United States enjoys a numerical edge over the Soviet Union in the total number of *strategic* warheads deployed, the Soviet Union has many more warheads overall. The *Bulletin of Atomic Scientists* estimated the total U.S. inventory at 23,400 warheads (June 1988 issue) and the Soviet inventory at 32,600 warheads (July 1988 issue).

10. According to the nuclear winter theory, darkness would fall over the entire Northern Hemisphere as a result of a large-scale countercity nuclear exchange, with smoke and ashes from the detonations blocking out the sun and cooling the earth dramatically. The Pentagon disputes the theory; nuclear winter, it said, will not result if a counterforce strategy is used. For a pro and con analysis of the theory, see Gary E. McCuen, *Nuclear Winter* (Hudson, WI: GEM Publications, 1987). See also Owen Greene, Ian Percival, and Irene Ridge, *Nuclear Winter: The Evidence and the Risk* (Cambridge, Eng.: Polity Press, 1985); and United Nations, *Climatic and Other Global Effects of Nuclear War: Summary of a United Nations Study*, United Nations Disarmament Fact no. 62 (New York, January 1989).

11. Nixon, *1999: Victory without War*, pp. 80–82.

12. Robert S. McNamara, *Blundering into Disaster: Surviving the First Century of the Nuclear Age* (New York: Pantheon Books, 1986), p. 45.

13. James Fallows, *National Defense* (New York: Random House, 1987), p. 141.

14. The same analogy could be made for a massive U.S. attack on the Soviet ICBM force.

15. Kaku and Axelrod, *To Win a Nuclear War*, p. 288.

16. McNamara, *Blundering into Disaster*, p. 29.

17. Each Trident (Ohio Class) submarine will be equipped to carry twenty-four D-5s, each with up to 14 warheads, for a total of 336 warheads.

18. U.S. General Accounting Office, *Navy Strategic Forces: Trident II Proceeding toward Deployment*, GAO/NSIAD–89–40 (Washington, DC: November 1988), p. 1.

19. *Time*, December 5 and December 12, 1988.

20. U.S. Department of Defense, *Soviet Military Power*, p. 46.

21. U.S. Department of Defense, Office of the Joint Chiefs of Staff, *Military Posture, FY 1989* (Washington, DC: U.S. Government Printing Office, 1988), p. 41.

22. McNamara, *Blundering into Disaster*, p. 49.

23. Fallows, *National Defense*, p. 148.

24. Harvard Nuclear Study Group, *Living with Nuclear Weapons* (Cambridge, MA: Harvard University Press, 1983), p. 139.

25. Helen Caldicott, *Missile Envy: The Arms Race and Nuclear War* (New York: Bantam Books, 1986), pp. 22–23.

26. McNamara, *Blundering into Disaster*, p. 98.

27. Kaku and Axelrod, *To Win a Nuclear War*, p. 242.

28. John Tirman, ed., *Empty Promise: The Growing Case against Star Wars* (Boston: The Union of Concerned Scientists, Beacon Press, 1986).

29. A major shortcoming of SDI would be its inability to defend against long-range bombers and cruise missiles carrying nuclear weapons. To close this gap, President Reagan ordered the Department of Defense in July 1985 to begin an "Air Defense Initiative Program." Its purpose is to develop the required technologies for an air defense system against low-penetrating air- and sea-launched cruise missiles.

30. Hans Mark, "Beyond Nuclear Terror: What's Wrong with Defending Our-selves?" *The Washingtonian*, February 1988.

31. Dennis Menos, "The Soviet SDI Moves Vigorously Ahead," *The Military Engineer*, January–February 1988, pp. 10–13.

32. For a detailed review of Soviet strategic defense programs, refer to U.S. Department of Defense publications: *Soviet Military Power: An Assessment of the Threat, 1988* (Washington, DC, 1988); and *Soviet Strategic Defense Programs* (Washington, DC, 1985).

33. U.S. Department of Defense, *Soviet Military Power*, p. 59.

34. Strategic Defense Initiative Organization, *Report to the Congress on the Strategic Defense Initiative* (Washington, DC, April 1988), p. 2–1.

35. U.S. Arms Control and Disarmament Agency, *Fact Sheet on INF Numbers Based on Updated Data* (Washington, DC, October 6, 1988).

36. Jesse James "Tactical Nuclear Modernization—the NATO Decision that Won't Go Away," *Arms Control Today*, December 1988; and, more recently, Robert McCartney: "NATO Allies Still Divided on Missiles," *Washington Post*, February 22, 1989; "Kohl Urges NATO to Delay Modernization Decision," *Washington Post*, February 11, 1989; "U.S. Bonn Accord Laid to One Word," *Washington Post*, May 31, 1989; and "NATO Arms Discord Seen Resurfacing," *Washington Post*, June 4, 1989.

37. The Committee on Foreign Affairs of the U.S. House of Representatives and on Governmental Affairs of the U.S. Senate regularly sponsor the publication of the *Nuclear Proliferation Factbook*. This is an excellent reference that collects in one volume many of the essential documents and data on the subject of nuclear non-proliferation. The *Factbook*'s fourth edition was published in June 1985.

38. The centerpiece of the world's nonproliferation regime, which the superpowers are committed to promoting, is the Non-Proliferation Treaty and its associated safeguards agency, the International Atomic Energy Agency. No one has ever accused the NPT of being unfair to the superpowers. Its terms favor the nuclear status quo in exchange for simple pledges on their part to promote the peaceful uses of nuclear energy (Article V) and to reduce and eventually eliminate their arsenals of nuclear arms (Article VI).

39. Committees on Foreign Affairs and Governmental Affairs, *Nuclear Proliferation Factbook*, p. 3.

40. Leonard S. Spector, "Nonproliferation—After the Bomb Has Spread," *Arms Control Today*, December 1988, p. 8. An excellent recent source is by David Albright and Tom Zamora, "India, Pakistan's Nuclear Weapons: All the Pieces in Place," *Bulletin of Atomic Scientists*, June 1989, pp. 20–26.

41. Leonard S. Spector, *Going Nuclear* (Cambridge, MA: Ballinger, 1987), pp. 76–77.

42. Spector, "Nonproliferation," p. 8.

43. Lewis A. Dunn, *Controlling the Bomb: Nuclear Proliferation in the 1980s* (New Haven: Yale University Press, 1982), pp. 48–49.

44. Mitchell Reiss, *Without the Bomb: The Politics of Nuclear Nonproliferation* (New York: Columbia University Press, 1988), p. 172.

2

The Superpowers

Given the enormous nuclear arsenals of the superpowers and the continuous acquisition of bigger and better weapons on both sides, the question logically arises: are the superpowers *really serious* about nuclear arms control? Are they dedicated to the goal of arresting the nuclear arms race?

If the superpowers are indeed serious about nuclear arms control, as their leaders wish us to believe, and are hard at work trying to reduce and stabilize the strategic balance, why have results to date been so meager? Why is the acquisition of nuclear arms progressing at a faster rate than are the efforts to eliminate them? On the other hand, if the superpowers have concluded that arms control is not for them, why the continued charade of negotiations, summits, proposals, and counterproposals? Why the hoax?

For the superpowers to be able to pursue arms control with a sense of purpose, they need above all a clear understanding of what it is that the process can do for them. Evidence suggests that, despite the superpowers' near-continuous preoccupation with the issue of containing nuclear arms, since the late 1940s, a wide gap still separates their stated goals. The Soviet Union, for instance, has repeatedly proclaimed the *abolition* of nuclear weapons as its ultimate arms control objective, even though common sense dictates that nuclear weapons can never really be abolished. The U.S. objective, equally flamboyant, aims to make nuclear weapons *impotent and obsolete*, a condition clearly unattainable. By their stated goals, the superpowers make evident their refusal to grasp the foremost rule of the nuclear age: nuclear weapons can neither be disinvented nor abolished—they are here to stay, and we must learn to live with them.[1] In this regard, the United States and the Soviet Union are imbued with a special burden: having themselves given birth to these weapons of awesome power, they now share in the responsibility for preventing their use and for regulating their ultimate disposition or control.

The years since Hiroshima have afforded the superpowers ample opportunity to ascertain the true essence of arms control, its potential, and also its limitations. The process cannot resolve the many ideological and political differences that divide them; neither can it correct in one big swoop the many problems that confront mankind. Arms control can, however, if carried out *responsibly*, enhance international stability by reducing the likelihood of accidental nuclear war; it can reduce and stabilize the strategic balance and prevent the further worldwide proliferation of nuclear weapons. Although these are the priority "musts" of the arms control agenda, the superpowers are finding them hard to adopt and pursue.

ARMS CONTROL POLICY

Since the dawn of the nuclear era, the nuclear arms race has been the superpowers' professed Enemy Number 1. The archives of Washington and Moscow are full of official pronouncements by U.S. and Soviet leaders of their nations' unfailing concern over the escalating arms race, the irrationality of nuclear war, and the need to reverse the process. Appropriate quotes could fill several volumes.

The official pronouncements and speeches could hardly have been intended to deceive mankind. In Moscow and Washington, arms control is uniformly regarded as the principal means for constraining the accelerated buildup of arms and for introducing a sense of order in the nuclear relationship of the superpowers. But the two powers differ greatly on what they expect arms control to accomplish. To the Soviet Union, the process is designed as a vehicle for bringing about *world disarmament*, a condition whereby all armaments, nuclear and conventional, will have been abolished and the world made safe for socialism. U.S. expectations are different. Arms control, according to the United States, to be successful must result in a world at peace and secure in its institutions, not one necessarily free of armaments. The United States is also committed to a nuclear-free world, but its heart is not really in it.

Soviet Policy

Arms control, like all other aspects of Soviet national security policy, is promulgated and controlled by a tiny group of dedicated Communists serving on the Politburo of the Soviet Communist party. In Moscow, as in Washington, there are hawks and doves constantly at odds with each other and in competition over specific policy choices.[2] But the Soviet governmental structure has one ingredient that is lacking in Washington: regardless of who the top man might be in the Kremlin at any time, Soviet arms control policy remains constant. World disarmament was the long-term goal of Lenin, Stalin, Khrushchev, and Brezhnev and continues to be that of present-day leader Mikhail Gorbachev.

An essential ingredient of Soviet arms control policy is the use of the nuclear issue for purposes of propaganda,[3] especially among the peoples of western Europe and in the Third World. On the continent, the approach is to charm the war-weary Europeans with a never-ending series of arms reduction proposals, coupled with assertions that the Soviet military threat to Europe no longer exists. The arms reduction proposals are clearly designed to lessen the nuclear fears of west Europeans, especially the Germans on whose territory a nuclear war (if it ever happens in Europe) is likely to be fought. An entirely different approach is used vis-à-vis the peoples of Asia, Africa, and Latin America. To the hungry and disadvantaged masses there, the message of world disarmament, with all of the images of material goods and prosperity that it conveys, is a lot more attractive than the concept of a world at peace and international security (the U.S. approach), which suggests more of the same. Moscow has been aware of this public relations opportunity for years. Its lofty pronouncements in support of world disarmament, dating from the earliest days of the Bolshevik Revolution, have been designed to exploit this opportunity.

At the United Nations, where the peoples of the Third World are able to observe the nuclear competition of the superpowers at close quarters, the Soviet Union has been especially adept at promoting a favorable image of itself as the leading opponent of the arms race and champion of the poor. The nuclear arms race, Soviet leaders have repeatedly emphasized, involves an enormous waste of national resources. These resources could more sensibly be applied to human needs, especially in the world's underdeveloped areas.

United States Policy

Until recently, two key factors have exerted paramount influence over U.S. arms control policy:[4] a deep distrust of the Soviets and widespread belief that world domination continues to be the Kremlin's principal foreign policy objective. Recurrent Soviet adventurism, such as in Nicaragua, Afghanistan, and Angola, aggravated these suspicions and eroded prospects for arms control. In 1968, for instance, the Senate delayed ratification of the Non-Proliferation Treaty (NPT) on news of the Soviet invasion of Czechoslovakia. A decade or so later, President Carter withdrew the Strategic Arms Limitation Talks (SALT) II Treaty from further Senate consideration when Soviet troops entered Afghanistan.

Since the advent to power of Mikhail Gorbachev, the long-standing U.S. distrust of the Soviet Union and its leadership has receded somewhat. The Soviet leader's many initiatives for withdrawing troops from Europe and for reducing nuclear weapons (many unilaterally and without compensatory U.S. reductions) have had the effect of reducing the perception of the Soviet threat and of swinging much of American public opinion away from fear of the "Evil Empire." There are many powerful U.S. voices, however, that counsel against a rush to premature conclusions. The Gorbachev proposals, they suggest, affect the margins of Soviet power. There is no evidence yet of a real desire by the Soviet leadership to alter its system (which is the crux of the problem) or to back up its many promises with action. The talk of the Cold War ending has been heard before—in the 1950s—only to have the Soviet army, soon thereafter, crush revolts in East Germany and Hungary. The United States would be foolhardy to base its arms control policy on the personality and continued political survival of one man.[5]

Distrust of Soviet arms control policies and goals is evidenced in a number of ways. It is demonstrated by the manner in which the United States responds to Soviet proposals, invariably labeling many of them as "propaganda,"[6] and the inordinate importance afforded the issue of verification as a precondition to any agreement. Distrust of the Soviets is also behind the recurrent U.S. charges of Soviet arms treaty violations, even on mini-issues of no strategic import. The multibillion dollar U.S. strategic modernization program itself is evidence of the direct relationship between American suspicion of Soviet intentions and official U.S. arms control policy.[7] To close an alleged window of vulnerability, the United States is acquiring weapons in numbers and capability far in excess of actual need, in the process dooming the viability of the SALT arms limitation regime and prospects for further arms limitations in the future.

To the Soviet Union, no aspect of U.S.–Soviet relations is more urgent and important than nuclear arms control. (At least, this is the official line from Moscow.) The United States does not agree, however.[8] Issues, such as the resolution of regional conflicts and violations of human rights, two areas in which the Soviet Union admittedly is vulnerable, demand equal time. The difference is not just a question of emphasis. It affects superpower agendas, determines the subjects to be discussed at summits, and, in the eyes of the United States, impacts on the priorities of the superpower relationship.[9]

Official Policy or Lofty Pronouncements?

Since gaining center stage in arms control in early 1985, Soviet leader Gorbachev has been extremely prolific, advancing one proposal after another, grabbing headlines, urging and at times pleading with the United States to join him in a whole series of major arms control initiatives.[10] His preoccupation with the issue has been so pronounced as to give the impression that there is no higher priority goal in his administration than reaching an accommodation with the United States to constrain nuclear arms.

Admittedly, because of the U.S. refusal to take them seriously, the majority of Gorbachev's initiatives have remained just that, mere "initiatives" for future generations of scholars to ponder. Many of these initiatives, however, have amassed for the Soviet leader considerable public relations benefit. Proposals such as the Year 2000 Disarmament Plan (announced on January 15, 1986); the nuclear test moratorium of 1985–1986, repeatedly, extended to induce United States adherence; his offer to eliminate all short-range nuclear weapons in Europe, a proposal resisted by Washington; and his efforts supporting continued superpower adherence to the ABM treaty have contributed enormously toward an image of Gorbachev as "the good guy," the one willing to take chances for peace, especially among the peoples of western Europe and in the Third World.

The Soviet leader's talent for blending arms control with propaganda cannot be disputed. In the case of the intermediate-range nuclear forces (INF) issue, for instance, he took over an American plan (the "zero" option first proposed by President Reagan in November 1981), gave it a twist favoring the Soviet Union, offered to eliminate some additional no-longer-needed shorter range delivery vehicles, and thus like a magician presented the world with its first arms control deal in more than eight years.

In contrast, Presidents Reagan and Bush are being looked at in many parts of the world, even in pro–U.S. western Europe, as the leaders primarily responsible for fueling the arms race. Of the various past actions that have given rise to this image, three are generally noted: (1) the decision to launch the Strategic Defense Initiative (SDI), (2) U.S. insistence that nuclear weapons remain in Europe for purposes of deterrence (despite major European opposition), and (3) the generally slow and cautious approach employed by the United States in all of its arms control dealings with the Soviet Union. Collectively, these actions have affected adversely the U.S. standing in world public opinion as an advocate of nuclear arms control.

The following statements on the subjects of nuclear arms and arms control were made by Presidents Reagan[11] and Bush and Soviet leader Gorbachev. Note these leaders' professed support for arms control and for the need to contain the nuclear arms race. But note also the continuing U.S. distrust of the Soviet Union as evidenced by President Reagan's statements and the strong propaganda flavor in the quotes from the Russian leader.

President Reagan

A nuclear war can never be won and must never be fought. (Speech to Japanese Parliament, Tokyo, November 11, 1983)

We want to reduce the weapons of war, pure and simple. All of our efforts... continue to be guided by that objective. (Remarks in Rose Garden, White House, October 4, 1983)

I have no higher priority than removing the threat of nuclear war.... Our current goal must be the reduction of nuclear arsenals, and I for one believe that we must never depart from the ultimate goal of banning them from the face of the Earth. (Radio Address to the Nation, July 16, 1983)

Since the dawn of the atomic age, we have sought to reduce the risk of war by maintaining a strong deterrent and by seeking genuine arms control. (Television Address to the Nation, March 23, 1983)

My duty as President is to insure that the ultimate nightmare never occurs, that the prairies and the cities and the people who inhabit them remain free and untouched by nuclear conflict. (Commencement Address, Eureka College, May 9, 1982)

Arms control requires a spirit beyond narrow national interests. (Address to the United Nations, September 26, 1983)

The record of Soviet behavior, the long history of Soviet brutality toward those who are weaker reminds us that the only guarantee of peace and freedom is our military strength and our national will. The peoples of Afghanistan and Poland, of Czechoslovakia and Cuba and so many other captive countries, they understand this. (Address to the Nation, February 26, 1986)

[At Geneva] I did not hesitate to tell Mr. Gorbachev our view of the source of that mistrust: the Soviet Union's record of seeking to impose its ideology and rule on others.... despite these differences, we resolved to work together for real reductions in nuclear arms. (Address to the United Nations, September 22, 1986)

We must remember that the Soviet Government is based upon and drawn from the Soviet Communist Party—an organization that remains formally pledged to subjecting the world to Communist domination.... I am convinced that we must take seriously the Soviet history of expansionism and provide an effective counter. At the same time, we must remain realistic and committed to arms control. (Statement in Glassboro, New Jersey, June 19, 1986)

President Bush

In the strategic arms reduction talks, we wish to reduce the risk of nuclear war. (Address to Texas A&M University, May 12, 1989)

We will not miss any opportunity to work for peace. The fundamental facts remain that the Soviets retain a very powerful military machine in the service of objectives which are still too often in conflict with ours.... Let us always be strong. (Address to Congress, February 9, 1989)

Our goals include a strategic arms agreement which will enhance strategic stability and security. (Meeting with press, February 25, 1989)

Mikhail Gorbachev

We consider it so important right now, immediately, before it is too late, to stop the "infernal train" of the arms race, to start the reduction of arms. (Address to the French Parliament, Paris, October 3, 1985)

The Soviet Union is proposing a step-by-step and consistent process of ridding the earth of nuclear weapons, to be undertaken and completed within the next 15 years, before the end of the century.... We propose that the third millennium should begin without nuclear weapons.... Instead of wasting the next 10 to 15 years on the development of new, extremely dangerous weapons in outer space, allegedly designed to make nuclear weapons unnecessary, is it not more sensible to start destroying those weapons and eventually reduce them to zero? (The Year 2000 Disarmament Speech, January 15, 1986)

We want the termination, and not continuation of the arms race and, therefore, offer a freeze of nuclear arsenals, and an end to further deployment of missiles. (Address as reported by *Tass*, March 11, 1985)

We have accumulated mountains of weapons, nuclear and all other kinds, yet the arms race is not slackening but picking up and there is now a danger that it may extend into space, while militarization in the United States and the entire NATO bloc is proceeding apace. (Statement on Soviet television, August 16, 1986)

It is time to realize to the full extent the harsh reality that nuclear weapons can produce a hurricane that would sweep the human race from the face of the Earth. ... Continuation of this race on Earth, let alone its spread to outer space, will accelerate the already critically high rate of stockpiling and perfecting nuclear weapons. (Address to Soviet Communist Party Congress, February 25, 1986)

It is hard to understand why our proposals have provoked such outspoken displeasure on the part of responsible U.S. statesmen. Attempts have been made to portray them as nothing but pure propaganda. (Interview with *Time*, September 9, 1985)

I am convinced that strategic military parity can be maintained at a low level and without nuclear weapons. We have clearly formulated our choice: to stop, then reverse the arms race. (Interview with the *Washington Post*, May 21, 1988)

ADVANCING NATIONAL INTERESTS

What is one to conclude from these quotes? To millions, they offer undisputed evidence that the U.S. president (or Soviet leader Gorbachev) is serious in his desire to end the planet-threatening nuclear arms race—if the other fellow will only cooperate. To millions of others, however, the words of the two leaders are just that, words, empty words designed for public relations effect.

The actual truth lies halfway between the two extremes. The superpowers are indeed serious in their support of arms control but only to the extent that it promotes their *national interests* and improves their position in the world. Evidence the manner in which the United States or the Soviet Union responds to specific initiatives of the other side. Their official pronouncements and alleged support of arms control notwithstanding, both nations will respond favorably only to initiatives that advance their own national interests. Mankind's concerns and hopes for a safe, secure world are hardly a consideration.

Recent arms control activities offer ample evidence. First consider some examples on which "progress" was made, because the basic goal of the initiative was consistent with or advanced the national interests of the superpowers.

The INF Agreement

The INF agreement, signed in Washington during the 1987 summit, was originally an American idea that was later adopted by the Soviet Union. The accord provides evidence that the superpowers will work hard at finding solutions, if the end result of the effort advances their national interests.[12] The fact that the agreement might also slow down the arms race is a mere fortunate coincidence.

In proposing in November 1981 an INF deal similar to the agreement that finally did materialize, the United States had a three-prong goal in mind: (1) to remove the threat posed on western Europe by the highly capable Soviet SS–20 system, (2) to retain intact its own nuclear battlefield weapons in Europe, and (3) to exclude from consideration in the agreement the French and British nuclear forces. In return, the United States was prepared to sacrifice its own INF forces (the Pershing II and Tomahawk ground-launched cruise missiles) and also some older INFs held by the Federal Republic of Germany. In the treaty the United States gained all that *and* the removal from Europe of a large arsenal of Soviet shorter range (300 to 600 miles) missiles: 846 U.S. delivery vehicles, as against 1,846 for the Soviet Union—definitely a good deal.

From Moscow's perspective, the INF treaty is likewise a good deal but for different reasons. First, it eliminates the threat posed on the Soviet command and control structure by the Pershing II missile. From its bases in western Europe, the American weapon could have reached Moscow within seven minutes of launch, hopelessly complicating Soviet retaliatory plans and decision making. Second, by eliminating all but battlefield nuclear weapons in Europe, the Soviet edge in conventional (nonnuclear) forces becomes more decisive. Finally, U.S. official pronouncements notwithstanding, the removal of the American INF forces from the continent is conveying a "decoupling" message to Europe, long a policy goal of Moscow.

Nuclear Risk Reduction Centers

This is a confidence-building initiative similarly designed to advance superpower interests. Its purpose is to reduce and ultimately eliminate the risk of outbreak of nuclear war, particularly as a result of misinterpretation, miscalculation, or accident. The original suggestion for Nuclear Risk Reduction Centers was made by two U.S. senators, and the idea was subsequently endorsed by the leaders of the superpowers at the Geneva Summit in November 1985.

Negotiations designed to implement the proposal were launched in Geneva in May 1986. Within a year, agreement was reached—evidence that when their national interests converge the superpowers can work with remarkable speed toward an understanding. Actually, there was never any doubt about the final outcome. The superpowers were dealing with an issue designed to enhance their own security and one that they obviously favored. The final document formalizing the establishment of the Nuclear Risk Reduction Centers was signed on September 15, 1987, during an official visit to Washington of Soviet Foreign Minister Edward Shevardnadze.[13]

Confidence and Security-Building Measures and Disarmament in Europe

On September 19, 1986, the nations of Europe, including the United States and Canada, signed an agreement designed to reduce the risk of military confrontation in Europe.[14] Its terms were anything but potent. They merely obligated the signatories to refrain from the threat or use of force and to provide advance notification on some of their military activities. The agreement had no impact on the nuclear arsenals of the superpowers, and neither did it limit their plans for the acquisition of more and bigger weapons. In short, it was an arms control success in name only.

The agreement became a reality because its basic provisions advance superpower interests by means of nonintrusive confidence-building measures. The superpowers hate surprises. Thus any measure designed to enhance knowledge and understanding of the other side's military capabilities and plans is supported by them.

Prevention of Dangerous Military Activities

The latest confidence-building measure concluded by the superpowers was signed in Moscow on June 12, 1989. The agreement aims to prevent future accidents (such as the straying of a plane into foreign territory) from escalating into open warfare through the use of improved communications between field commanders. This is another instance of the superpowers concluding an agreement primarily to protect themselves. The agreement codifies procedures that a sensible military field commander would have followed anyway if confronted with a situation likely to escalate to a shooting war. An obvious shortcoming of the agreement is its failure to prohibit the first use of nuclear or other weapons of mass destruction in any superpower crisis resulting from accident, equipment malfunction, or misunderstanding.

The Superpowers and the NPT

At the heart of international efforts to prevent the further spread of nuclear weapons is the NPT. The superpowers like the treaty; after all, it preserves the nuclear status quo by making it difficult for nonnuclear states to acquire nuclear weapons. True, the treaty requires also that the superpowers negotiate in good faith on "effective measures relating to the cessation of the nuclear arms race . . . and to nuclear disarmament," but this is one pledge that Washington and Moscow have never taken very seriously.

The greater the number of nations possessing nuclear weapons, the greater the threat to international peace and security. The United States and the Soviet Union are in complete agreement on this issue. Accordingly, consistent with their national interests, which do not always converge on the issue of nuclear nonproliferation, both have collaborated in efforts to encourage holdout nations to remain nuclear-free and to adhere to the treaty.

The NPT requires that its signatories meet every five years to review the implementation of the treaty. The third such Review Conference, held in Geneva during August and September 1985,[15] again found the superpowers on the defensive over their failure to achieve the NPT's disarmament goals. Unperturbed, the superpowers turned a deaf ear to the complaints of the nonnuclears, and after reaffirming their commitment to the International Atomic Energy Agency (IAEA) and its safeguards system, they departed for home. From their perspective, nuclear nonproliferation and nuclear disarmament were in as good a shape as could be expected.

The superpowers display a similar apathy twice each year, during their regularly scheduled one-on-one meetings, which address issues relating to the "integrity of the nuclear nonproliferation regime." These consultations, states the U.S. government, are for the purpose of reinforcing the common interests of the United States and of the Soviet Union in nuclear nonproliferation. They are, obviously, strictly superpower affairs.

The Search for a Chemical Nonproliferation Regime

On several instances during the past few years, the superpowers have expressed concern over the growing problem of worldwide chemical proliferation.[16] Soviet leader Gorbachev is even on record as favoring the conclusion of a formal chemical nonproliferation agreement patterned after its nuclear counterpart.

Superpower concern with this issue is understandable. Seventy years ago, during World War I, chemical weapons claimed at least 1 million casualties, 100,000 of which were fatal. This occurred with chemical warfare agents and delivery systems that were primitive in comparison to those presently in the arsenals of nations. The chemical weapons club, then, included no more than four nations. Today, perhaps as many as fifteen countries produce and stockpile chemical warfare agents.

In 1986 and again in 1987 and 1988, representatives of the superpowers held talks on the issue. Reportedly, there is a general convergence of the views, but many technical details still remain. The most serious of them entails enlisting the support of the international community in yet another nonproliferation agreement. To expect 130 or so nations that are parties to the nuclear NPT also to join a chemical counterpart without loud voices of protest is unrealistic. The great majority of the nuclear havenot nations feel cheated by the superpowers' nonfulfillment of Article VI of the NPT. This is the article, noted earlier, that calls upon the nuclear-weapon states to pursue negotiations toward a "treaty on general and complete disarmament."

The other side of the coin concerns arms control initiatives on which no progress was achieved because of a clash of superpower interests.

Nuclear Testing

The superpowers are sharply divided on the issue of nuclear testing.[17] For reasons of its own, the Soviet Union favors an immediate end to all testing and is prepared to sign a Comprehensive Test Ban Treaty (CTBT) to this effect right now. The United States, however, is opposed. A CTBT, it believes, should be signed only after major arms reduction agreements have been concluded and procedures have been agreed upon for verifying underground nuclear tests.[18] The statement sounds hopeful, but in fact it is not. In official circles in Washington there is strong support for continued nuclear testing as a means of sustaining the strategy of deterrence and for proceeding with weapons development under the U.S. strategic modernization program and SDI.[19]

Throughout the years, both superpowers have tried to resolve the nuclear test issue to their advantage. They have advanced initiatives and made "goodwill gestures," all so one-sided as to insure their rejection from the outset. On the Soviet side, initiatives have included repeated offers by Soviet leader Gorbachev to meet President Reagan at the locale of his choosing for the purpose of negotiating a CTBT. They also have included the announcement in August 1985 of a nuclear test moratorium, extended repeatedly in an effort to induce the United States to follow suit. In light of U.S. policy, however, which mandated that nuclear testing be continued, the offers were shallow exercises in public relations. Not surprisingly, the United States simply ignored them, proceeding instead with its scheduled nuclear test series.

The United States followed up on the Soviet initiatives with some of its own. In moves designed to bring the Soviet Union around to its point of view (i.e., that nuclear testing cannot be suspended until a fool-proof regime has been agreed upon for verifying compliance) it invited representatives of the Soviet Union to visit here for the purpose of observing a nuclear test and to share in the technology used for overseeing nuclear explosions.[20] The Soviet Union initially characterized the proposal as a "political gimmick." Later, however, it consented to the conduct of a Joint Verification Experiment[21] under which nuclear explosions (one each in the United States and the Soviet Union) were observed by scientists of both nations for the purpose of improving verification capabilities. Undoubtedly, the U.S. promise to resume nuclear test negotiations led the Soviet Union to reverse its position and to agree to the U.S. proposal. On several occasions since 1986 experts from the United States and the Soviet Union have met in Geneva for the purpose of addressing the issue. But nothing has ever come of the effort. The superpowers could not even agree on the subject of the talks, with the United States arguing for better verification of underground tests (i.e., continued nuclear testing), the Soviet Union for an end to all testing. The events proved again that on issues having a direct bearing on their national interests, the superpowers have an uncanny ability to talk past each other and to refuse giving ground on even the most minute of terms.

Strategic Arms Reductions

Although the superpowers are in general agreement on the need to reduce their strategic arsenals, and thus hopefully lessen the risk of nuclear war, little has come of their extended negotiations of the past two decades.[22] The absence of concrete results is proof that the superpowers are still searching for the elusive formula, one that will result in fewer nuclear armaments on the other side and greater security to themselves. As in the case of nuclear testing, the driving force behind the negotiations for arms reductions is not the desire to free mankind from the threat of nuclear terror but to advance U.S. and Soviet national interests.

The positions taken by the superpowers at the negotiations in Geneva, during the four Gorbachev-Reagan summits and elsewhere, provide ample evidence. The Soviet Union, for instance, favors across-the-board reductions in *all* strategic systems (land-based missiles, bombers, strategic submarines, and long-range cruise missiles), with all such systems dismantled within ten years. Additionally, it supports continued compliance with the ABM treaty for at least a period of ten years, with development of defense systems during that period permitted only if carried out subject to the limitations of the traditional (i.e., narrow) interpretation of the treaty.

The first of these provisions aims to eliminate the weapons that the Soviet Union perceives as posing the greatest threat to its security. They include the U.S. strategic submarine force (especially the upcoming Trident II D-5), the future generation of stealth technology bombers, and the growing arsenal of sea- and air-launched cruise missiles, which make it possible for every

American warplane, ship, or submarine to serve as a nuclear launching platform against the Soviet Union. The second provision in the Soviet plan is designed to stop the development and testing of U.S. space-based weapons for SDI.

The United States likewise favors arms reductions but initially only for intercontinental ballistic missiles (ICBMs). The reason is understandable. The Soviet Union has an overwhelming lead in land-based missiles (including the SS-18, a monster of a weapon). On the ABM treaty, the United States favors a very limited compliance period, with enough flexibility allowed during that period to experiment and test space-based weapons for SDI as well as the freedom to deploy the system at the conclusion of the adherence period. In effect, the United States wants (1) to eliminate the most threatening weapons of the Soviet Union; (2) to retain fairly intact the weapons (bombers, cruise missiles, and submarine-launched ballistic missiles [SLBMs]) in which it maintains the upper hand; and (3) authority to proceed unchallenged with the development, testing, and deployment of weapons for ballistic missile defense.

At the summits in Geneva, Rekjavik, Washington, and Moscow the superpowers have been exploring a compromise, halfway between the opposing views. But considering the long history of U.S.–Soviet negotiations on this issue and their competing goals, can one really be optimistic?

Third Zero

On the matter of the nuclear battlefield weapons—popularity designated as "third zero"—an enormous gap still separates the two sides. At issue are the nearly 10,000 short-range missiles, artillery, and nuclear capable aircraft now deployed on the European continent. The Soviet Union proposes that these weapons be eliminated, but the North Atlantic Treaty Organization (NATO), except for the Federal Republic of Germany, is opposed. The Soviet position is not driven by altruism. Removal of nuclear battlefield weapons from Europe would definitely strengthen Moscow's hand. It would shatter NATO's strategy of flexible response and severely weaken the West's capability to defend against the numerically superior Warsaw Pact conventional forces.

The United States is unyielding on this issue[23]—if its troops are to remain in Europe, so will be its tactical nuclear weapons. Still, for reasons of alliance unity and to acquiesce to German demands for talks, the United States agreed in May 1989 to NATO holding such talks with the other side but only after the Soviet conventional forces superiority in Europe had been checked by means of an arms control agreement, very optimistically expected to occur in the 1992–1994 time frame. Even then, the NATO–Warsaw Pact talks would aim only at a partial (not total) elimination of nuclear battlefield weapons. Considering, however, the experience of the last superpower attempt at reaching an agreement on the conventional forces in Europe—the mutual and balanced forces reductions (MBFR) negotiations—when the two sides talked past each other and without success for fifteen years, can one really be hopeful? Not really, unless the Soviet Union agrees to withdraw "unilaterally" some of its nuclear forces from Europe, a move which the United States has been actively encouraging.[24]

Tinkering with Existing Treaties

Until the mid-1980s, two agreements epitomized the U.S.–Soviet arms control relationship: the ABM treaty and SALT II. Both are now seriously threatened and their future is uncertain.[25] The ABM treaty, already violated by the Soviet Union through the erection of a major ABM installation in Krasnoyarsk, is further menaced by efforts in the United States to redefine its purpose and principal provisions. SDI-related research and development here and in the Soviet Union, unless limited by some type of superpower accord or informal understanding, would before too long mortally wound the treaty. SALT II has already been crippled by Soviet actions and the adoption in May 1986 by the Reagan administration of the "proportionate response" policy. (For more on both treaties, see Chapter 4.)

NEGOTIATING TACTICS

The tactics that the superpowers employ while ostensibly negotiating reductions in their nuclear arsenals are driven always by the same goal: to promote and advance their own "national interests" while skillfully manipulating the negotiating process for maximum public relations effect. The escalating nuclear arms race, the issue that the two nations are supposedly addressing, is all but forgotten.

Proposals

Denying the other side a political advantage is an obvious goal in any East–West contact. In the arms control arena this is practiced with great skill and finesse by both superpowers.[26] Almost always it takes the form of turning a deaf ear to the other side's initiatives or, when the other side has come up with something obviously good and worthwhile, to acknowledge it briefly, praise it as a positive move "worthy of careful study," and then simply ignore it. Examples abound.

Early in 1986 Soviet leader Gorbachev announced that his nation was prepared to renounce formally the targeting or use of nuclear weapons against Great Britain or any other country that removes nuclear armaments and bases from its territory. The nations of NATO for whose benefit the proposal had been formulated did not even honor it with a formal response.

Not long thereafter, Moscow by way of its Warsaw Pact allies launched a major troop reduction plan. Its goal, it said, was to reduce by 500,000 men the troops stationed in the area from "the Atlantic to the Urals." For over a year, the United States and NATO looked the other way, pretending that the proposal had never been made.

In contrast, because of the exigencies of the moment, the United States took special pains to praise Soviet arms control initiatives. Such was the case with the Year 2000 Disarmament Plan by Soviet leader Gorbachev. In Washington the plan was not only officially acknowledged but was even graced with the term *constructive*; President Reagan is "grateful" for the proposals said the official communique.[27] This was the response even though the Soviet leader's plan contained a definite link between SDI and nuclear arms reductions, the very issue that later caused the Iceland stalemate. Apparently, the United States chose to overlook the imperfection in the proposal, somehow hoping to lure the Soviets into an early INF agreement, delinked from SDI. Washington's response to Moscow made this goal abundantly clear. The United States was prepared to accept some portions of the plan (i.e., those parts that advanced its national interests) but was in no mood to sacrifice SDI or allow the Soviets to provide the blueprint for mankind's arms control future. As far as the American government was concerned, the Year 2000 Disarmament Plan had already outlived its usefulness.

Later Soviet proposals similarly were praised when first announced, even though they called for a fifteen-year adherence to the ABM Treaty in exchange for major reductions in strategic systems, a position opposed by the United States. The proposals have merit, commented a White House spokesman, and they are not being taken for propaganda. Added President Reagan: "The Soviet Union has begun to make a serious effort to negotiate reductions in nuclear weapons."[28] Actually, Gorbachev's proposals contained very little that was new and continued to insist that SDI be limited to the laboratory. Why the favorable U.S. response? The U.S. enthusiasm was politically motivated: it was designed to send "positive" signals to Moscow when the administration still had high hopes for a 1986 summit in Washington. (Disagreements between the superpowers forced postponement of the Washington summit to December 1987.)

The Soviet proposals of February 1987, delinking the INF issue from SDI and thus increasing the possibility of an INF agreement, likewise were profusely praised when first announced. U.S. response again was politically motivated. The proposals opened the door for the Reagan administration to conclude a "major" arms control accord (something that had elluded it during its first six years of office). It mattered little that there was major opposition to the plan both at home and in Europe and that numerous technical details remained to be resolved. The prospective INF accord made political sense by positioning President Reagan alongside previous presidents who had concluded arms control accords with the Soviet Union. The fact that the agreement did not eliminate all nuclear weapons in Europe (thousands of battlefield weapons would still remain) was a minor flaw that the general public would hopefully overlook.

The transition from the Reagan to the Bush administration brought forth little perceptible change in the manner that the United States is responding to Soviet arms control proposals. When in May 1989 Soviet leader Gorbachev advised Secretary of State Baker of plans to reduce Soviet short-range nuclear forces in Europe by 500 warheads, the secretary's only response was: "It is a good step, but a small step."[29] Commented the president's chief spokesman Fitzwater a few days later: "The Soviet leader is throwing out, in a kind of drugstore cowboy fashion, one arms control proposal after another."[30] Vice-president Quayle had even harsher words: "There is a bit of phoniness about the Gorbachev proposals. His offers amount to little more than PR gambits."[31]

For their part, despite *glasnost* and other promises of greater future openness, the Soviets have been turning a deaf ear to many of President Bush's arms control initiatives. The president's proposal for an open-skies regime, for instance, made early in his administration to enhance confidence building between the superpowers, might as well never have been made. Moscow ignored it completely. The president's next initiative—his call for Soviet troops to be withdrawn from Poland—did not fare much better. "It is propaganda," commented Soviet leader Gorbachev, dismissing outright the Bush proposal.[32]

Linkage as a Delaying Tactic

When all else fails, the superpowers use "linkage" to block legitimate arms control proposals that are in conflict with their national interests.[33] Some examples have already been cited. The U.S. insistence that improved verification and reductions in strategic arms precede the conclusion of a CTBT and the Soviet demand that arms reductions be held hostage to SDI limitations both are powerful "linkages" introduced by the superpowers in a never-ending pursuit of advantage. A summit in Washington during 1986, previously agreed to in Geneva, also fell victim to linkage. It was not enough, suggested the Soviets, merely to meet and talk. An agreement would have to result from a summit or there could be no meeting of the two leaders.

In the case of INF weapons control, the Soviet Union repeatedly used linkage to put pressure on the United States and force it to grant Moscow favorable terms. During 1985 Soviet spokesmen let it be known that there could be no deal on this issue unless the United States agreed first to ban weapons development under SDI. After the Geneva summit, the Soviet Union announced that it was no longer insisting that SDI be banned as a precondition to INF (i.e., the linkage was removed). But in October 1986

Moscow changed signals again, and SDI linkage became one more time part of the INF picture. Finally, in February 1987 another change occurred in Soviet policy. The SDI and INF issues were again delinked, a condition that allowed the two sides to finalize the INF accord.[34]

The principal victim of linkage was the Iceland Summit and the associated Geneva arms control negotiations. It is still not clear what specific reductions the two leaders considered seriously in Reykjavik, but little doubt exists that the minisummit suddenly confronted them with the type of agreement they were both ill prepared to conclude.[35] Linkage provided both sides with a graceful exit from the dilemma. To the Soviets, linkage was the future course of the U.S. space defense program—SDI would have to remain in the laboratory for a period of ten years or there could be no major arms reductions. To the United States, SDI likewise was the linkage, but SDI in the form of an insurance policy (after arms have been reduced), to protect against a potential madman or terrorist who succeeds in obtaining nuclear arms. As expected, the offense–defense linkage is also obstructing progress at the Geneva Nuclear and Space Talks (NST). Despite numerous rounds of talks, draft treaties, and agreements in principle at the Geneva, Washington, and Moscow summits, a wide gulf still separates the two sides, on the ABM/SDI issue, on mobile missiles, on how to account for cruise missiles, and on the issues of verification and arms treaty compliance.

Verification as an Excuse for Not Negotiating

The U.S. government is the principal practitioner of the verification tactic. Since the beginning of arms control negotiations, the United States has maintained (and rightly so) that an agreement concluded with the Soviet Union must be verifiable or there could be no agreement. Underlying this policy has been the continuing U.S. distrust of the Russians and the fear that they might trick the United States into disarming while they themselves would continue to accumulate weapons. The U.S. verification policy enjoys greater bipartisan support than probably any other foreign policy pronouncement. Every president since Dwight D. Eisenhower has religiously applied it in his relations with the Soviets: simple pledges would not do. Our intelligence must be able to verify Soviet compliance of a potential agreement or there can be no agreement.[36]

No sensible person can fault the U.S. policy. It is prudent and logical. The stakes in the nuclear age are so high that an arms control agreement to be credible must be verifiable. There is, however, another less known side to the U.S. verification policy. In the past, the United States has used verification also as a negotiating tool—as an excuse for stalling or for not considering an arms control initiative if it was not in the national interest to do so. The easiest way for not playing with the other side was to claim that the proposal is "not verifiable." Thus proposals for a U.S.–Soviet nuclear weapons freeze in the early 1980s were alleged to be "not verifiable"; an accord restricting the development of antisatellite (ASAT) weapons would be "not verifiable"; a comprehensive nuclear test ban would also be "not verifiable," thus not a candidate for negotiation. Although in all of these instances, significant verification issues were also involved, the U.S. position was motivated by more strategic considerations. The proposals considered were not in the national interest to pursue, considering either content or time. The United States, for example, is presently in the process of expanding its strategic forces and is developing weapons designed to defend against ballistic missiles. Both programs require extensive nuclear weapons testing, which would not be permissible under the terms of a CTBT. Therefore, the U.S. claims that underground nuclear testing cannot be verified and that an agreement with the Soviets on a CTBT cannot be consumated. Actually, the issue is more one of the national interest than of verification.

Claims of verification difficulty also provide the basic rationale for two U.S. negotiating positions at the Strategic Arms Reduction Talks (START). In Geneva, the United States favors banning mobile ICBMs "because they cannot be verified" but wants sea-launched cruise missiles (SLCMs) retained similarly "because they cannot be verified." A contradiction? Of course. What the United States is attempting to accomplish by the contrary policies is to eliminate the threat posed by the Soviet mobile ICBM systems (the SS-24s and SS-25s) while retaining the SLCMs, a weapons area in which it has an overwhelming lead over the Soviet Union. Undoubtedly, determining the precise location of mobile missiles is an extremely complicated task and so is the differentiation between nuclear-armed and conventional SLCMs. But to ban one weapon system because of these difficulties while retaining the other makes a mockery of nuclear arms control and perverts verification from the deadly serious issue that it is to a simple game.

Shifting of Priorities

Early in 1989 the United States and the Soviet Union made a monumental shift in their arms control priorities. The shift involves a sudden and highly publicized emphasis on conventional (i.e., nonnuclear) arms control at the detriment of superpower efforts to reduce strategic weapons and end nuclear testing. Whether the shift in superpower priorities, from nuclear to conventional arms control, was by chance or design, no one is sure at this stage. The superpowers may be pursuing this initiative in all seriousness because they sense an opportunity to eliminate the threat of a conventional war in Europe. Then again, the shift may be merely a maneuver—a ploy—designed to spare the United States and the Soviet Union the hard decision making that confronts them in the START and CTBT talks.

The superpower shift from nuclear to conventional arms control began in earnest in December 1988 with the appearance of Soviet leader Gorbachev before the U.N. General Assembly. His nation, he noted, was prepared to make unilateral cuts amounting to half a million men and 10,000 tanks. During the ensuing months, the Soviet Union followed up with several additional initiatives before the negotiations on conventional forces in Europe (CFE) in Vienna and elsewhere. Emphasis in each case was on major mutual troop reductions (10 to 15 percent below present NATO levels initially; 25 percent later) and with the remaining forces on both sides converted to strictly defensive character.[37] Even more massive reductions in conventional forces are called for in the U.S. plan, which was presented by President Bush early in June 1989, including a ceiling of 275,000 each for U.S. and Soviet troops in Europe. (The Soviet Union would have to slash its troop strength nearly in half to reach this figure.)

It would serve no useful purpose here to speculate on the likely success of the superpowers' latest initiative. The last time that the two nations attempted to address the issue of conventional forces, during the MBFR negotiations, they talked past each other for fifteen years before finally recognizing the futility of the effort. One aspect of conventional arms control, however, that does bear keeping in mind is its certain adverse impact on the search for START and for an agreement limiting nuclear testing. There simply is no way that the superpowers can pursue all three initiatives concurrently.

UNDERLYING CONSIDERATIONS

The failure of the superpowers to achieve major arms control success can be attributed to many factors. Advancing national interests, as we have seen, is a paramount consideration. Other factors, perhaps equally significant, result from the status of the United States and the Soviet Union as the unquestioned superpowers of the present.

The fact that the United States and the Soviet Union are superpowers means that they cannot be coerced to accept solutions they do not wish, and that includes an arms control deal that they judge to be inimical to their interests.[38]

Yet often this is precisely what both nations are attempting to do. During the Iceland Summit, for instance, the Soviet Union repeatedly confronted the United States with sweeping proposals and offers. Soviet leader Gorbachev even proposed, and President Reagan agreed to, the total elimination within ten years of *all* strategic nuclear arms, including ballistic missiles, bombers, and long-range cruise missiles. The Soviet strategy was to exert pressure on the president. Not until the second day of the talks did the Soviet leader make it clear that the euphoria of terms was conditioned on keeping SDI in the laboratory for ten years. When the president balked at the suggestion, the meeting broke up.

The type of tactics employed in Iceland eventually work against the superpowers and against the prospects for arms control. In the United States the sudden realization that the president had considered in earnest, and could possibly have agreed to, the elimination of *all* strategic delivery systems within ten years caused great consternation among key members of the Congress, NATO allies, and others who believe that the route to nuclear arms sanity is not by means of broad sweeping plans but by carefully crafted small steps. Reportedly, the Iceland stalemate had the opposite effect in the Soviet Union. Disarmament advocates in Moscow (in the party and the military) found themselves being challenged by hawks, advocating increased expenditures to shore up Soviet security against the threat from the U.S. SDI.

A second consideration affecting East–West arms control relations involves the fact that neither superpower *must have* arms control to survive.[39] Their status as superpowers makes that merely a desirable option. In theory, the United States and the Soviet Union can go on building weapons forever. As long as they can prevent the occurrence of a major nuclear accident or do not direct these weapons against each other, arms control is not essential to their survival.

Since arms control, then, is merely a desirable option, neither superpower has an incentive to accede to a treaty that is not a "good" one. By superpower definition a "good" treaty is one that advances national interests, one that is characterized by fairness, and one in which both sides give up something equally.

Fair and equal treaties presuppose terms that are fair and equal, an area in which neither superpower can lay claim to significant accomplishment. Again and again, the United States and the Soviet Union have confronted each other with proposals that have been so one-sided as to preclude the possibility of agreement or even serious negotiation.[40] What conclusions could one reach, for instance, from the Soviet proposal in 1983 for an ASAT moratorium as a precondition to talks on space weapons control? It was made when the Soviet Union possessed an operational ASAT weapon while the United States did not. Why would a U.S. president accept such an offer? In the same nonstarter category were early Soviet proposals at the START talks that defined as "strategic" any delivery system able by virtue of its location to strike the territory of the other side. Applied to the European area, this definition would have reduced in half the great majority of the U.S. planes and missiles stationed in the NATO area (because of their capability to reach Soviet territory) while excluding from the same cuts most of the Soviet weapons.

The superpowers have little to show for their arms control efforts of the past twenty years. Success will continue to ellude them until they begin applying in their arms control dealings "a spirit beyond national interests" (the quote is from President Reagan's 1983 address before the U.N. General Assembly) and they abandon the game playing and search for unilateral advantage that now occupies so much of their time.

In summary, the superpowers are pursuing arms control only when it serves their own long-term interests. The worldwide outcry for an end to the arms race, the marches and peace demonstrations, are irrelevant to the process. So is Article VI of the NPT, which calls upon them to pursue negotiations toward a treaty on general and complete disarmament. Arms control must serve the superpowers' *own* interests or it serves no purpose.

The superpowers are aware that the odds are extremely low that areas of potential agreement will ever be found. Accordingly, while pursuing the search for illusive deals, they also act to convey to the world an earnest effort at finding solutions. For the benefit of world public opinion: they publicize their unfailing opposition to the nuclear arms race but continue to build bigger and better weapons;[41] they warn of the irrationality of nuclear war but blindly pursue actions likely to increase the risk of nuclear war; they preach of the need to reverse the process but refuse to take even the most minute risks on the route to nuclear sanity.

In many ways, the superpowers are playing games with nuclear arms control, the kind in which points are scored for gaining national advantage rather than for practical measures to end the nuclear arms race.

NOTES

1. Richard Nixon, *1999: Victory without War* (New York: Simon & Schuster, 1988), p. 66; and Harvard Nuclear Study Group, *Living with Nuclear Weapons* (Cambridge, MA: Harvard University Press, 1983), p. 5. For the opposite view, that nuclear weapons can be totally "eliminated," see George F. Kennan, *The Nuclear Delusion* (New York: Pantheon Books, 1982), p. 72.

2. Jerry F. Hough, "Soviet Decision Making on Defense," *Bulletin of Atomic Scientists*, August 1985, pp. 84–88; George G. Weickhardt, "The Military Consensus Behind Soviet Arms Control Proposals," *Bulletin of Atomic Scientists*, September 1987, pp. 20–24.

3. Harvard Nuclear Study Group, *Living with Nuclear Weapons*, p. 195.

4. George Shultz, "Realism and Responsibility: The U.S. Approach to Arms Control," in U.S. Department of State, Bureau of Public Affairs, *Realism, Strength, Negotiation: Key Foreign Policy Statements of the Reagan Administration* (Washington, DC: U.S. Government Printing Office, 1984).

5. Robert M. Gates, "The Uneven Cycles of Kremlin Reform," *Washington Post*, April 30, 1989. See also Interview with Gen. John Galvin, NATO commander, "Keep the Power Dry," *Time*, May 29, 1989.

6. U.S. Department of State, Bureau of Public Affairs, *Security and Arms Control: The Search for a More Stable Peace* (Washington, DC: U.S. Government Print-

ing Office, 1984), p. 23. For a recent example of the U.S. labeling a Soviet unitiative as "propaganda," see Helen Dewar, "Secretary of Defense Calls Soviet Attack on NATO Arms Plans "Propaganda," *Washington Post*, February 2, 1988.

7. U.S. Department of State, Bureau of Public Affairs, *Fundamentals of U.S. Foreign Policy* (Washington, DC: U.S. Government Printing Office, 1988), p. 12.

8. Edward L. Rowny, *Negotiating with the Soviet Union: Then and Now*, Current Policy no. 1088 (Washington, DC: U.S. Department of State, Bureau of Public Affairs, June 30, 1988); idem, *Effective Arms Control Demands a Broad Approach*, Current Policy no. 955 (Washington, DC: U.S. Department of State, Bureau of Public Affairs, April 27, 1987); idem, *Principles and Initiatives in U.S. Arms Control Policy*, Current Policy no. 975 (Washington, DC: U.S. Department of State, Bureau of Public Affairs, June 9, 1987).

9. The United States lists its arms control objectives as strengthening security, promoting and defending freedom, and resolving disputes peacefully. In contrast, notes the United States, Soviet objectives are to challenge U.S. vital interests, promote socialism, create division within the West, and support insurgent movements designed to replace friendly governments with authoritarian/totalitarian regimes.

10. Jonathan Dean, "Gorbachev's Arms Control Moves," *Bulletin of Atomic Scientists*, June 1987, pp. 34–40.

11. White House Digest, *President Reagan on Peace, Arms Reductions, and Deterrence* (Washington, DC, November 18, 1983).

12. George Shultz, *The INF Treaty Strengthening U.S. Security*, Current Policy no. 1038 (Washington, DC: U.S. Department of State, Bureau of Public Affairs, January 25, 1988) and idem, *The INF Treaty: Advancing U.S. Security Interests*, Current Policy no. 1057 (Washington, DC: U.S. Department of State, Bureau of Public Affairs, March 14, 1988).

13. The Nuclear Risk Reduction Centers in Moscow and Washington became operational in April 1988.

14. U.S. Arms Control and Disarmament Agency, *Annual Report to the Congress, 1986* (Washington, DC: U.S. ACDA, January 17, 1987), pp. 55–58. See also John Borawski, "Accord at Stockholm," *Bulletin of Atomic Scientists*, December 1986.

15. "Nuclear Proliferation: The Third Review Conference on the NPT," *Disarmament*, Winter 1985. See also Congressional Research Service, *The Treaty on the Non-Proliferation of Nuclear Weapons: The 1985 Review Conference and Matters of Congressional Interest* (Washington, DC: April 22, 1985).

16. On September 22, 1988, President Reagan, in an address before the U.N. General Assembly, called for an international conference to "put teeth" in the 1925 Geneva Protocol. The conference was held in Paris in January 1989 but was mired in controversy over the relationship between chemical and nuclear weapons.

17. Refer to Chapter 6 for a detailed discussion of U.S.–Soviet negotiations relating to the cessation of nuclear testing.

18. For a brief statement of U.S. nuclear test policy, refer to U.S. Department of State, Bureau of Public Affairs, *U.S. Policy Regarding Limitations on Nuclear Testing*, Special Report no. 150 (Washington, DC: August 1986).

19. In a report to the Congress late in September 1988, the Reagan administration expressed the view that it does not regard "nuclear testing as an evil to be curtailed." Nuclear testing, it added, would be even more important should a START agreement come into being.

20. Presidential Statement, March 14, 1986.

21. Jesse James, "Nuclear Test Agreement Signed at Summit," *Arms Control Today*, January/February 1988, p. 25. See also R. Jeffrey Smith, "Soviet Team to Monitor H-Bomb Test," *Washington Post*, August 16, 1988.

22. Refer to Chapter 6 for a detailed discussion of U.S.–Soviet negotiations relating to strategic reductions.

23. Editorial, "The NATO Impasse," *Washington Post*, May 4, 1989; see also Don Oberdorfer and R. Jeffrey Smith, "U.S. Reaffirms Opposition to Bonn Arms Talk Demand," *Washington Post*, May 3, 1989; Rowland Evans and Robert Novak, "Missile Misery," *Washington Post*, April 28, 1989.

24. David B. Ottaway, "Baker Asks Soviets to Cut Short-Range Atom Arms," *Washington Post*, June 9, 1989.

25. Mary McGrory, "Treaty Trashing," *Washington Post*, February 12, 1987.

26. Rowny: *Negotiating with the Soviet Union*; Soviet tactics are reviewed in Congressional Research Service, Library of Congress, *Fundamentals of Nuclear Arms Control* (Washington, DC: U.S. Government Printing Office, 1986), pp. 277–80. See also M. Scott Davis and Leon Sloss, eds., *A Game of High Stakes* (Cambridge, MA: Ballinger, 1986).

27. George J. Church, "A Farewell to Arms?" *Time*, January 27, 1986; David Hoffman, "President Grateful; Aides Cautious on Soviet Arms Control Proposal," *Washington Post*, January 17, 1986.

28. David Hoffman, "President Says Soviets Serious on Arms Cuts," *Washington Post*, June 20, 1986.

29. George J. Church, "Madison Avenue, Moscow: As Baker Sits Tight, Gorbachev Wins Another Public Relations Round," *Time*, May 22, 1989.

30. David Hoffman, "Gorbachev Gambits Challenged," *Washington Post*, May 17, 1989.

31. Ann Devroy, "Quayle Labels Gorbachev's Offers PR Gambits," *Washington Post*, May 20, 1989.

32. David Hoffman, "Bush Again Rejects Missile Cut," *Washington Post*, July 7, 1989.

33. Albert Carnesale and Richard N. Haass, eds., *Superpower Arms Control: Setting the Record Straight* (Cambridge, MA: Ballinger, 1987), Chapter 10.

34. U.S. Arms Control and Disarmament Agency, *Annual Report to the Congress for 1987* (Washington, DC: U.S. ACDA, February 24, 1988), pp. 7–19.

35. U.S. Arms Control and Disarmament Agency, *Annual Report to the Congress, 1986*, pp. 14–16 and 19–20. See also Committee on International Security and Arms Control, National Academy of Sciences, *Reykjavik and Beyond* (Washington, DC: National Academy Press, 1988), p. 2.

36. Dennis Menos, *World at Risk: The Debate over Arms Control* (Jefferson, NC: McFarland, 1986), p. 53.

37. Jill Smolowe, "Let's Count Down: The Superpowers Want to Shrink Conventional Arms, but Don't Agree How," *Time*, March 20, 1989.

38. Committee on International Security and Arms Control, National Academy of Sciences, *Nuclear Arms Control: Background and Issues* (Washington, DC: National Academy Press, 1985), p. 20.

39. Paul C. Warnke, "Is Arms Control Possible?" *Washington Post*, October 6, 1985.

40. Strobe Talbott, *Deadly Gambits* (New York: Knopf, 1984), is an excellent source on the process used by the United States in formulating proposals and developing negotiating positions for INF and START.

41. On January 13, 1989, the White House released a report that recommends spending $81 billion over twenty years to modernize and upgrade the nation's nuclear weapons complex.

3

The Impotent Opposition

Standing by helplessly, watching the superpowers' never-ending quest for bigger and better weapons, are the world's billions—the nuclear havenots.

FRUSTRATION AT THE UNITED NATIONS

Nowhere is frustration greater than at the United Nations. It is hardly surprising. For more than forty years, the international organization has pursued the cause of nuclear disarmament with the greatest of urgency.[1] It has pleaded with the superpowers to control their nuclear arms, beseeched them to place mankind's interests ahead of their own, offered plans and proposals designed to translate words into action—but to no avail.

The superpowers are not really adverse to having the nuclear issue discussed before the United Nations provided that the U.N. role is limited to discussion, not to concrete measures likely to affect their national interests. The need to arrest the arms race, the hopes of mankind, are secondary considerations. The superpowers' only objective at the United Nations is to protect their own special status in the world and to advance their national interests.

The world received its first lesson in superpower disarmament politics as early as 1946, when both the United States and the Soviet Union submitted proposals[2] before the international organization for ending the production of nuclear weapons and the destruction of existing stockpiles. There was a major difference, though, in the two plans: the U.S. proposal called for international controls and sanctions to be effectively in place before production of nuclear weapons could cease; the Soviet plan would go into effect immediately on entry of the agreement into force—no controls, nothing.

Neither plan succeeded; respective national interests would not allow it. The United States, which already possessed nuclear weapons, would not trade its nuclear monopoly for an empty Soviet promise not to produce in the future. Neither was the Soviet Union prepared to accept the status of a second-rate power, which, clearly, acceptance of the U.S. plan implied.

The world organization confronted its first major failure by reorganizing its resources for disarmament negotiation. A new organization was created, the Disarmament Commission, consisting initially of the members of the U.N. Security Council and Canada.[3] But despite successive reorganizations and a plethora of proposals before it for the regulation and reduction of nuclear armaments, the commission accomplished little during the five years it served as the primary U.N. disarmament body. The superpowers intimidated its every effort, in the process insuring for themselves the freedom to continue exploiting the atom in support of their national interests.

In an effort to break the impasse, the U.N. General Assembly voted in 1959 to place on its agenda an item entitled "general and complete disarmament under effective international control."[4] This was a big order and one that the world organization, considering its record of nonaccomplishment, was foolhardy to want to undertake. Concurrently, the Ten-Nation Committee on Disarmament was established, the predecessor of the current Conference on Disarmament.

Nothing came of "general and complete disarmament under effective international control" or of the work of the Ten-Nation Committee. Next the U.N. General Assembly tried a different approach: it proclaimed the 1970s as the First Disarmament Decade,[5] a period for nations and governments to "intensify their efforts to achieve effective measures relating to the cessation of the nuclear arms race."

From a public relations perspective, the First Disarmament Decade did fairly well. There were conferences and workshops and lofty pronouncements by world leaders on the pressing need to slow down and eventually reverse the nuclear arms race. But to no one's surprise, not one nuclear device was eliminated. During that period, the superpowers were busy perfecting their latest generation of weapons: intercontinental ballistic missiles (ICBMs) equipped with multiple independently targeted reentry vehicles (MIRVs).

Throughout the 1970s, U.N. frustration persisted and so did the search for an approach likely to bring about a favorable superpower response to the nuclear issue. With the arms race becoming increasingly more threatening, the General Assembly even decided to do a little soul searching of its own. In 1975 it asked the opinion of all of its members on what the U.N. role should be in the field of disarmament; in typical fashion, it also created a new body to address the problem, the Committee on the Review of the Role of the United Nations in the Field of Disarmament.[6]

There was never any doubt how the nuclear havenots would respond to the U.N. inquiry. In near unison they demanded a greater involvement of the international organization in disarmament affairs and an end to the nuclear arms race. At the urging of several members, a call went out for a "Special" Session of the U.N. General Assembly dedicated to the issue of disarmament. The session was to signal the beginning of a new era for mankind, one no longer threatened by nuclear arms.

As U.N. conferences go, the first Special Session on Disarmament held during the summer of 1978 was a success. (In contrast, the second Special Session four years later was a flop. The third session held in June 1988 was an outright embarrassment, despite the attendance of almost sixty heads of state, presidents, and prime ministers from 158 nations). All U.N. members attended the first session and approved its Final Document,[7] a comprehensive although grossly idealistic framework of the international community's disarmament goals for the years ahead. Included in the Final Document was also a *Program of Action*, replete with priorities and measures that member states were to undertake.

Because of superpower reluctance to take action on any disarmament issue, unless it also advanced their own national interests, the Final Document of the first Special Session rapidly became a footnote in history. Nothing ever came of it. To be sure, the U.N. General Assembly did try to salvage it during its second Special Session by unanimously reaffirming its validity, but the Final Document launched with such great hopes in 1978 is for all practical purposes dead.

The superpowers' true colors were displayed once again during the second Special Session.[8] Totally preoccupied with their own interests, they refused to give serious consideration to any of the sixty proposals placed before the conference or to the thousands of communications, petitions, and appeals that reached U.N. Headquarters in connection with the session. Without superpower support and cooperation, not a single substantive proposal could be adopted. As a consolation prize, the conference managed to launch another disarmament forum, the World Disarmament Campaign.[9] Its orders were to "inform, educate, and generate public understanding and support for disarmament." The action hardly caused a stir of excitement. The general public had no need for additional information on the potential benefits of disarmament. What it did need was fewer nuclear weapons in the arsenals of the superpowers. On this, the key issue before it, the United Nations was unable to deliver.[10]

In fairness to the superpowers, their participation in the United Nations during the past forty years has not been entirely in vain. In between foot dragging and obstruction, they did manage to agree on half a dozen disarmament initiatives (all of them, incidentally, fairly worthwhile). Naturally, no reductions in nuclear armaments were involved, and neither did the resulting agreements constrain the superpowers from expanding their nuclear forces. But by their action, the United States and the Soviet Union appeared to be heeding mankind's calls for nuclear restraint—and that was a welcome beginning.

Five of the initiatives involved the conclusion of agreements prohibiting the introduction of nuclear weapons into certain areas of our planet heretofore nuclear-free, that is, the Antarctica, outer space, the moon, the seabed, and Latin America.[11] The superpowers welcomed these accords, not only because they involved no real sacrifices on their part but also because they enhanced their own security. The Outer Space Treaty, for example, bans nuclear and other weapons of mass destruction from the Earth's orbit or their stationing in outer space.[12] It also prohibits the military use of celestial bodies or the placement of nuclear weapons on them. The treaty makes both superpowers more secure in the knowledge that the other side cannot threaten them by placing weapons in outer space, against which no defense presently exists.

The remaining two initiatives to which the superpowers became parties are the Limited Test Ban Treaty (LTBT), signed in 1963, and the Treaty on the Non-Proliferation of Nuclear Weapons (NPT) (1968). Although both of these accords were negotiated and signed under U.N. auspices and as such are generally included in the international organization's record of accomplishments, their existence today is more due to the efforts of the superpowers than those of the United Nations. In retrospect, both the United States and the Soviet Union do not regret having taken an active role in the development of the LTBT and the NPT. The two treaties have advanced superpower interests and security and, undoubtedly, have resulted in a safer world for everyone.

General and Complete Disarmament

From the outset, the United Nations has been enamored with the idea of "general and complete disarmament" (not *arms control*, which is a fairly recent term of U.S. origin). In fact, the first resolution ever adopted by the U.N. General Assembly dealt with this issue.[13] It called for the elimination of all nuclear and other weapons of mass destruction and the assurance that atomic energy would be used only for peaceful purposes.

Since general and complete disarmament was a major U.N. goal, it is not surprising that the organization would devote enormous time and energy in search of an adequate definition for the process. Both superpowers actively collaborated in this, presumably, there being no risk in talking. In 1961, for instance, representatives of the United States and of the Soviet Union met to establish ground rules for future disarmament negotiations. Their conclusions were recorded in a Joint Statement (the McCloy/Zorin Agreement[14]), which was subsequently adopted by their respective governments and the United Nations as the foundation for future negotiations toward general and complete disarmament.

Admittedly, the McCloy/Zorin Agreement was years ahead of its time. It spoke of disestablishing the armed forces of all nations; the dismantling of military bases; the elimination of stockpiles of nuclear, chemical, bacteriological, and other weapons of mass destruction; the cessation of military training; and much more. Few persons today share this vision. But in 1961 general and complete disarmament "under effective international control" (the words in quote were added at U.S. insistence) was official American and Soviet policy. To underscore their support for this policy, both superpowers submitted soon thereafter elaborate proposals for disarmament based on the principles of the McCloy/Zorin agreement.

It is extremely doubtful that the superpowers had really intended to translate the lofty pronouncements of McCloy/Zorin into real action. It is equally doubtful that many nations of the world expected them to. A total stalemate in U.S.–Soviet negotiations soon developed, convincing even the most ardent of U.N. disarmament activists of the utter impossibility of achieving general and complete disarmament by means of a single, sweeping, comprehensive plan. By the mid-1960s most persons in and outside the U.N. organization had come to realize what the superpowers had known all along: general and complete disarmament was no more than a long-term goal and a very long-term goal at that.

Still, interest in designing a master plan for general and complete disarmament persisted in the halls and corridors of the United Nations. In 1969 the General Assembly decided to act. Presumably the fact that the superpowers had failed to solve the problem was no reason for the United Nations not to try. The Assembly turned to the Conference on Disarmament, its subsidiary organization based in Geneva,[15] and directed it to draft a "comprehensive program"[16] for dealing with all aspects of the cessation of the nuclear arms race, with a view toward general and complete disarmament under international control.

Twenty years later, the "comprehensive program" is still in work at the conference,[17] and despite repeated efforts by the General Assembly to resuscitate the process, little of any real substance has been produced. The underlying problem is the superpower confrontation. The United States and the Soviet Union differ not only on procedural aspects of disarmament (for instance, the timing of specific actions) but more importantly on the very nature of the disarmament commitment that is expected of them.

Nuclear Disarmament

Despite the lack of accomplishments at Geneva and elsewhere, U.N. dedication to the goal of nuclear disarmament remains unabated. The accelerated arms race, the ever-growing threat of a nuclear holocaust due to error or accident, and predictions of a nuclear winter likely to engulf the planet after a large-scale nuclear exchange all have contributed to raising public consciousness of the nuclear issue. All nations have a vital interest in negotiations on nuclear disarmament, because the existence of nuclear weapons jeopardizes the security of all, nuclear and nonnuclear nations alike.

At no time do these feelings become more evident than during the annual U.N. General Assembly meetings, when the havenots normally field a sustained lobbying effort for nuclear disarmament.[18] But the results are always the same: a lot of talk, feeble excuses by the superpowers why proposals cannot be implemented now, and vague promises of future unspecified action.

Two resolutions on the subject, considered by the U.N. General Assembly during its forty-second session, illustrate the point. On October 26, 1987, China submitted a draft resolution entitled "Nuclear Disarmament."[19] Its purpose, it explained, was to urge the two superpowers to carry out negotiations on nuclear disarmament in earnest and to create the conditions under which the smaller nuclear weapon states could participate. How did the superpowers respond? The Soviet Union "welcomed" the resolution as proof of the awareness of the world community of the need for practical decisions on matters of nuclear disarmament. The United States asserted that it recognized its responsibilities as a nuclear power, as evidenced by the fact that it was negotiating with the Soviet Union in Geneva on measures for the reduction of nuclear arms. So much for Resolution 42/38H of the forty-second session.

Likewise, on October 27, 1987, twenty-one nations (including several U.S. allies: Australia, Canada, Denmark, Greece, Japan, the Netherlands, Norway, and the Philippines) submitted a draft resolution on the prohibition of the production of fissionable material for weapons purposes.[20] Cessation of the production of fissionable materials, argued the resolution's drafters, would advance the cause of nuclear disarmament by ending the vertical and horizontal proliferation of weapons. On November 30, 1987, the General Assembly adopted the resolution by a vote of 148 to 1 (France) with 6 abstentions. The abstentions were all from nuclear weapons states, or nations at the nuclear threshold, and included the United States, the United Kingdom, China, India, Argentina, and Brazil. The Soviet Union, the only nuclear weapons state to vote for the resolution, did so reluctantly and with the understanding, it said, that the issue would be reexamined later by all nuclear weapons states.

Throughout the years, literally hundreds of resolutions dealing with the issue of nuclear disarmament have been debated before the U.N. General Assembly. The United States has generally responded to them with indifference, the Soviet Union with a lot of political savvy, seeing in them an opportunity for public relations benefit. The U.S. position reflects national policy and the belief that nuclear disarmament cannot be separated from conventional arms control. Both must be carried out simultaneously, since the elimination of nuclear weapons, without proper adjustment in the size and composition of conventional forces, would destroy deterrence and increase the likelihood of war.[21] The best way for nations to enhance international stability and their own security, the United States believes, is for all nations to live up to their obligations under the U.N. Charter.

The Soviet Union is displaying a lot of "street smarts" when responding to U.N. proposals for nuclear disarmament. Its usual posture is to draw attention to Soviet plans previously offered, even if irrelevant. The cessation of nuclear weapons production, their reduction, and their ultimate elimination, argues the Soviet Union, should be done on a stage-by-stage basis, with the strategic balance being maintained during the period that stockpiles are being lowered.

Nonuse of Nuclear Weapons

As expected, the likely use of nuclear weapons, either during a confrontation between the superpowers or as a result of accident or other unforeseen circumstance, is a cause of considerable anxiety to the nuclear havenots. It supports their contention that nuclear weapons, because of their extreme devastating effects (irrespective of international boundaries) are a threat to all nations, not merely to those against whom they are being employed.[22]

Throughout the years the United Nations has addressed this issue on numerous occasions, searching for practical measures to guard against the threat of use of nuclear weapons. Proposals considered have ranged from outright prohibition of use to a restriction on first use only.[23] But despite repeated condemnations of nuclear weapons as instruments of war and characterization of their use as a "crime against mankind and civilization," a formal agreement on the issue is still eluding the world organization.

Leading the international effort to ban the use of nuclear weapons is India, itself a nuclear power but one that presumably is prepared to forego the nuclear option if everyone else does. The vehicle chosen by India to make its case is a resolution offered on the opening day of every U.N. General Assembly session. The Indian resolution[24] is brief and to the point: use of nuclear weapons would threaten the survival of mankind, would be a crime against humanity; the U.N. has debated the issue long enough—the time for action is now. The specific action that India proposes is the adoption of an International Convention on the Prohibition of the Use of Nuclear Weapons, a proposal supported by most nuclear havenots.

The resolutions by India usually follow the same route. The great majority of U.N. members support them, the United States and some Western nations oppose them, and there are generally a few abstentions. Approval of the resolutions implies that the buck is passed back again to the Conference on Disarmament in Geneva (the General Assembly's debating society) for another try at developing a consensus. India and most of the other supporters of the nonuse initiative are aware that little if anything can be accomplished in Geneva as long as the superpower positions on the issue continue to be diametrically opposed.[25]

In 1978, when India first proposed its nonuse resolution, the Soviet Union pointedly abstained, because the prohibition, so it claimed, was being considered in isolation from the larger problem of the nonuse of force in international relations. The Soviet Union, however, no longer takes this position. During the forty-second session of the U.N. General Assembly it joined 135 other nations in voting in the affirmative on the Indian resolution, "in recognition of the urgent need for action to save human civilization and to rid society of the nuclear threat."[26] In contrast, the United States and several Western nations continue to oppose any restrictions on the use of nuclear weapons. Opposition flows from deterrence, the underlying U.S. strategy for reducing the risk of nuclear war. Deterrence can work only if the threat of the use of nuclear weapons remains credible to the other side.

The superpowers are likewise divided on the related issue of *first* use of nuclear weapons. The United States has never renounced the option of being the first nation to use nuclear weapons in a time of conflict, but China and the Soviet Union have. Supporters of the first-use policy maintain that it is needed to deter nuclear war; opponents argue that first use would violate the principles of human morality. The gap separating the two sides is so wide that no amount of U.N. debate or intercession can ever expect to bridge it.

Cessation of Nuclear Testing

Throughout some forty years of disarmament efforts one fundamental issue has preoccupied the United Nations: how to end nuclear testing and in the process bring about a slowdown in the nuclear arms race. The international organization has devoted enormous time and energy toward this goal, providing appropriate forums for debate, creating specialized organizations to address particularly sticky issues (such as verification), and offering its good offices whenever an agreement between the superpowers appeared likely.[27] But this has all been to no avail.

It would be grossly unfair to blame the United Nations for the discouraging record of the past forty years. Responsibility for continued nuclear testing rests with the world's nuclear weapon states—primarily the United States,[28] France, and the United Kingdom—and their national security policies, which demand that such testing be continued. If the United Nations is to share the blame, it is for its refusal to recognize its own impotence. No matter how many conferences the United Nations convenes or how extensive the debate, a comprehensive nuclear test ban treaty will not come about until the military and civilian leaders in Moscow and Washington decide that such a treaty is in their national interest. The Limited Test Ban

Treaty signed in 1963 is a good case in point. Despite sustained U.N. negotiating efforts continuing more than ten years; despite the drafting of proposals and compromises likely to appeal to the superpowers; and despite the international uproar over the radioactive fallout resulting from U.S. and Soviet nuclear weapons tests, the LTBT became a reality only after the superpowers discovered a formula designed to advance their national interests.[29] The formula has allowed them to continue nuclear testing while muting international protests by suspending atmospheric testing. The superpowers lost absolutely nothing by signing the LTBT.

The complete record of U.N. efforts directed at the conclusion of a nuclear test ban agreement is far too voluminous for inclusion here. It dates from the early 1950s, when Jawaharlal Nehru, then prime minister of India, proposed a convention to end all nuclear testing as the first step of worldwide nuclear disarmament.[30] At the superpower level, the record is replete with years of bickering, delays and subterfuge, deadlocked negotiations, and a near-total preoccupation with the next generation of weapons that would need testing and, therefore, make a treaty impractical. For the nuclear have-nots, the record is one of frustration but always thrust in hope that perhaps the next plan will prove to be acceptable to the superpowers.

For a great many years after signing the LTBT, the superpowers walked away from the issue of a total test ban, leaving it up to the United Nations to pick up the pieces. Within the international organization the task fell on the Conference on Disarmament meeting in Geneva. Twice each year, since 1963, the conference has placed the question of a total nuclear test ban on its agenda, has debated the merits of the various plans before it, has stumbled against the uncompromising positions of the superpowers, and has promptly retreated. The cycle has been repeated with ironic similarity for twenty-five years.[31]

The failure of the conference to achieve any measure of success reflects the diametrically opposed views of the superpowers, compounded by vacillation and shifts in policy in Washington and Moscow. During the 1960s, for instance, the United States did in fact favor a ban on nuclear testing but felt compelled to resist Soviet overtures at signing an agreement because of concerns over the issue of verification.[32] Any such ban, the United States insisted, would have to include on-site inspections (OSI) of Soviet territory in addition to whatever black boxes or other scientific instruments were used. The demand for OSI was unacceptable to the Soviet Union, and an agreement did not materialize. Incidentally, the Soviet Union is no longer opposed to OSI, as evidenced by the terms of the INF treaty and of the Joint Verification Experiment, signed in December 1987, which allowed experts from both countries to observe each other's nuclear tests.[33]

Policy shifts in Moscow and Washington during the mid- and late 1970s twice helped break the deadlock. In 1974–1976, while the international community in Geneva was busy debating the pros and cons of a total test ban, the superpowers working outside the conference came up with two partial agreements: the Threshold Test Ban Treaty (TTBT) and the Peaceful Nuclear Explosions Treaty (PNET).[34] The action did not amount to a great deal, as evidenced by the fact that fifteen years later neither treaty had legally entered force. In 1977 following private talks between the Soviet Union and the United States, trilateral negotiations (with the participation of the United Kingdom) began for the ostensible purpose of achieving a comprehensive test ban. Several rounds of talks took place, but national interests on all sides demanded that the effort soon be abandoned.

The United States has never officially said so, but it has always acted as if it considered the U.N.'s Conference on Disarmament preoccupation with the nuclear test issue to be meddling in superpower affairs. The Soviet Union has taken the opposite view, judging the conference as an ideal forum for advancing Soviet negotiating positions and for criticizing those of the United States. Especially during the Reagan administration, the United States has stubbornly resisted all conference initiatives designed to break the superpower deadlock leading to a test agreement. In the administration's view, continued nuclear testing was essential[35] to maintain the reliability of the nuclear stockpile, to develop state-of-the-art warheads for new systems, and to research new sophisticated weapons for possible application in ballistic missile defenses.

Throughout the 1980s, and despite the highest priority afforded the nuclear test issue, lack of progress has continued to characterize the work of the conference. A draft treaty, proposed by Sweden,[36] has been awaiting action since 1983. Its verification provisions are more than ample, providing, among other things, for exchanges of seismological data, international OSI, and appropriate machinery for resolving compliance disputes. Next on the conference's agenda (not expected to go very far) is the creation of a multilateral body to negotiate the treaty.

In the meantime, back at the U.N. General Assembly where basic policy on the nuclear test issue is supposed to be formulated, frustration and the annual battle of resolutions continue unabated.[37] During 1987 the Assembly adopted four resolutions but not one by consensus. As always, the great majority of nations support the immediate suspension of nuclear testing; the United States, France, and the United Kingdom oppose it; and about a dozen U.S. allies abstain out of deference to the U.S. position.[38]

By far the most direct of the resolutions considered by the General Assembly in 1987 was one submitted by New Zealand.[39] Titled appropriately "Urgent need for a comprehensive nuclear test ban," the resolution reaffirmed that a treaty to achieve the prohibition of all nuclear test explosions by all nations, in all environments, and for all time, was a matter of fundamental importance to mankind. The General Assembly listened, debated, and voted (143 for, 2 against, and 8 abstentions). Once more it instructed the Conference on Disarmament to begin practical work toward a nuclear test ban treaty beginning with its 1988 session.

What is the likelihood that the Conference on Disarmament will succeed soon where it has failed during the past twenty-five years? Practically nil. Of the three largest nuclear weapon states only the Soviet Union favors an early beginning of negotiations on the conclusion of a comprehensive test ban treaty. The United Kingdom is opposed because it believes the technical and practical problems involved in establishing an international seismic monitoring system for purposes of verification have not yet been resolved. The United States is likewise opposed to a treaty. Its policy is to seek verification improvements in the existing TTBT and PNET treaties first and then to engage the Soviet Union in direct talks on ways to implement a step-by-step program of limiting and ultimately ending nuclear testing. (The United States obviously considers the nuclear test ban to be a superpower problem, one to be resolved by them in direct talks, without the meddling of the forty-member Conference on Disarmament.)

Preventing an Arms Race in Outer Space

Preventing the nuclear arms race now threatening Earth from engulfing outer space as well is another issue that has preoccupied the world organization for many years.[40] In fact, two of the few U.N. accomplishments in the area of disarmament, the Outer Space Treaty and the Agreement Governing the Activities of States on the Moon and Other Celestial Bodies, are direct results of sustained U.N. concern with the issue and active intercession on its behalf with the superpowers.

Despite the unusual success, the threat to mankind posed by space weapons now in the laboratories of the superpowers remains at the forefront of U.N. concerns. Three reasons account for the continued anxiety: (1) increased development by both sides of weapons capable of destroying or incapacitating satellites, (2) initiation in 1983 by the United States of its Strategic Defense Initiative (SDI) program (the Soviet Union has had an SDI of its own for many years), and (3) radically differing perceptions of the issue by the superpowers, making all U.N. efforts at a compromise utterly useless.

The situation is no different than in the disarmament initiatives previously reviewed. In the judgment of the majority of U.N. members, a real threat exists; the superpowers are at odds on how to address it; the international organization lacks the punch to impose a solution. Meanwhile, the dimensions of the threat are increasing. The situation is no different, too, with respect to the individual positions taken by the superpowers: the Soviet Union, dazzling its fellow U.N. members with resolutions, draft treaties, and proposals for action; the United States continuing to be the odd man out resisting any changes in the status quo. In 1986, and again in 1987, the United States was the single opposing or abstaining vote on U.N. General Assembly resolutions calling for development of an international agreement on the issue.[41] All other U.N. nations present (154 in 1987, 151 in 1986) supported the resolutions.

At the Conference on Disarmament in Geneva,[42] where the issue resides between sessions of the General Assembly, an ad hoc working group was established in 1985. Its mandate, however, is not to develop the desired treaty but merely to examine issues "relevant to the prevention of an arms race in outer space." As of this writing, the working group's only accomplishment is the fact that it exists and that it provides a forum where the nuclear havenots can let off steam.

Is There Hope?

For forty years, on issues of disarmament, the international organization has been extravagant in oratory but fairly limited on accomplishments. The question arises: what is it about the United Nations, its structure, or the manner in which it approaches disarmament that makes results so difficult?

The international organization, undoubtedly, has numerous shortcomings. Most of them, however, are not of its own making. The majority of problems that cause the organization's impotence have their roots in the policies of the governments that make up its membership, primarily those of the superpowers.

It is not uncommon for the superpowers to blame each other, in public, over the prevailing stalemate. In private, however, their views bear great similarity. The international community, they admit, can coax and cajole, but there is little it can do to advance agreements in the nuclear field until the main elements of these agreements have been agreed to by the superpowers. Their comment applies especially to the Conference on Disarmament, which increasingly, during the past decade, has been assuming negotiating as opposed to debating responsibilities. The superpowers are prepared to grant the conference the role of a booster or cheerleader of superpower interests, but a role resulting in the loss of their most prized possessions—never.

THE FIVE CONTINENT PEACE INITIATIVE

Until the early 1980s, the U.N. General Assembly and its subsidiary disarmament agencies have provided the only forums for nonnuclear nations to make their views known on the nuclear issue. But nothing much has resulted from such oratory. The superpowers listen politely to the customary admonitions of the havenot nations, respond briefly with assurances of hope, and then revert to business as usual.

In 1984 a new player was added to the international scene, a sort of megalobby for disarmament known as the Five Continent Peace Initiative. Formed by the leaders of India, Tanzania, Mexico, Argentina, Greece, and Sweden, the Peace Initiative is designed to serve as the voice of the nuclear havenots and the means by which they hope to convince the superpowers that a global crisis, which the nuclear arms race is, demands a global solution.

The message of the Five Continent Peace Initiative is simple: the escalating arms race is increasing the risk of nuclear war; a war fought with nuclear weapons would bring death and destruction to all peoples; nonnuclear nations are no less threatened by nuclear war than are the nuclear weapons states; responsibility for preventing nuclear war belongs to the superpowers, but the problem is far too important to be left to them alone. It is a sensible message and one that every nuclear havenot can subscribe to, regardless of ideological orientation or political encumbrances.

The leaders of the Five Continent Peace Initiative have no illusions about the enormity of the task before them. They are aware also that the superpowers do not welcome advice on how to handle their affairs, especially when such advice comes from nations the size of Greece and Sweden. It is to the credit of these leaders that they have launched the initiative and that they are persisting at it, despite the obvious annoyance of one of the superpowers (the United States) and the attempts by the other (the Soviet Union) to manipulate their effort for propaganda purposes.

The initial declaration of the Five Continent Peace Initiative was issued on May 22, 1984, six months into the total breakdown of U.S.–Soviet negotiations that followed the deployment of the first Pershing II missiles in Europe. "The rush towards global suicide must be stopped," stressed the declaration. "The survival of mankind is in jeopardy. We urge as a necessary first step, the United States and the Soviet Union, as well as the United Kingdom, France and China, to halt all testing, production and deployment of nuclear weapons and their delivery systems, to be immediately followed by substantial reductions in nuclear forces."[43]

Seven months later, the six leaders met in person in New Delhi, India, to repeat their basic message to the superpowers. Recent atmospheric and biological studies, they noted, indicated that in addition to causing blast, heat, and radiation, nuclear war, even on a limited scale, would trigger an arctic nuclear winter that could transform the earth into a darkened, frozen planet, posing unprecedented peril to all nations, even those far removed from the explosions. This makes it even more pressing that nuclear weapons never be used and nuclear war never be fought.

In the formal declaration, which was issued at the conclusion of the New Delhi meeting,[44] the six leaders once again challenged the superpowers to bring the arms race to a halt. "We reiterate our appeal for an all-embracing halt to the testing, production and deployment of nuclear weapons and their

delivery systems," they wrote. "Such a halt would greatly facilitate negotiations. Two specific steps today require special attention: the prevention
of an arms race in outer space and a comprehensive test ban treaty."

The nuclear weapons freeze, called for by the New Delhi Declaration,
failed to materialize and so did the nuclear test ban. But eventually, in their
slow, reluctant way, the superpowers found it in their hearts to resume arms
control negotiations in Geneva after a sixteen-month hiatus, even planning
a summit for later that year. The auspicious events prompted the leaders
of the Five Continent Peace Initiative to draft yet another message.

"The world's highest expectations are focused on your meeting at Geneva
next month," read the declaration.[45] "You know that the growing stockpiles
of nuclear weapons, if used, even though by accident or miscalculation, will
engulf us all in complete destruction. No interest can justify this threat to
present and future generations. Hence the prevention of nuclear war is a
key not only for your peoples and their destinies but for all people on every
continent." Suspend nuclear testing, implored the six leaders. If verification
is an obstacle, we are prepared to assist in the establishment of effective
arrangements, including the positioning of verification mechanisms on our
territories. Considering the geographic locations of the six nations in the
Five Continent Peace Initiative, the offer had some merit. Sweden, India,
and Greece are strategically located for monitoring test activity in the Soviet
Union; so, theoretically, are Mexico and Argentina with respect to U.S.
nuclear tests.

Four months later, the six principals of the Five Continent Peace Initiative
were again dispatching a joint message to President Reagan and General
Secretary Gorbachev. Noting that the Geneva Summit had passed without
producing a single breakthrough on the issue of arresting the nuclear arms
race, they again implored the superpowers in the interest of humanity and
the survival of our planet.[46] "As long as nuclear weapons exist," they declared once more, "there can be no security for the world. We all live
confronting the awful possibility of our extinction in a nuclear holocaust,
whether by design or accident.... You have a major responsibility for ensuring our common survival." The message concluded with another appeal
for the cessation of nuclear testing and reiteration of the earlier offer to
assist in the verification process by means of on-site inspection or other
required monitoring activity.

Benign silence, as usual, greeted the message in Washington. In Moscow,
however, still smarting from President Reagan's refusal to join in the Soviet
nuclear test moratorium, policymakers saw major opportunities for political
advantage in the message of the six leaders. At a minimum, the message
provided the Kremlin with the opportunity to draw together a camp of test
ban proponents outside the Soviet bloc (including Greece, a NATO member)
and to embarrass the Reagan administration for its stance on nuclear testing.
Thus on receipt of the six-nation message of February 28, 1986, Moscow

set out to do what it probably had intended all along—it extended its test moratorium "until such time the United States conducts a nuclear test" but cast the action as a concession to the six nations comprising the Peace Initiative.

Despite their obvious lack of success, the leaders of the Peace Initiative were ready to try again. Meeting this time in Ixtapa, Mexico, in August 1986,[47] they again focused on the failure of the superpowers to come to grips with the nuclear issue. Since Hiroshima, they reminded the leaders of the United States and of the Soviet Union that "we have lived on borrowed time. All that is previous and beautiful, all that human civilization has reached for and achieved, could, in a short time be reduced to radioactive dust."

Then, in a formal declaration, the six leaders of the Peace Initiative decided to tell it like it is:

For four decades, the nuclear-weapon states have had almost sole responsibility to end the nuclear arms race, while the rest of the world has been forced to stand anxiously on the sidelines. The nuclear arms race has continued and become more intense. In the face of the consequent danger of common annihilation, the distinction between the powerful and the weak has become meaningless. We are therefore determined that countries such as ours which possess no nuclear arsenals will be actively involved in all aspects of disarmament. *The protection of this planet is a matter for all people who live in it; we cannot accept that a few countries should alone decide the fate of the whole world.*

They were harsh words but words that needed to be said.

This, in effect, is where the Five Continent Peace Initiative finds itself at present.[48] The initiative is driven by a noble goal, has good leadership, and has a world following probably in the billions. But in terms of actual results, it can claim none. Should this failure lead one to write off the initiative as just another movement, another voice in the wilderness? It is hard to tell. A great deal will depend on how the superpowers will respond to its future pronouncements. If recent history teaches us anything, the more powerful its voice becomes, the greater the opposition it is likely to encounter from the superpowers. The possibility, however, of the initiative ever becoming a full-pledged partner in the superpower disarmament negotiating process, which is its not-so-secret desire, is extremely remote.

THE PEACE MOVEMENT AND THE CHURCHES

Equally impotent in terms of their ability to influence superpower disarmament policy have been the American and European peace (antinuclear) movements.

The Nuclear Freeze Campaign

In the United States, an organized antinuclear movement with a voice strong enough to be heard in the Congress, but unfortunately not sufficiently powerful to influence administration policy, did not come into being until the early 1980s. To be sure, there had been peace movements before, and occasionally certain causes, such as the need to suspend atmospheric testing in the 1960s, did galvanize widespread public support. But most of the pre-1980 efforts lacked continuity, were uncertain as to their basic objectives, and suffered from poor overall direction and coordination.

The U.S. antinuclear movement of the 1980s was not the result of Ronald Reagan's policies, as it is commonly believed. The president's strategic modernization program undoubtedly provided a strong stimulus, as did many of his hawkish statements on the Soviet Union and its policies. But the concept of a nuclear freeze had been around long before Reagan and his conservative friends achieved power in Washington.[49] It was being debated by antinuclear activists in the days of Jimmy Carter, amid alarm that the superpowers were confronting each other with growing belligerence and suspicion.

Soon Americans, ordinary citizens, in all walks of life became attracted to the idea.[50] Here was a concept that was easily understood and seemed to make a lot of sense. It required no treaty to enter into effect. All that was needed for solving the world-threatening problem was for the two sides to freeze their nuclear armaments, that is, to stop testing, developing, or buying additional nuclear weapons. For the first time in thirty years, there was hope that nuclear war could be averted. Before long, millions across the land were signing petitions in support of a mutual freeze, colleges were sponsoring teach-ins, and hundreds of public officials and legislators were competing for the opportunity to place the issue before their voters. In retrospect, their anxiety was understandable. All polls taken during that period showed a deep and sustained support for the concept of a nuclear freeze, with support registering strongest among the better educated, more affluent, young Americans, that is, the ones likely to vote.

Eventually, one or both houses in the legislatures of twenty-three states endorsed the freeze, and so did sixty state and local freeze referendums held across the nation. In the U.S. House of Representatives a resolution favoring an "immediate, mutual, and verifiable freeze" was passed by a vote of 278 to 149.[51] But decisions affecting nuclear weapons are not made in county bodies, town meetings, or even by House of Representatives resolution. In the White House, the National Security Council, and the Pentagon, where arms control policy is made, the nuclear freeze idea was anathema. It will lock forever the strategic superiority presently enjoyed by the Soviet Union, went the argument; besides, it will be enormously difficult to verify. Eventually, skillful congressional lobbying, assurances by a very popular president that he, too, favored reduced levels of armaments, and a confused public that seemed to favor both a halt in nuclear arms but also a tougher stance toward the Soviets helped kill the freeze idea. In the United States, the antinuclear movement has not been heard since.

The European Peace Movement

While the United States was debating the merits of a nuclear freeze, an entirely different issue (the proposed deployment in Europe of 108 Pershing IIs and 464 Tomahawk cruise missiles) was driving the European peace movement. The action, coupled with statements by President Reagan on the possibility of a limited nuclear war on the continent, convinced many Europeans that the United States was more interested in deploying its weapons there than in removing the Soviet SS-20s that had been given as the reason for the U.S. deployments.[52]

The results were massive demonstrations in numerous European cities. Even one nuclear weapon, argued opponents, can cause havoc in densely populated western Europe. Why add to the more than 10,000 nuclear weapons already in place? Fear of the bomb, however, was only one of the reasons that led Europeans to the streets. There was also frustration and a feeling of helplessness that weapons were being deployed in their midst for which no European had a finger on the nuclear trigger. Disarmament, they contended, is the ultimate solution. Relying on an increasing number of nuclear weapons for peace and security is an invitation for disaster, especially in a world that regularly produces unstable and demented leaders (Stalin, Hitler, Mussolini, to cite a few).

By the end of 1981 movements against the proposed missile deployments had emerged in almost every European nation, including France, which has traditionally abstained from antinuclear protests. Especially vociferous were the West German, British, and Dutch movements.[53] In West Germany, the antideployment call was led by a coalition of religious pacifists, political centrists, and the Greens (a new political coalition dedicated to a clean environment and disarmament). In the United Kingdom, spearheading the opposition was the Campaign for Nuclear Disarmament, Europe's oldest peace organization. Its support came from laborites, church groups, trade union members, and feminist organizations. In the Netherlands, the Interchurch Peace Council, which has always stood at the vanguard of the opposition to nuclear weapons in Europe, served not only as the standard-bearer for local activists but as a leader for many other European peace organizations.

What came of the movement? Nothing. Many of the same factors that helped defeat the Nuclear Freeze movement in the United States caused also the demise of the effort to block deployment of the American weapons in Europe. Strong U.S. pressure in favor of deployment and conservative victories in West Germany and Great Britain in 1983 literally took the wind out of the sails of the antideployment movement. This occurred despite millions of protesters and the findings of all opinion polls of the period, which clearly documented an overwhelming European opposition to the proposed deployments but not to withdrawal from the North Atlantic Treaty Organization (NATO).

The Churches

Churches in the United States and Europe have always been steadfast in their support of nuclear arms control. There has hardly been a protest, demonstration, or rally against the nuclear arms race and the threat to human life and civilization it poses that did not include a generous contingent of clergy or other religious leaders. But despite their willingness to help, churches seldom if ever have spoken out with a unified voice on the issue of nuclear arms or assumed a leadership role in the antinuclear movement.

A major change occurred in the early 1980s, when the three largest U.S. faiths issued formal declarations condemning nuclear weapons as instruments of war, in the process staking out for themselves a leadership role in the U.S. antinuclear movement. First to speak out on the issue was the National Conference of Catholic Bishops, which in May 1983 issued a Pastoral Letter entitled *The Challenge of Peace: God's Promise and Our Response*. It was followed by the publication of the *Nuclear Dilemma: A Search for Christian Understanding*, the Episcopal Church's statement on nuclear war, and later by the Pastoral Letter of the United Methodist Council of Bishops, *In Defense of Creation: The Nuclear Crisis and a Just Peace*.

The three declarations have much in common. The increasing accumulations of nuclear weapons by the superpowers, they note, threaten the future of mankind; ours is the first generation since Genesis that has the power to threaten the created order (in effect, to destroy Creation); a nuclear war would clearly be contrary to the Will of God. The three documents are also in agreement on the policies that could reverse the trend: a total ban on nuclear testing; a multilateral, mutually verifiable nuclear weapons freeze; reductions and the ultimate dismantling of all nuclear weapons.

Of the three declarations, by far the strongest and most poignant is the pastoral letter from the United Methodist Council of Bishops. "We write in defense of creation," note the bishops:

and we do so because creation itself is under attack. Air and water, trees and fruits and flowers, birds and fish and cattle, all children and youth, women and men live under the darkening shadows of a threatening nuclear winter. . . . It is a crisis that threatens to assault not only the whole human family but planet earth itself. . . . We say a clear and unconditioned No to nuclear war and to any use of nuclear weapons. We conclude that nuclear deterrence is a position that cannot receive the church's blessing.

On the issue of deterrence, the Methodist and Catholic viewpoints differ. Methodists reject the concept as unacceptable; Catholics accept deterrence but only as a transitional strategy on the route to disarmament.

Although the principal thrust of the Methodist letter is on man's ability to undo Creation by his never-ending acquisition of weapons of mass destruction, the Roman Catholic letter focuses on the weapons themselves:

We do not perceive any situation, in which the deliberate initiation of nuclear war, on however restricted a scale, can be morally justified.... Under no circumstances may nuclear weapons or other instruments of mass slaughter be used for purposes of destroying population centers or other predominantly civilian targets.... The whole world must summon the moral courage and technical means to say no to nuclear conflict; no to weapons of mass destruction; no to an arms race which robs the poor and the vulnerable.

Admittedly, neither the two church letters nor the Episcopal statement on nuclear war have made any difference in the formulation of U.S. nuclear policies. They have influenced the Kremlin's policies even less. But for millions of Catholics, Episcopalians, and Methodists, the three documents represent official statements of moral principle. To date, the church statements have posed no major moral dilemma to our citizens, probably because no specific action is required of them other than opposition to the arms race, which most of them share anyway. By addressing the moral and theological dimensions of the nuclear arms race, however, the churches of America in effect are warning the U.S. government that they are urging their faithful in formulating their positions on nuclear issues to consider religious convictions along with official policy. Pushed to extreme, this may confront citizens with a major religious–political clash when they must choose between loyalty to their nation and having to uphold the dictates of their faith.

NOTES

1. For a history of U.N. efforts in the area of disarmament, refer to United Nations, Department for Disarmament Affairs, *United Nations and Disarmament: A Short History* (New York, 1988).

2. Lawrence D. Weiler, "General Disarmament Proposals," *Arms Control Today*, July/August 1986, p. 6.

3. The Disarmament Commission is still in existence, but its importance is overshadowed by the Conference on Disarmament, the United Nations' principal body for negotiating arms control and disarmament issues. The Disarmament Commission meets in New York, the conference in Geneva.

4. United Nations, Department for Disarmament Affairs, *The United Nations Disarmament Yearbook. Vol. 12, 1987* (New York: United Nations, 1987), p. 74.

5. United Nations, Department for Disarmament Affairs, *United Nations and Disarmament 1945–1985* (New York: United Nations, 1985), p. 3.

6. Ibid., pp. 3–4.

7. The full text of the Final Document has appeared in numerous U.N. publications, including United Nations, Department for Disarmament Affairs, *Final Document, First Special Session of the General Assembly on Disarmament, 1978* (New York: United Nations, February 1981).

8. "U.N. General Assembly, Second Special Session on Disarmament, June 7 to July 9, 1982," *Disarmament*, November 1982.

9. For information on activities carried out under the banner of the World Disarmament Campaign, refer to United Nations, *The World Disarmament Campaign: Questions and Answers*, U.N. Information Paper (New York: United Nations, June 1985); see also United Nations, *The World Disarmament Campaign* U.N. Fact Sheets nos. 24 and 36 (New York, August 1982 and June 1984).

10. The U.N.'s impotence on the nuclear issue was revealed once again in the summer of 1988 during the Third Special Session on Disarmament. Little was accomplished, despite four weeks of debate, an agenda replete with issues demanding priority consideration, and attendance at the session of representatives from all U.N. members. See Archelaus R. Turrentine, "The U.S. Stands Alone: The Third U.N. Session on Disarmament," *Arms Control Today*, June 1988, pp. 5–7; and Peter Herby, "U.N. Disarmament Fizzles," *Bulletin of the Atomic Scientists*, September 1988, pp. 6–7.

11. Texts and brief histories on all multilateral agreements are in U.S. Arms Control and Disarmament Agency, *Arms Control and Disarmament Agreements: Text and Histories of Negotiations* (Washington, DC: U.S. Government Printing Office, 1982).

12. Article V of the "Treaty on Principles Governing the Activities of States in the Exploration and Use of Outer Space, Including the Moon and other Celestial Bodies."

13. United Nations, Department for Disarmament Affairs, *United Nations and Disarmament 1945–1985*, p. 11.

14. The complete text of the agreement is included in an undated pamphlet by the World Federalist Association, Washington, DC, entitled *Peace is Possible*.

15. The organization and functions of the *Conference on Disarmament* and of the other organs within the U.N. system dealing with disarmament and arms limitation are provided in United Nations, *Disarmament Machinery*, U.N. Fact Sheet no. 35 (New York, United Nations, May 1984).

16. Dennis Menos, *Arms Control Fact Book* (Jefferson, NC: McFarland, 1985), p. 11.

17. Conference on Disarmament, *Report of the Conference on Disarmament to the General Assembly of the United Nations* (Geneva, September 20, 1988).

18. "Disarmament Resolutions Adopted by the General Assembly at its 42nd Session, 15 September to 21 December 1987," *Disarmament*, Winter 1987–1988.

19. United Nations, Department for Disarmament Affairs, *The United Nations General Assembly and Disarmament 1987* (New York: United Nations, 1988), pp. 54–55.

20. Ibid., pp. 61–62.

21. For a current statement of U.S. national security and arms limitations policy, refer to U.S. Department of State, Bureau of Public Affairs, *Fundamentals of U.S.*

Foreign Policy (Washington, DC: U.S. Government Printing Office, 1988), pp. 11–23.

22. This is the rationale behind the Five Continent Peace Initiative discussed later in this chapter.

23. "Report to the Conference on Disarmament from the Ad Hoc Committee on Effective International Arrangements to Assure Non-Nuclear Weapons States Against the Use or Threat of Use of Nuclear Weapons," in U.S. Arms Control and Disarmament Agency, *Documents on Disarmament, 1984* (Washington, DC: U.S. Government Printing Office, 1986) pp. 581–88.

24. United Nations, Department for Disarmament Affairs, *United Nations and Disarmament, 1945–1985,* pp. 40–43; and idem, *United Nations General Assembly and Disarmament, 1987,* pp. 73–74.

25. Conference on Disarmament, *Report of the Conference on Disarmament to the General Assembly of the United Nations,* pp. 231–39.

26. United Nations, Department for Disarmament Affairs, *The United Nations General Assembly and Disarmament, 1987,* pp. 73–74.

27. United Nations, Department for Disarmament Affairs, *United Nations and Disarmament,* pp. 41–44.

28. For a brief statement of U.S. nuclear test policy, refer to U.S. Department of State, *U.S. Policy Regarding Limitations on Nuclear Testing,* Special Report no. 150 (Washington, DC, August 1986).

29. The events leading to the conclusion of the LTBT are summarized in U.S. Arms Control and Disarmament Agency, *Arms Control and Disarmament Agreements,* pp. 34–40; and in Committee on International Security and Arms Control, National Academy of Sciences, *Nuclear Arms Control: Background and Issues* (Washington, DC: National Academy Press, 1985), Chapter 7.

30. United Nations, Department for Disarmament Affairs, *United Nations and Disarmament, 1945–1985,* p. 59.

31. Conference on Disarmament, *Report of the Conference on Disarmament to the General Assembly of the United Nations,* pp. 15–21.

32. U.S. Arms Control and Disarmament Agency, *Arms Control and Disarmament Agreements,* pp. 35–38.

33. Jesse James, "Nuclear Test Agreement Signed at Summit," *Arms Control Today,* January/February 1988, p. 25.

34. U.S. Arms Control and Disarmament Agency, *Arms Control and Disarmament Agreements,* pp. 164–89.

35. U.S. Department of State, *U.S. Policy Regarding Limitations on Nuclear Testing.*

36. United Nations, Department for Disarmament Affairs, *United Nations and Disarmament,* p. 50.

37. William Epstein, "U.N. Presses Superpowers on Test Ban," *Bulletin of Atomic Scientists,* March 1988, pp. 7–8.

38. United Nations, Department for Disarmament Affairs, *The United Nations General Assembly and Disarmament, 1987,* p. 75.

39. Ibid., pp. 80–83.

40. Conference on Disarmament, *Report of the Conference on Disarmament to the General Assembly of the United Nations,* pp. 215–30.

41. United Nations, Department for Disarmament Affairs, *The United Nations General Assembly and Disarmament, 1987*, pp. 116–21.

42. United Nations, Department for Disarmament Affairs, *The United Nations Disarmament Yearbook. Vol. 12, 1987*, pp. 276–91.

43. Joint Declaration, May 22, 1984.

44. New Delhi Declaration, January 28, 1985.

45. Joint Declaration, October 24, 1985.

46. Joint Declaration, February 28, 1986.

47. Mexico City Declaration, August 7, 1986.

48. The initiative's latest pronouncement came in January 1988, within a month of the Washington Summit. It appealed to the superpowers to finalize during 1988 agreements to end nuclear testing and reduce strategic armaments.

49. For a detailed account of the Nuclear Freeze campaign, refer to Douglas C. Waller, *Congress and the Nuclear Freeze: An Inside Look at the Politics of a Mass Movement* (Amherst: University of Massachusetts Press, 1987); see also Paul M. Cole and William J. Taylor, *The Nuclear Freeze Debate: Arms Control Issues for the 1980s* (Boulder, CO: Westview Press, 1983); and Adam M. Garfinkle, *The Politics of the Nuclear Freeze* (Philadelphia: Foreign Policy Research Institute, 1984).

50. Randall Forsberg, "A Bilateral Nuclear Weapon Freeze," *Scientific American*, November 1982.

51. "House Approves Altered Version of Arms Freeze," *New York Times*, May 5, 1983.

52. Riverside Church Disarmament Program, *The Arms Race and Us* (New York, 1982), especially Mary Kaldor's article, "A Nuclear Free World," pp. 36–42.

53. For a detailed account of the European Peace Movement refer to Congressional Research Service, Library of Congress, *European Opposition to INF Deployment*, IB 83174 (Washington, DC, December 8, 1983).

4

Tearing Down the Few
Past Accomplishments

Until the mid-1980s, the superpowers have kept arms control under *their* complete control through a combination of irrelevant policies, lots of hype and game playing (especially at the United Nations), and a generally lack-luster attitude when confronted with a serious arms control challenge. About that time, however, the superpowers' approach to arms control took an ominous turn. No longer satisfied with their role as casual bystanders, the superpowers have embarked on a policy of arms control "self-destruct," a conscientious effort to withdraw from the process and to undo the few positive accomplishments of the past forty years. Notwithstanding the successive series of Reagan–Gorbachev summits and conclusion of the INF treaty[1]—all, skillfully designed to convey the impression of arms control "momentum"—the self-destruct policies of the superpowers continue to occupy center stage. Evidence the unceremonious termination of the SALT II treaty and the not-so-secret plans of Moscow and Washington soon to also discard the ABM treaty.

The policies adopted by the superpowers to discredit and bring about the demise of arms control have a great deal in common. As usual, those of the Soviet Union are a lot more circumspect and devious. Moscow's game plan is to infuse so much propaganda and uncertainty into its arms limitation agenda as to bring about a total U.S. disenchantment with arms control, eventually leading to a formal American withdrawal from the process. Enormous public relations benefit would accrue to the Soviet Union from such a U.S. action. For its part, the American side has built its entire case of arms control disengagement on the issue of Soviet arms treaty noncompliance.[2] Especially during the Reagan years, allegations of Soviet treaty violations have been used and abused with such finesse as to injure fatally the Soviet

Union's image as a negotiating partner and its sincerity in coming to grips with the world's most pressing problem.[3] The arms treaty compliance issue has also been used by the United States to justify and rationalize its own arms control "self-destruct" actions, as was the case in May 1986, when it unilaterally terminated adherence to the SALT II treaty[4] because of Soviet "cheating."

ARMS TREATY COMPLIANCE

According to the U.S. government, Soviet noncompliance with existing agreements is the primary cause for the regressive state of nuclear arms control in the world. Arms control, the United States claims, cannot exist unless both partners comply with the terms and spirit of signed agreements. Noncompliance destroys confidence in the process and poisons the environment for further negotiations.[5]

U.S. charges of Soviet noncompliance logically give rise to two questions: (1) To what extent and how serious are the Soviet violations of agreements signed thus far? (2) What about the United States? Is it keeping up its part of the bargain? To a layperson, not privy to the supersecret files of the Pentagon or the Kremlin, an authoritative answer to either question is not only difficult but impossible.

True or False?

Because of the secrecy with which the superpowers surround their military activities, a layperson in the United States or the Soviet Union is for all practical purposes at the mercy of his government on the issue of arms treaty compliance. The government side (here and in Moscow) is big: it has military experts, intelligence analysts, and lots of public relations people. In Washington it also has respected Kremlinologists and highly paid consultants to help with analysis. More important, it has access to extensive supersecret and supersensitive intelligence concerning the other side's military plans and operations.

It is not even a contest. In regard to the specifics of arms treaty compliance, all a layperson can do is contemplate his or her government's story. There is no practical way to confirm or deny the charges. Repeatedly, for instance, since January 1984, the United States has charged the Soviet Union with arms treaty violations. The charges each time were made by means of classified reports provided to the Congress, accompanied by brief unclassified press releases for use by the public at large. "True or false" is a game between an all-powerful government insisting that the other side is violating agreements wholesale and a lot of laypersons remaining skeptical but being unable even to identify the basis for their skepticism.

The alleged Soviet violation of the 1972 Biological and Toxin Weapons

Convention,[6] a charge repeatedly made by the United States, is a case in point. Reportedly, the Soviet Union has violated its legal obligations under the convention by maintaining an offensive biological warfare program and capability. No specific proof has ever been provided regarding this violation, at least not on an unclassified basis. Since the Soviets do not give access to their biological laboratories and facilities[7] for the purpose of refuting the U.S. charges, a layperson has two options: accept the charges as given or shrug off the entire matter for lack of evidence.

Escalating the Arms Treaty Compliance Issue

With approximately twenty-five bilateral and multilateral arms control agreements to which the United States and the Soviet Union are signatories,[8] it was only natural that sooner or later problems concerning compliance would arise. Until the early 1980s, all such problems were considered through direct diplomatic contact between the two sides and, in the case of disputes involving the Strategic Arms Limitation Talks (SALT) I and II, at regularly scheduled sessions of the Standing Consultative Commission (SCC).[9] The commission was established by the SALT I treaty as a forum for considering compliance questions and for resolving issues flowing from treaty provisions judged to be ambiguous.

Until early 1984 Americans were only vaguely aware of the diplomatic dialogue between the superpowers on the issue of arms treaty compliance, even less so regarding the specific issues considered. Diplomacy and discretion kept most such information away from public view. Beginning in 1984, however, the situation changed drastically. Soviet arms treaty violations were no longer to be kept secret, and the U.S. government went public on the issue in anger. The decision added yet another quarrelsome problem in relations between the superpowers and provided also the rationale for several U.S. unilateral actions inimical to arms control.

The escalation of arms treaty compliance was undoubtedly politically motivated, and the Reagan administration was gratified by the praise it received from its conservative supporters. There was, however, and continues to be considerable criticism from opponents, many in the Congress, who charged that the Reagan administration had intentionally distorted the compliance picture[10] by exaggerating the importance of the alleged violations while ignoring the many areas of Soviet compliance. In the view of these critics, the publicity surrounding Soviet arms treaty noncompliance had a more sinister purpose: to undermine U.S. public confidence in arms control and to diminish prospects for a future accord.

Ambiguous Terms

All arms control agreements, no matter how carefully prepared, contain ambiguous language. Ambiguity is the source of many of the disagreements encountered in arms treaty compliance,[11] and many actions claimed to be perfectly legitimate by one nation are challenged by the other as violations.

It is utopian to expect the superpowers not to take advantage of ambiguities. Both nations exploit loopholes in treaty language. As part of their weapons development process, for example, both superpowers do extensive flight testing of new missiles. During such testing, information from the missiles in flight is radioed to the ground by means of coded signals known as telemetry. The radio signals are designed for the eyes and ears of the nation conducting the test, but it is not uncommon for the other side also to receive and read them. To deny outsiders the opportunity to eavesdrop on its tests, a nation may resort to "encryption" of telemetry, that is, to scramble the radio signals so as to conceal the true character of the data being radioed.

According to the provisions of the SALT I and II treaties, encoding of telemetry is legal, but "encryption" to impede verification is not. Both parties are prohibited by treaty language from using deliberate concealment measures that impede verification.[12] Ambiguity becomes an issue with the meaning of the word *impede*, since it can be variously defined (i.e., to "obstruct," "hinder," but also to "make slower"). What was the intent of the treaties?

The United States has repeatedly accused the Soviet Union of extensive encryption of telemetry during tests of strategic missiles.[13] The Soviet Union denies the charge. Soviet telemetry is undoubtedly being encrypted, but the U.S. government has never specified the extent or complexity of the encryption. If the encryption was so sophisticated as to have prevented the verification process, a major treaty violation has occurred. If, on the other hand, the Soviet encryption practices merely hindered or made it more difficult for U.S. intelligence to understand the technical characteristics of Soviet missiles, the charge hardly deserves consideration as an arms treaty violation. Ambiguity in treaty language never leads to clear-cut answers. It is all a matter of interpretation and perspective.

Existing Agreements

The United States and the Soviet Union are signatories to approximately twenty-five arms control agreements. The majority of them are "bilateral" accords, regulating relations between the two nations only. The remaining agreements are "multilateral," meaning that they were negotiated and concluded under the aegis of the United Nations with many other nations participating.

A listing of the agreements follows. Bilateral accords are identified with a (B), multilateral with an (M). The asterisk (*) preceeding certain treaties and accords denotes those agreements that, according to the U.S. government, the Soviet Union has violated:

Hot Line Agreement (B)

Hot Line Improvement and Modernization Agreement (B)

Agreement on Measures to Reduce the Risk of Outbreak of Nuclear War (B)

Agreement on Prevention of Incidents on and over the High Seas (B)

*Antiballistic Missile (ABM) Treaty (B)

*Interim Agreement on the Limitation of Strategic Offensive Arms (SALT I) (B)

Memorandum of Understanding Regarding Establishment of a Standing Consultative Commission (SCC) (B)

Protocol on the Prevention of Incidents on and over the High Seas (B)

Agreement on Prevention of Nuclear War (B)

Protocol to the ABM Treaty (B)

*Threshold Test Ban Treaty (TTBT) (B)

Peaceful Nuclear Explosions Treaty (PNET) (B)

*Treaty on the Limitation of Strategic Offensive Arms (SALT II) (B)

Agreement for Improving the Hot Line (B)

Agreement Establishing Nuclear Risk Reduction Centers (B)

*Intermediate-range Nuclear Forces (INF) Treaty (B)

Antarctic Treaty (M)

*Limited Test Ban Treaty (LTBT) (M)

Outer Space Treaty (M)

No Nuclear Weapons in Latin America (M)

Non-Proliferation Treaty (NPT) (M)

Seabed Arms Control Treaty (M)

*Geneva Protocol (M)

*Biological and Toxin Weapons Convention (M)

Environmental Modification Convention (M)

Nuclear Material Convention (M)

*Helsinki Final Act (M)

Since January 1984, when the United States began to escalate the arms compliance issue, seven administration reports have been published,[14] including one produced by the General Advisory Committee on Arms Control and Disarmament (this is an independent advisory body that periodically advises the president on issues of arms control). Comparable Soviet reports on U.S. treaty noncompliance, if any, are not available. On several occasions in the past, however, as part of the superpower game of charges and countercharges, the Soviet Union has similarly accused the United States of engaging in dubious compliance activities.

The latest U.S. report on Soviet arms treaty noncompliance was issued in December 1988.[15] This and previous reports have accused the Soviet Union of violating eight arms control accords (the ones marked with an asterisk in the above list). By implication the Soviets are complying with all remaining treaties and agreements. The question logically arises: if the Soviet Union is bent on gaining a military advantage over the United States by means of arms control cheating, why is it complying with so many agreements? Certainly, accords such as the Outer Space Treaty, the Seabed Arms Control Treaty, and the NPT offer a great many more incentives and opportunities for military gain than does the Helsinki Final Act or the TTBT, which the Soviet Union is accused of violating. The suspicion is that many of the U.S. accusations are motivated more by a desire for political gain than by concern over the military implications of the Soviet actions. In the case of the alleged Soviet violations of the INF treaty, the U.S. government admits that the violations have been resolved to its satisfaction or are being resolved.

The ABM Treaty Violations

The U.S. government is charging that the Soviet Union "may be preparing an ABM defense of its national territory" in violation of the ABM treaty.[16] The accord bans deployment of ABM systems, except that each party is permitted to deploy one ABM system to defend its national capital area (the Soviet Union is maintaining one around Moscow)[17] or, alternatively, at a single ICBM deployment area. The United States deployed an ABM system in Grand Forks, North Dakota, during the 1960s but has since abandoned the site.

Six specific findings are offered by the United States in support of the ABM treaty charge. The evidence is hardly devastating. In fact, five of the six findings are based, by U.S. admission, either on "insufficient evidence" or are "ambiguous." In the case of another violation (certain ABM components in Gomel) the United States admits they are not likely to "support an ABM defense at that locality."[18] The one exception where a Soviet violation is evident concerns the construction of a large phased-array radar in the Siberian city of Krasnoyarsk. The radar's siting, orientation, and capability[19] support the conclusion that the installation is designed for ballistic missile detection and tracking; that is, the radar has an ABM role and is not designed for space-tracking purposes as originally claimed by the Soviet Union. (The U.S. government has been insisting that the Krasnoyarsk violation must be corrected and that failure to do so will adversely affect conclusion of the Strategic Arms Reduction Talks [START]. This view was shared by the Congress.[20] For its part, the Soviet Union, after denying for years that a violation had occurred in Krasnoyarsk, reversed itself in September 1989, admitted that the radar facility in question was inconsistent with the guidelines of the ABM Treaty and promised to dismantle it.)

The five "suspect" activities (above) all deal with Soviet actions for which the United States has obvious difficulty determining their true nature and scope.[21] There is the case of the *mobile land-based ABM systems or components* whose development, testing, or deployment is prohibited by the treaty. The evidence on this is "ambiguous," but Soviet activities represent a "potential violation," according to the U.S. government. Next is the case of the concurrent testing of ABM and air defense components, similarly prohibited by the treaty. The evidence of Soviet actions in this area again is "insufficient," but the Soviets probably have violated the treaty's prohibition on testing air defense components in an ABM mode. The evidence of Soviet actions with respect to SAM upgrades is likewise "insufficient," but, claims the U.S. government, this and other ABM-related activities suggest that the Soviets may be preparing for an ABM defense of their territory.

What is one to conclude from these and the related ABM treaty charges based on "insufficient evidence" or "ambiguity?" The issue has profound East–West strategic balance implications. Are the charges part of the superpower game or, possibly, worst threat estimates on the part of supercautious Pentagon planners? The evidence presented by the Reagan administration in its unclassified press releases certainly does not allow for an informed judgment. A unilateral Soviet territorial ABM capability, acquired in violation of the ABM treaty, would indeed erode the U.S. strategic deterrent. Conversely, unfounded charges or mere illusions of Soviet violations of the ABM treaty place unbearable burdens on the already frail environment of arms control negotiations and make achievement of credible accords extremely difficult.

Nuclear Testing Violations

Repeatedly during the past four years and again in December 1988, the U.S. government has accused the Soviet Union of violating its commitments under the LTBT and the TTBT. Reportedly, the LTBT violations flow from Soviet test practices that allow the release of nuclear debris into the atmosphere beyond the borders of the USSR, a practice banned by the treaty.[22] The debris from these tests, admits the United States, does not pose calculable health, safety, or environmental risks, and the infractions have no apparent military significance. So what is the problem? It appears, quoting from an earlier U.S. report on Soviet arms treaty noncompliance, that "the Soviet Union has failed to take the precautions necessary to minimize the contamination of man's environment by radioactive substances despite numerous U.S. demarches and requests for corrective action."[23] Also, since the resumption of Soviet underground testing in February 1987, the United States has protested to the Soviet Union on two occasions when unambiguously attributable venting occurred.

Prior U.S. reports on Soviet noncompliance accused the Soviet Union of "likely violating" the TTBT.[24] The treaty prohibits underground nuclear tests having yields in excess of 150 kilotons.[25] Specific charges are not given in the December 1988 report, but the "totality of evidence," claims the U.S. government, "strengthens the previous findings and the United States continues to find that the Soviet Union has likely violated its legal obligations under the TTBT."[26]

SALT II Violations

In January 1984, when the United States first went public with the arms compliance issue, it made Soviet violations of SALT II the centerpiece of its case. The situation changed radically in 1986 when, because of alleged Soviet noncompliance, the Reagan administration declared the treaty null and void. Presently, the Soviet SALT II violations (if any) are officially being ignored, the United States not wishing to accuse the Soviets of violating a treaty that it, too, is violating.

Were the Soviet violations of SALT II of such a magnitude as to warrant U.S. rejection of the treaty? A definitive answer is impossible. The entire case, pro and con, rests exclusively on U.S. government reports and Soviet denials, both obviously colored to prove different points of view. There are no independent sources available, and security on both sides makes an informed judgment on the alleged violations impossible.

The last U.S. formal report on Soviet noncompliance in which SALT II was considered was dated February 1, 1986.[27] It cited two specific violations and half a dozen other Soviet actions, some "probable violations," some "ambiguous," which reportedly were inconsistent with the terms of SALT II.

The first of the alleged violations concerned Soviet telemetry encryption practices.[28] This is a case of the Soviets taking advantage of ambiguities in the language of the treaty that fails to spell out the criteria for determining when encryption impedes verification. No one denies that the Soviet Union has used encryption in its missile tests, but the extent to which such encryption has prevented the verification process, which would constitute a treaty violation, still has to be proven. Judging from the discussion on the SS-25 that follows, the intelligence information obtained by the United States from Soviet missile tests does not seem to suffer from lack of telemetry. The United States would not have been able to make its case on the SS-25 if Soviet telemetry had been truly encrypted to impede verification. The second of the alleged violations, the SS-25 issue, is equally controversial, and ambiguity in treaty language might again be the culprit.[29]

In an attempt to constrain the modernization and proliferation of new, more capable types of intercontinental ballistic missiles (ICBMs), the provisions of SALT II permitted each side to "flight test and deploy" only *one* new type of light ICBM.[30] A new type was defined in the agreement as one that differed from an existing type by more than 5 percent in length, largest diameter, launch-weight, and throw-weight or in the number of stages or the type of propellant used (i.e., liquid or solid). The Soviets have declared the SS-24, a large solid-propellant ICBM approximately the size of our MX, to be their allowed one new type of ICBM. By also flight testing and deploying the SS-25, however, they have violated the treaty—so charged the United States.

The case is different from the viewpoint of the Soviets. The SS-25 is not a new ICBM, they maintain, but the modernization of an existing type (the SS-13) and, therefore, is permitted under the treaty. The argument obviously is based on the 5 percent rule and other SALT II treaty provisions that define a "new" ICBM. These provisions are complicated and at times ambiguous. The Reagan administration was convinced that the Soviets had committed a violation. A great many persons outside the administration did not share this view. The Soviet actions, they suggested, did not add up to an unequivocal violation but rather to a skillful manipulation of ambiguous treaty language.

U.S. Treaty Violations

On the other side of the coin, a presidential directive, late in 1986, placed the United States on a collision course with the provisions of SALT II. In December 1986 President Reagan ordered the Department of Defense to proceed with full-scale development of the Small ICBM (popularly known as the Midgetman). The Small ICBM was the second ICBM that the United States would be developing, MX being the first one. Development of a second ICBM would not have been prohibited by the terms of SALT II, but its subsequent flight testing and deployment would. The test, when it did occur in May 1989, signified a major U.S. violation of the provisions of SALT II.

We noted earlier treaty-language ambiguities that the Soviet Union is quick to exploit. The United States is no different. Whenever opportunities arise for unilateral advantage due to ambiguous treaty language, the United States responds with similar eagerness while professing to remain within the letter of the treaty.

The large U.S. radar in Fylingdales, England, illustrates the point. The radar is being "modernized," an action permitted under the terms of the ABM treaty. The modernization effort[31] however, is giving the installation enormously enlarged capabilities, a fact that has not escaped the notice of Moscow, which repeatedly has charged the U.S. with treaty violation. At issue is the language in the treaty that does not precisely define parameters for the modernization of radars, a weakness the United States is eagerly exploiting.

THE END OF SALT

When the SALT II treaty was signed by President Carter in June 1979, he heralded the event as a "truly national accomplishment." Within months, however, the president's accomplishment was gasping for air, victim of the Soviet invasion of Afghanistan and opposition by powerful senators who made ratification extremely uncertain. During the early 1980s, an accommodation of sorts between the superpowers infused some life into the treaty, and there was even optimism that the treaty's moment in history perhaps had not passed. Subsequent events proved such optimism wrong. By the summer of 1986, SALT lay dead, the result of dubious activities by the Soviet Union and inconsistent arms control policies by a hawkish Reagan administration.[32]

Who Is to Blame?

In retrospect it is easy to blame the United States for the demise of SALT. It was, after all, the United States that in the summer of 1986 formally declared the SALT structure (meaning SALT I and SALT II) to be null and void. Careful examination, however, of the events preceeding the U.S. action makes it apparent that both superpowers share blame for destroying their most significant arms control accomplishment of the past three decades.

From the outset the Reagan administration's opposition to SALT II was hardly a national secret. (The treaty is "flawed," declared then candidate Reagan.) Still, on March 3, 1981, and again on May 31, 1982, the new administration announced that it would take no action that would undercut the existing SALT agreements "as long as the Soviet Union exercises the same restraint." The Soviet Union answered in kind on June 21, 1982. It, too, said the formal announcement from Moscow was prepared to comply by SALT I and II to the "same degree as the United States."[33]

Before considering what the United States did to SALT and why, a brief comment on the key provisions of SALT I and II is necessary. Much of the rationale for the U.S. action is imbedded in these provisions.

SALT I, the interim agreement with the Soviet Union, preceeded SALT II by seven years. As its name implies, SALT I was intended as a holding action, an "interim" arrangement, until a more comprehensive accord limiting the strategic arsenals of the superpowers could be developed. From the U.S. point of view, SALT I was not a particularly good deal.[34] The treaty froze at existing levels the number of strategic land-based missile launchers on each side (1,054 for the United States; 1,618 for the Soviet Union) and permitted an increase in submarine-launched ballistic missile (SLBM) launchers up to an agreed-upon level of 710 for the United States and 950 for the Soviet Union.[35] Modernization or replacement of ICBMs and SLBMs was to be accompanied by the dismantling or destruction of a corresponding number of older launchers.

There undoubtedly were some good features about SALT I, but the imposed ICBM and SLBM numerical ceilings were not one of them. In fact, looking at numbers alone, the treaty appeared to be highly inequitable. This fact did not escape the notice of Congress, which in the Joint Resolution approving SALT I advised the president to seek in SALT II an agreement that "would not limit the U.S. to levels of strategic forces inferior to those of the Soviet Union."[36]

SALT II, when it did come, was "equitable," but it did *not* reduce a single weapon in the arsenals of the superpowers. Neither did it impose major restrictions on the development of many new weapons or the modernization of existing systems. On the U.S. side, for instance, SALT II had no impact on the development of the MX ICBM, the D-5 SLBM cruise missiles, the B-1B, or the B-2 Stealth bomber. It would have prohibited however, the testing and deployment of the Small ICBM or Midgetman in addition to the MX.

SALT II imposed an overall ceiling of 2,400 in strategic delivery vehicles on each side. This ceiling would have been lowered to 2,250 by the end of 1981. Within these limits each party was limited to:

1. 1,320 multiple, independently targeted reentry vehicle (MIRVed) ICBMs, SLBMs, and air-to-surface ballistic missiles (ASBMs) and heavy bombers equipped for cruise missiles capable of a range in excess of 600 kilometers
2. 1,200 MIRVed ICBMs, SLBMs, and ASBMs
3. 820 MIRVed ICBMs[37]

In line with their earlier pledges, both superpowers complied with the SALT I and II ceilings and subceilings between 1972 (the date of the signing of SALT I) and the end of 1986. They did so by repeatedly deactivating ICBMs, SLBMs, and nuclear submarines to remain within the limits imposed by these agreements.[38] This fact notwithstanding, the United States announced on May 27, 1986, its "Interim Restraint Policy."

The Interim Restraint Policy

The policy came in the form of a statement by President Reagan. The United States, it reported, had completed a comprehensive review of the required response to the continuing pattern of Soviet noncompliance with arms control agreements. Based on this review it has determined that the Soviet Union has not, as yet, taken those actions that would indicate a readiness to join the United States in an interim framework of truly mutual restraint.[39] Accordingly, "given the lack of Soviet reciprocity, the President has decided that in the future the United States must base decisions regarding its strategic force structure on the nature and magnitude of the threat posed by Soviet strategic forces and not on standards contained in SALT II or SALT I."[40] U.S. noncompliance was scheduled to start late in 1986. It actually occurred on December 7 of that year with the deployment of the 131st B-52 heavy bomber with cruise missiles but *without* dismantling U.S. systems as compensation. Not wishing to alarm the Soviets unduly, the presidential statement concluded by stating that the United States would continue to exercise utmost restraint in its strategic programs and that no appreciable numerical growth in the number of U.S. strategic offensive forces was anticipated. Instead, the United States would seek agreement on a new and more durable arms control framework, one built on deep, equitable, and verifiable reductions in the offensive nuclear forces of the superpowers.

Thus with the mere stroke of a pen, SALT I and SALT II, for all practical purposes the only U.S.–Soviet agreements actually regulating nuclear arms, lay dead, victims of an alleged Soviet failure to comply with their terms and the promise of a future arms accord.

Two questions arise: Did it make sense for the United States to seek a new arms control accord with the Soviet Union (which it is actually now doing by means of the START negotiations) while discarding existing agreements because of Soviet failure to comply? Either the Soviet Union is a reliable arms control partner or it is not. If it has indeed violated the SALT I and II agreements, or has taken advantage of ambiguities in treaty language, what is there to stop it from repeating this performance under the terms of a START agreement? Why take a chance with yet another arms accord that is likely to work to the detriment of U.S. security? Similarly, if the sole purpose of arms control agreements is to enhance the national security of their signatories, was Soviet national security in such peril as to induce Moscow to undertake the type of dubious activities (telemetry encryption, the deployment of the SS-25, and so on) that aroused the U.S. anger and in the process helped kill SALT?

Despite its vast public relations network, the Reagan administration was never able to respond convincingly to the first question. Even if SALT II was, as the Reagan administration contended, "expired, flawed, violated, unratified, and unratifiable," this still did not explain what specific provisions in a new treaty would prevent the Soviets from violating it, assuming their determination to do so. Neither can a rational explanation be found for Moscow's urge to further increase its otherwise all-powerful ICBM force by means of additional SS-25s. The entire SALT exercise seems to have been one of superpower self-destruct. SALT I and II undoubtedly advanced U.S. and Soviet interests when first concluded, by allowing each side to advance its own nuclear programs while placing some constraints on those of the other. By the mid and late 1980s, however, the agreements were no longer able to constrain the military threats confronting the superpowers. This realization led them to cooperate in discarding both treaties to the detriment of their own security and of future international stability.

A Terrible Blunder?

In the United States, considerable opposition developed to the administration's action. The demise of SALT II,[41] supporters of the treaty claimed, was a terrible blunder and one that would severely damage prospects for a new U.S.–Soviet strategic arms accord. Supporters offered four arguments in favor of retaining SALT:

1. Throughout the years, the treaty had served U.S. security interests well by constraining the growth of Soviet strategic forces (evidence the dismantling by the Soviet Union of hundreds of ICBM and SLBM launchers to remain within SALT restraints). The argument was not entirely cogent, since most of the dismantled Soviet weapons were old and would have been dismantled anyway, whether or not SALT existed.

2. Continued adherence to SALT II would have required the Soviet Union to dismantle many more strategic nuclear vehicles than the United States, that is, the numbers favor this side.[42] Again, the argument was only partly true. Beginning with the late 1980s, as a result of the acquisition of the D-5 and cruise missiles, the United States would have to dismantle an equal number of older systems to remain within the constraints of SALT.

3. In the absence of SALT II constraints on strategic launchers and warheads, the Soviets would be in a better position than the United States to expand their strategic forces. The argument reflects concern that, by taking advantage of the greater throw-weight capability of its missiles, the Soviet Union can deploy many more missile warheads than can the United States. The Soviet SS-18, for example, was restricted by SALT II to only 10 warheads; without SALT II constraints, the missile could be deployed with up to 30 warheads—an enormous increase in nuclear firepower considering that the Soviet Union has an inventory of 308 SS-18s.

4. SALT II had added predictability and stability in the strategic equation. The verification provisions of the treaty (i.e., noninterference with national technical means (NTM) and prohibitions against deliberate concealment to impede verification), if denied, would seriously complicate military planning on both sides.

By far the most vocal response to the termination of SALT was in the Senate, with treaty supporters urging President Reagan to bring the United States back into compliance and opponents threatening to give the treaty its final *coup de grace* by formally calling for its ratification and defeat on the Senate floor. The full Senate never did have the opportunity to vote for or against SALT II, although it had conducted extensive hearings on most aspects of the treaty. Senate approval in 1979 had been doubtful; in 1986 it would have been highly improbable.

Despite the ratification-vote threat, supporters of the treaty inside and outside the government continue to exert major pressure on the Congress to force treaty compliance through the use of "the powers of the purse."[43] A start of sorts was made in the fall of 1986 when Congress enacted binding legislation that prohibited the funding of programs violating the terms of SALT II. The effort, however, was soon aborted in view of the impending Iceland summit, the Congress not wishing to appear as restricting the president's freedom of action at the summit. Instead, a nonbinding Sense of the Congress resolution was substituted, affirming that it was in the "national security interests of the United States to continue voluntary compliance with the numerical sublimits of SALT II."

The exercise was repeated in the fall of 1987 as part of the FY 1988 DOD authorizations bill. Again the Congress requested that the president comply with the weapons limits of SALT II, and again it was forced to back off when confronted with another summit and the threat of a presidential veto. In a compromise, the Congress dropped its insistence that the president observe the strategic weapons limits in SALT II. In return, the administration agreed to dismantle 16 launchers on a Poseidon nuclear missile submarine[44] and also not to increase the rate of conversion of B-52 bombers to carry air-launched cruise missiles. The net effect of these actions was to place a cap on the U.S. MIRVed vehicles, one slightly higher than the ceiling of 1,320 called for by the treaty.[45] This again placed the United States in compliance with the SALT II limits, although not entirely.

THE ABM TREATY UNDER SIEGE

Having for all practical purposes wrecked SALT, the superpowers are next zeroing in on the ABM treaty, their only other major bilateral arms control accomplishment of the post–World War II era. Long the high-water mark in their efforts to contain the nuclear arms race, the treaty's remaining time in history is extremely short. The ABM treaty stands in the way of the superpower race for strategic defenses, and since the development of strategic defenses and the ABM treaty cannot coexist, the superpowers have elected to go with the former.

As in the case of SALT, it is easy to blame the United States as the party responsible for the pending emasculation of the ABM treaty. After all, it was the U.S. government that first questioned the precise meaning of the treaty and the extent that it might interfere with the development of strategic defenses (i.e., the Strategic Defense Initiative [SDI]). What this argument overlooks is the fact that both superpowers are busy developing strategic defenses; in fact, the Soviet SDI program might exceed that of the United

States in scope and dimension.[46] Although both superpowers have set out to build ballistic missile defenses, the United States in its never-ending search for legalism has questioned the impact of the treaty on its plans; the Soviets, in contrast, have proceeded with their work, treaty or no treaty.

Reinterpreting the Treaty

The crux of the ABM controversy involves one central question: What restrictions does the ABM treaty place on the development and testing of strategic defenses based on advanced technologies, that is, lasers, particle beam, and other "exotic" weapons? The question is not merely academic. It is crucial in determining how far development and testing may proceed under SDI (U.S. and Soviet).[47]

The treaty, unfortunately, does not provide clear-cut answers.[48] Two separate provisions are involved. "Each party," states Article V, "undertakes not to develop, test or deploy ABM systems or components which are sea-based, air-based, space-based, or mobile land-based." Note, however, Agreed Statement D: "the parties agree that in the event ABM systems based on other physical principles and including components capable of substituting for ABM interceptor missiles, ABM launchers, or ABM radars are created in the future, specific limitations on such systems and their components would be subject to discussion."

Until about 1984, when U.S. interest in exotic technologies began to be increasingly more pronounced, because of their possible application to SDI, Article V provided the sole basis for determining what could or could not be accomplished under the provisions of the treaty. The prohibition was precise and clear-cut; there were no exceptions or gray areas: ABM systems and components (except those of a *fixed, land-based* type) could *not* be developed, tested, or deployed.

What about the ABM systems and components of SDI interest, those futuristic space-based weapons based on physical principles unknown in 1972 (the year the treaty was signed)? What about Agreed Statement D? Two interpretations have been advanced: a traditional or narrow interpretation and a broad or permissive one.

The *traditional* interpretation, oldest of the two, holds that the ABM treaty bans the development, testing, and deployment of ABM systems and components of any type that are "sea-based, air-based, space-based, or mobile land-based." However, research ("research" only) may be carried out on any technology aimed at defending against ballistic missiles. Additionally, ABM systems and components, based on exotic technologies (such as lasers), may also be developed and tested, as long as they are fixed and land based (the sea-based, air-based, space-based, or mobile land-based prohibition remaining). But to deploy such fixed and land-based systems, an amendment to the treaty would be needed. This, supporters claim, is the correct interpretation of the ABM treaty that one gets from reading the appropriate provisions. It is also the one given to the Senate by Nixon administration officials when they sought its advice and consent on the treaty in 1972.

In contrast, the *broad* interpretation of the ABM treaty[49] holds that the treaty's restrictions on development and testing apply only to defensive technologies that existed in 1972. Therefore, systems based on physical principles unknown then can be developed and tested in any basing mode, including a space-based mode, although their deployment would still be subject to treaty amendment. The interpretation has the effect of permitting, for instance, laser tests in space. Supporters of the broad interpretation make their case by referring to the words "are created" in Agreed Statement D, which they interpret as meaning "are developed and tested." They also recall the treaty's negotiations during which the Soviet Union allegedly refused to consider any limitations on future weapons, arguing that it would be inappropriate for the two sides to agree on systems and components that at the time of the treaty's signing were neither defined nor understood.

To summarize the ABM controversy:

1. It does not concern ABM systems and components as we know them today (i.e., interceptor missiles, launchers, and radars). Development, testing, and deployment of such systems are permitted as long as the systems are fixed and land based. All others are prohibited.

2. The controversy arises from the language of the treaty, which is ambiguous in its treatment of certain advanced technologies being investigated by both superpowers in their SDI programs (i.e., lasers, particle beam, kinetic energy devices, and so on). For these advanced technologies, the controversy is limited only to the "development and testing" of mobile, including space-based systems and not to "research," which is permitted, or "deployment," which is not.

Reflecting a decision by President Reagan, the U.S. government formally ruled early in February 1987 that the *broad* interpretation of the treaty is the correct one.[50] There is considerable opposition to this view, especially in the U.S. Senate.[51] For reasons of international policy, however, and as long as the traditional interpretation of the treaty does not interfere unduly with progress under the SDI program, the United States intends to comply with that interpretation. There is logic in the U.S. position, regardless of one's feelings on the issue: why pursue openly the broad interpretation as long as SDI is still in the research phase and, therefore, permissible under the traditional interpretation?

The conflicting interpretations are a cause of great consternation to lawmakers, especially during the annual SDI appropriations cycle. Is the program, they ask, for which funds are requested permissible under the traditional interpretation or is the technology on which the experiment is based "new" (i.e., unknown in 1972). If the proposed program is prohibited by the traditional but allowed by the broad interpretation, at which point of development would the United States be in conflict with the traditional interpretation of the treaty?

Examining the Record

Since announcement by the Reagan administration of its support for the broad interpretation, partisans of both points of view have attempted to document the validity of their position. In the process every conceivable source bearing on the issue has been looked at: the record of the negotiations, the Senate ratification proceedings, and the practice of the two parties to the agreement during the ensuing years. As of this writing, the findings of the two groups can at best be described a "draw," with the negotiating record seeming to support the broad interpretation, but the ratification proceedings and superpower practices since 1972 suggesting that the traditional interpretation is the correct one. During the Reagan years, the Department of State, specifically its legal counsel,[52] carried the brunt of the effort to "sell" the broad interpretation to the Congress. He was supported by Paul Nitze,[53] the Reagan administration's senior statesman for arms control matters. Two powerful Democratic senators led the opposition: Sam Nunn of Georgia[54] and Carl Levin of Michigan.[55]

The first of the sources on the treaty's intent—the negotiating record—provides at best a fuzzy view. The record itself is still classified, and evidence on what actually transpired is generally based on the memory of the persons who participated in the proceedings.[56] During the diplomatic exchanges leading to the conclusion of the treaty the Soviet Union, they insist, consistently opposed any restrictions on futuristic weapons. By implication, the Soviets favored the broad interpretation. Eventually, Agreed Statement D was drafted prohibiting the "deployment" of weapons based on new physical principles but not their "creation" (i.e., their development and testing). There is an important question, however, that these reports do not answer. If the Soviets, in 1972, were supportive of the broad interpretation, what caused them suddenly to become the champions of the narrow or traditional interpretation, as they now claim to be?

The second source on the treaty's intent—the ratification proceedings—is no less confusing, and support for both points of view can be found in the committee hearings and the ensuing Senate debate. Partisans of the broad interpretation insist that the proceedings support unequivocally their point of view. Opponents claim that the record of the ratification proceedings is being misrepresented by selective editing of statements by Nixon administration officials supportive of the traditional interpretation. They also cite the case of a senator who in 1972 voted against ratification of the ABM treaty, allegedly because it prohibited the development and testing of laser weapons in space.

Finally, superpower practices since the treaty came into being clearly support the contention that the traditional interpretation is what the superpowers had agreed to in 1972.[57] The Moscow ABM complex, for instance, has been steadily upgraded by the Soviets during the past decade through the introduction of greater capability interceptors and radars. These activities, being fixed and land based, have been consistent with the provisions of Article V of the treaty. Similarly, Soviet SDI research into advanced technologies has not been taken past the limits of research permitted by the treaty. By not engaging in SDI development and testing the Soviets are signaling their support of the traditional interpretation.

Early SDI Deployment

Early in 1987 the issue over the treaty's proper interpretation made headlines again, when the Reagan administration let it be known that sufficient progress had been made in SDI research to justify early deployment of a limited SDI defense.[58] There was a major problem, though, with the administration's announcement. The proposed early deployment was not based on some exotic laser weapon or other directed-energy technology but on space-based interceptors, hardly a technology that qualified under the treaty's Agreed Statement D as a physical principle unknown in 1972. Specifically, what the administration was proposing was to use kinetic energy to intercept and destroy incoming ballistic missiles with ground-based and space-based nonnuclear weapons. (*Kinetic* energy weapons destroy targets simply by hitting them.[59])

To treaty supporters, the proposed early deployment of a limited SDI defense provided additional evidence that the dismantlement of the ABM treaty was near.[60] A limited SDI deployment, based on space-based kinetic vehicles, besides its enormous cost[61] would violate the treaty on two accounts: (1) by using space-based in lieu of fixed, land-based interceptors, prohibited by Article V; and (2) by basing the entire program on old technology, which is prohibited under Agreed Statement D. (How could hitting something with a rock be considered a new physical principle?[62])

Strong protests from Capitol Hill were immediately voiced.[63] A unilateral reinterpretation of the treaty by the executive branch, which would be different from the one on which the Senate had given its advice and consent, warned Senator Nunn (chairman of the Armed Services Committee), would "provoke a constitutional crisis of profound dimensions."[64] The intensity of the congressional opposition eventually forced the administration to agree to an SDI program for FYs 1988 and 1989 that remained well within the bounds of the traditional interpretation but without actually saying so.[65]

In evaluating the U.S. actions (above) vis-à-vis the ABM treaty, a fundamental question arises.[66] If the United States is determined to abandon the treaty, why doesn't it renounce it outright and be finished with it, as it did with SALT? Article XV allows each party to the treaty, in exercising its national sovereignty, to withdraw after giving a six-month notice. Would this not be preferable to the slow chipping away at the treaty, which the United States now seems to be engaged in?

The same question applies to the Soviet Union, with its record of treaty violations, especially with regard to the Krasnoyarsk radar.[67] The answer should be obvious. Despite its many drawbacks, when viewed from the perspective of superpower national interests, the treaty is useful to the superpowers for a while longer. Their SDI programs have not yet reached the point at which development and testing will be required. When they do, and unless the treaty can be modified beforehand in a way to suit superpower interests, it will surely be discarded. The reasons that led the superpowers in 1972 to conclude the agreement—that a dangerous and expensive superpower competition would occur without ABM restraints, that strategic defenses invariablly cause increases in offensive arms, that the risk of a nuclear war increases as each side fears that the other is developing ABMs as part of a first-strike strategy—have long been forgotten. In the 1990s, given a choice between developing their strategic defenses and having an ABM treaty, the superpowers will unfailingly choose the former option.

Specific proposals made by Soviet and U.S. leaders over the past three years provide ample evidence of the superpowers' long-term goal to eliminate the treaty in its present form. In July 1986, for instance, the U.S. proposed superpower adherence to the treaty for a period of five years, while performing development and testing that "is permitted by the ABM treaty" (i.e., the broad interpretation). The offer was extended at the Reykjavik summit to a longer period, after which either party could move out of the treaty and begin deploying its SDI defenses (i.e., the ABM treaty would no longer apply). Both U.S. offers presupposed major reductions in offensive strategic systems, including the elimination of all ballistic missiles on both sides. By its proposals, the United States wanted the best of both worlds: zero ballistic missiles in the Soviet Union and plenty of SDI defenses here. There was one question, though, that the U.S. proposals were unable to explain. In a world of no ballistic missiles, what useful purpose would SDI serve?

The Soviet strategy for terminating the ABM treaty is different from that of the United States, but the goal is the same. The Soviet approach is to make proposals that are totally unacceptable to this side, such as the one for "strengthening" the treaty by renegotiating what could and could not be done under SDI. To the U.S. side, this plan is designed to impose constraints on the SDI program that are more severe than those imposed by the traditional interpretation of the treaty. Such additional constraints, said the Reagan administration, would kill the SDI program. Another Soviet suggestion is for the superpowers to waive for a period of ten years their rights under Article XV (i.e., the right to give notice and withdraw from the treaty). This, too, is judged by the United States as a Soviet ploy designed to deny it the option of deploying SDI.

During the Washington Summit in December 1987, the superpowers confirmed once again their desire to hang on to the ABM treaty a while longer but, they hope, not for very long. They did this by using the most ambiguous language ever in their final communiqué. Evidence also the title of a space treaty proposed by the United States soon after the summit: Treaty between the United States and the Soviet Union on Certain Measures to Facilitate the Cooperative Transition to the Deployment of Future Strategic Ballistic Missile Defenses.[68]

NOTES

1. A principal goal of the INF treaty was to convey to the world an aura of arms control momentum. The treaty addressed none of the critical arms control issues of the day, left the strategic arsenals of the superpowers intact, and even allowed the removal and reuse of the nuclear warheads from the delivery vehicles that were eliminated. See also George F. Will, "Is This Arms Control?" *Washington Post*, September 24, 1987.

2. White House, Office of Press Secretary, *The President's Report to the Congress on Soviet Noncompliance with Arms Control Agreements* (Washington, DC, January 23, 1984), and subsequent reports.

3. Kenneth L. Adelman, *Is Arms Control at a Dead End?* Current Policy no. 837 (Washington, DC: Department of State, Bureau of Public Affairs, May 16, 1986).

4. The SALT II proportionate response decision of May 1986, which in effect killed the SALT II treaty, was defended by the United States exclusively on the Soviet record of arms treaty noncompliance.

5. U.S. Arms Control and Disarmament Agency, *Annual Report to the Congress, 1987* (Washington, DC: U.S. ACDA, February 24, 1988), pp. 69–71; and U.S. Department of State, Bureau of Public Affairs, *Soviet Noncompliance with Arms Control Agreements: The President's Report to the Congress*, Special Report no. 175 (Washington, DC, December 2, 1987), pp. 2–3.

6. U.S. Department of State, Bureau of Public Affairs, *Soviet Noncompliance with Arms Control Agreements*, p. 6.

7. In line with their policy of greater openness, the Soviets have been easing some of their formerly very restrictive rules governing travel to sensitive military areas. Thus on September 5, 1987, a U.S. congressional delegation was allowed to inspect the radar facility in Krasnoyarsk; a month later another U.S. delegation was permitted to visit and observe the Soviet chemical facility at Shikhany.

8. Listed in U.S. Arms Control and Disarmament Agency, *Arms Control and Disarmament Agreements: Texts and Histories of Negotiations* (Washington, DC: U.S. Government Printing Office, 1982).

9. Michael Krepon, "How Reagan Is Killing a Quiet Forum for Arms Talks," *Washington Post*, August 31, 1986.

10. R. Jeffrey Smith, "Soviet Arms Violations Disputed: House Panel's Democrats Call Evidence of Cheating Inconclusive," *Washington Post*, November 21, 1987.

11. Congressional Research Service, Library of Congress, *Verification: Soviet Compliance with Arms Control Agreements*, IB 84131 (Washington, DC, October 1987), p. 11.

12. SALT I, Article V; SALT II, Article XV.

13. U.S. Arms Control and Disarmament Agency, *Annual Report to the Congress, 1985* (Washington, DC: U.S. ACDA, January 30, 1986), p. 45; and Arms Control Association, "Analysis of the President's Report on Soviet Noncompliance," *Arms Control Today*, April 1987.

14. The U.S. reports on Soviet noncompliance were dated January 1984, February 1985, December 1985, December 1986, March 1987, December 1987, and December 1988.

15. White House, *Soviet Noncompliance with Arms Control Agreements: The President's Report to the Congress* (Washington, DC: December 1988).

16. Ibid., p. 6

17. Until the late 1970s, the Moscow ABM complex consisted of sixty-four above-ground launchers. Since 1980, the complex has been upgraded. When modernization is completed, one-hundred launchers, the maximum permitted under the ABM treaty, will be on station.

18. A delegation of eight persons, including one from the U.S. Embassy in Moscow, visited the Gomel site in December 1987. The U.S. government maintains that deployment of radar components in Gomel constitutes a violation of the ABM treaty.

19. Until September 1989, when the Soviet Union formally admitted that the Krasnoyarsk radar was in violation of the ABM treaty, the purpose of the Krasnoyarsk facility was a major irritant in U.S.–Soviet relations. See R. Jeffrey Smith, "Soviets Rebuff U.S. Complaint on Missile Radar," *Washington Post*, September 1, 1988. See also Ralph Earle II and John B. Rhinelander, "The Krasnoyarsk Radar— A Material Breach of the ABM Treaty?" *Arms Control Today*, September 1988, pp. 9–11.

20. The Senate on September 16, 1988, unanimously declared that the Krasnoyarsk violation must be corrected before the conclusion of any future agreement on strategic arms. A House resolution a year earlier similarly declared the Krasnoyarsk radar as a Soviet violation of its legal obligations under the ABM treaty. In the opinion of the three U.S. congressmen who visited the radar in September 1987, the installation, not being completed as yet, technically does not violate the ABM treaty. See Congressmen Thomas J. Downey, Bob Carr, and Jim Moody, "Report from Krasnoyarsk," *Bulletin of Atomic Scientists*, November, 1987, pp. 11–14. For the official U.S. government position, see the Department of State statement of November 2, 1988.

21. White House, *Soviet Noncompliance with Arms Control Agreements*, December 1988, pp. 15–18.

22. LTBT, Article I, paragraph 1 (b).

23. U.S. Department of State, Bureau of Public Affairs, *Soviet Noncompliance with Arms Control Agreements*, Special Report no. 136 (Washington, DC, December 23, 1985), p. 8.

24. The view is not shared by the Congressional Office of Technology Assessment.

25. TTBT, Article III.

26. White House, *Soviet Noncompliance with Arms Control Agreements*, p. 11.

27. U.S. Arms Control and Disarmament Agency, *Soviet Noncompliance* (Washington, DC: U.S. Government Printing Office, February 1986).

28. Ibid., p. 11.

29. Ibid., pp. 7–8.

30. SALT II, Article IV, paragraph 9.

31. Karen De Young, "Aging British Radar Site Complicates Arms Talks: Soviets Say Modernization Foreshadows SDI," *Washington Post*, June 13, 1988. See also Peter Zimmerman, "The Thule, Fylingdales, and Krasnoyarsk Radars: Innocents Abroad?" *Arms Control Today*, March 1987, pp. 9–11. The author suggested that both the United States and the Soviet Union are constructing large phased-array radars that violate the ABM treaty.

32. Jack Mendelsohn, "Proportionate Response: Sense or Nonsense?" *Arms Control Today*, January/February 1986, pp. 7–11.

33. Congressional Research Service, Library of Congress, *Fundamentals of Nuclear Arms Control* (Washington, DC: U.S. Government Printing Office, 1986).

34. Ibid., pp. 63–140.

35. U.S. Arms Control and Disarmament Agency, *Arms Control and Disarmament Agreements: Texts and Histories of Negotiations* (Washington, DC: U.S. Government Printing Office, 1982), p. 153.

36. Congressional Research Service, Library of Congress, *Fundamentals of Nuclear Arms Control*, p. 140.

37. Ibid., pp. 33–34.

38. A detailed listing of U.S. and Soviet weapons deactivations to remain within the numerical ceilings of SALT I and II is provided in Arms Control Association and the Ploughshares Fund, *Countdown on SALT II: The Case for Preserving SALT II Limits on U.S. and Soviet Strategic Forces* (Washington, DC: Arms Control Association, 1985), pp. 13–14.

39. U.S. Department of State, Bureau of Public Affairs, *U.S. Interim Restraint Policy: Responding to Soviet Arms Control Violations*, Special Report no. 147 (Washington, DC, May 27, 1986); see also idem, *Interim Restraint: U.S. and Soviet Force Projections*, Special Report no. 151 (Washington, DC, August 5, 1986).

40. U.S. Department of State, Bureau of Public Affairs, *U.S. Interim Restraint Policy: Responding to Soviet Arms Control Violations*, p. 3.

41. Arms Control Association and the Ploughshares Fund, *Countdown on SALT II*, makes an excellent case for SALT II and includes the text of the treaty. See also Arms Control Association, *The Case for Preserving SALT II*, Background Paper (Washington, DC, May 1986).

42. Congressman Lee Hamilton, "Soviet Compliance and the Future of SALT," *Arms Control Today*, July/August 1986, pp. 3–5.

43. Senators Dale Bumpers, John Chaffe, and Patrick Leahy, "Salvaging SALT: The New Congressional Compromise," *Arms Control Today*, December 1987, pp. 3–6.

44. Marcel A. Bryar, "Congress, Administration Reach Arms Control Compromise," *Arms Control Today*, December 1987, pp. 23–24.

45. Helen Dewar, "Senate Defense Bill Sent to the White House, Arms Control Compromise Included," *Washington Post*, November 20, 1987.

46. U.S. Department of Defense and U.S. Department of State, *Soviet Strategic Defense Programs* (Washington, DC: U.S. Government Printing Office, 1985). See also U.S. Department of Defense, *Soviet Military Power: An Assessment of the Threat, 1988* (Washington, DC: U.S. Government Printing Office, 1988), pp. 55–62.

47. A good overview of U.S. SDI testing, past and planned, is by Matthew Bunn, "Star Wars Testing and the ABM Treaty," *Arms Control Today*, April 1988, pp. 11–19.

48. U.S. Arms Control and Disarmament Agency, *Arms Control and Disarmament Agreements*, pp. 132–44.

49. A good statement on the broad interpretation is by Paul H. Nitze, *Permitted and Prohibited Activities under the ABM Treaty*, Current Policy no. 886 (Washington, DC: U.S. Department of State, Bureau of Public Affairs, October 31, 1986).

50. Dusko Dodel and R. Jeffrey Smith, "Shultz Accepts Broad View of ABM Treaty," *Washington Post*, February 9, 1987.

51. R. Jeffrey Smith, "Foreign Relations Panel Denounces Reinterpreting of ABM Treaty," *Washington Post*, September 21, 1987.

52. Senator Joseph R. Biden and John B. Ritch III, "The End of the Sofaer Doctrine: A Victory for Arms Control and the Constitution," *Arms Control Today*, September 1988, pp. 3–8. But see also Don Oberdorfer, "Two New Studies Back Permissive ABM View," *Washington Post*, May 14, 1987.

53. Paul H. Nitze, *Interpreting the ABM Treaty*, Current Policy no. 936 (Washington, DC: U.S. Department of State, Bureau of Public Affairs, April 1, 1987).

54. Sam Nunn, "ABM Reinterpretation Fundamentally Flawed," *Arms Control Today*, April 1987, pp. 8–14. See also R. Jeffrey Smith, "Nunn Takes Strict View on ABM: Broad Interpretation of Pact to Allow SDI Work Is Termed Absurd," *Washington Post*, March 12, 1987.

55. Carl Levin, "Administration Wrong on ABM Treaty," *Bulletin of Atomic Scientists*, April 1987, pp. 30–32.

56. John B. Rhinelander and James P. Rubin, "Mission Accomplished: An Insider's Account of the ABM Treaty Negotiating Record," *Arms Control Today*, September 1987, pp. 3–14.

57. Raymond L. Garthoff, "History Confirms the Traditional Meaning," *Arms Control Today*, September 1987, pp. 15–19.

58. George C. Wilson, "Reagan May Pick an SDI System Soon," *Washington Post*, January 14, 1987; Strobe Talbott, "A Shield Against Arms Control: Weinberger Calls for Early Deployment of SDI," *Time*, February 2, 1987.

59. For a description of the technologies now being explored under the SDI program, refer to U.S. Department of Defense, Strategic Defense Initiative Organization, *Report to the Congress on the Strategic Defense Initiative* (Washington, DC, April 1988). See also Matthew Bunn, "What Is Phase One Defense?" *Arms Control Today*, May 1988, pp. 20–21; and R. Jeffrey Smith, "Early SDI Deployment Unfeasible, Experts Say," *Washington Post*, April 24, 1987.

60. Arms Control Association, *Early Dismantlement of the ABM Treaty: Experts Criticize the Administration's Move toward Treaty Reinterpretation and Early SDI Deployment*, Press Briefing (Washington, DC, March 1987).

61. Early SDI deployment (or Phase I as it is officially known) was originally estimated to cost $115 billion; its cost has since been scaled down to $69 billion.

62. Bruce van Voorst, "From Star Wars to Smart Rocks," *Time*, February 23, 1987.

63. Helen Dewar, "Administration Warned on SDI Tests," *Washington Post*, February 25, 1987.

64. Helen Dewar, "Senator Nunn Warns Reagan on Shift in Missile Treaty," *Washington Post*, February 7, 1987. The senator does support, though, a modest defense against ballistic missiles to guard against an accidental launch. More on this in Michael Krepons' "Nunn's Modest SDI," *Bulletin of Atomic Scientists*, April 1988, p. 5.

65. Tom Kenworthy, "House Votes to Restrict the Missile Defense Program," *Washington Post*, April 28, 1988; see also Thomas Halverston, "House Passes Defense Bill Endorsing Traditional Interpretation," *Arms Control Today*, June 1988, p. 6.

66. Harold Brown, "Too Much, Too Soon: National Decision on SDI Should Wait Until 1990s," *Arms Control Today*, May 1987, pp. 2–3.

67. Congressional Research Service, Library of Congress, *Arms Control: Negotiations to Limit Defense and Space Weapons*, IB 86073 (Washington, DC, March 1988). See also, R. Jeffrey Smith, "U.S. ABM Treaty Complaint Imperils START, Soviet Says: USSR Radar Site is Focus of Dispute," *Washington Post*, July 16, 1988; idem, "U.S. Reasserts Concern over Soviet Radar," *Washington Post*, August 13, 1988.

68. Arms Control Association, *Defense and Space Talks: Background and Negotiating History*, Background Paper (Washington, DC, April 1988), p. 10.

5

The Politics of Arms Control

On most major arms control issues, the United States does not speak with a single voice. There is the official U.S. government position adopted by the administration, but invariably, there is also a second very powerful voice, that of the Congress. The pluralism (which must delight but also confuse the other superpower) is evidence of the increasing breakdown in executive-congressional relations on many aspects of arms control, compounded by partisan political bickering. Despite some recent "accommodations" (such as the compromise agreements on the defense budgets concluded just before the Iceland and Washington summits and the Senate's overwhelming ratification of the intermediate-range nuclear forces [INF] treaty), a bipartisan and constitutionally correct concensus on U.S. arms control policy simply does not exist.[1]

SOURCES OF FRICTION

Few issues in recent times have caused a deeper schism between the president and the Congress than nuclear arms control. The reasons are not hard to discern. Arms control is an issue that neither the president nor the Congress can handle alone. To formulate and implement a truly integrated national arms control policy, one that the American people will support and the Soviets respect, requires extremely close ties and collaboration between the two responsible branches of our government. In actual practice, the very opposite has been happening, especially during most of the decade of the 1980s.

Recalling the basic constitutional prerogatives involved, on arms control as in all aspects of foreign policy, the president speaks for the nation. He determines which particular weapon systems we ought to buy, when to negotiate with the Soviet Union, and which agreements to conclude.[2] But in the exercise of these duties, the president's powers are not absolute. Under our system of checks and balances, his weapons-procurement plans are subject to congressional approval as are most of the international agreements that he signs. The same system of checks and balances requires that the Congress work with the president, not at cross-purposes with him. Stated briefly, the president and the Congress share responsibility[3] for the conduct of the nation's arms control agenda. Neither can carry it out alone. Both are essential to the process.

Sharing responsibility requires a great deal of give and take, qualities not in great abundance either on Capitol Hill or in the executive mansion. It is not uncommon, therefore, for perfectly legitimate congressional actions to be rejected by the president as "power grabbing" exercises and "crude interferences" into his prerogatives.[4] Neither is it unusual for the Congress openly to rebel against the president's arms control policies and to deny him programs that he as the commander-in-chief considers essential to national security. On several occasions during the past decade, the Congress even attempted to seize from the president the lead in arms control policy by openly pursuing policies diagonally opposed to those of his administration. To the president, such congressional activism gives the Soviets perceptions of major U.S. internal dissention and greatly undermines his negotiating position at summits and in Geneva.[5]

Approval of Treaties

A common source of friction between the president and the Congress is the requirement for Senate or congressional approval of international arms control agreements. International agreements take the form of either formal treaties or executive agreements.[6] Treaties, as Article II, Section 2, of the Constitution specifies, can only take force on "the advice and consent of the Senate," provided that two-thirds of the senators present concur. Executive agreements, on the other hand, require the approval of both houses of the Congress, but by a simple majority vote. Throughout the years, the Congress has insisted that all important arms control agreements be in one of the two forms, except for lesser accords (such as the type of "confidence building" measures that established the Hot Line between Washington and Moscow and, more recently, the Nuclear Risk Reduction Centers) that do not require congressional approval. To sustain this requirement, the Congress even wrote appropriate language into the Arms Control and Disarmament Act. Section 33 of the Act specifies that "no action can be taken which obligates the United States to reduce its armaments, except pursuant to the treaty-making power or unless authorized by further affirmative legislation of the Congress."

In an age when the great majority of the members of the Congress have strong views on arms control, the requirement for congressional approval of international arms control agreements provides the Congress with a powerful clout. The Congress has repeatedly taken advantage of its authority in this regard, as it did for instance when considering the Strategic Arms Limitation Talks (SALT) I Interim Agreement. Noting numerical limits in the agreement that appeared to favor the Soviet Union, the Congress mandated that the president negotiate a follow-on agreement that would entail equal numerical limits on both sides. The resolution approving SALT I was explicit in this regard. The president was to seek a future treaty that, among other things, "would not limit the United States to levels of intercontinental strategic forces inferior to the limits proposed for the Soviet Union."[7]

Administrations, regardless of political orientation, regard with extreme annoyance any congressional effort to tamper with a treaty once it has been negotiated and signed. The introduction of amendments that would necessitate the reopening of negotiations is especially troublesome. (The SALT II treaty would most certainly have resulted in such amendments, had it come to a final vote. In approving the treaty, the Senate Foreign Relations Committee did so subject to twenty reservations, understandings, and declarations.[8]) In an effort to minimize the possibility of such troubling amendments, members of both houses of the Congress now periodically attend arms control negotiations either as advisers or simply as observers. By working with the Congress while agreements with the other side are being negotiated, an administration stands a far better chance of neutralizing opposition to the final agreement once it has been signed.

Congressional participation in arms control talks is a fairly new practice, having been adopted first by the Carter administration in 1977 in connection with the SALT II talks. But as evidenced by the fierce opposition that the resulting treaty eventually encountered in the Senate, the presence of congressional observers during negotiations does not necessarily insure approval of the completed document. The arrangement does provide the Congress, however, with greater information on the specific issues being debated and opens up a useful channel of communications between the executive and legislators. The arrangement represents a definite improvement over the situation that prevailed earlier, when the Congress was left in the dark along with everyone else on the fine print of arms control agreements until after the president had signed them. SALT I was one such case.

Whether an international arms control agreement is eventually submitted to the Congress in the form of a treaty or as an executive agreement is a decision that the president alone can make. A major consideration in his judgment is the anticipated reception of the treaty in the Senate, where a minority of one-third of the senators present plus one can defeat it. If the president elects to submit the accord in the form of an executive agreement, his odds for success are increased in the Senate (there he would need only a simple majority), but he now has to contend also with the entire House of Representatives. The two houses have different institutional interests in the issue, the Senate preferring treaties and the House executive agreements. In this context, a risk always exists that the president may anger several senators and even cause the defeat of an agreement if he chooses to submit it as an executive agreement rather than a treaty. This was probably the rationale behind President Carter's decision to process the SALT II as a "treaty." When in August 1978 he inquired of the Congress' desires on this matter, he was advised by the Senate leadership in no uncertain terms that the proposed accord should be a treaty "sound in every respect and able to withstand the constitutional test of advise and consent."[9]

Once a president has made his determination in favor of processing an international agreement as a treaty, the Congress cannot unilaterally change that decision. The issue surfaced in the early 1980s, when supporters of SALT II in the Senate Foreign Relations Committee attempted to secure a de facto ratification of the treaty through the passage of a Senate Joint Resolution.[10] The action would have required a simple majority in the Senate and the House of Representatives to take effect. Critics of the action complained that the president had not requested approval of SALT II and that, therefore, it was improper to require him to accept an international agreement that he had not sought. In the opinion of the treaty's opponents, the resolution before the Senate Foreign Relations Committee was an attempt to give binding effect to the obligations of a treaty, which had never received the requisite approval by two-thirds of the Senate; therefore, it was a constitutionally impermissable intrusion by the Congress into the treaty-making powers of the president.[11]

Reporting Requirements

Congressional reporting requirements are another source of friction between president and Congress in the conduct of the nation's arms control policy.[12] As the name implies, reporting requirements are requests by congressional committees or individual members appended to key pieces of legislation for the purpose of obtaining information from the president or to coerce him to pursue a specified course of action. As many as thirty such congressional requirements may be in effect at any time.

By far the largest number of reporting requirements are simple requests for information, that is, the Congress asking to be provided with data on issues of current interest, such as Soviet compliance with arms control agreements, the status of U.S. civil defense programs, or worldwide nuclear proliferation developments.[13] Such requests seldom cause controversy. More contentious, however, are "presidential certification" requirements, which deal with specific policies that the Congress wishes the president to pursue. Under the "presidential certification" rule, the president must certify to the

Congress *before* taking a specified action that the planned action is in the national interest. Requirements for "presidential certification" cause great hardship on an executive, especially when they constrain him from carrying out policies he favors but that the Congress opposes.

Persons in and out of the government often complain of the futility of the reporting requirements imposed by the Congress. Information requirements, they charge, hardly ever influence national arms control policy, and the reports they generate are not read by more than a handful of committee members or staff. Why then, waste the government's time and money? Similar criticisms are levied against "presidential certification" requirements. These requirements are nothing but trouble—the Congress is never able to make them stick and presidents forever subvert them for their own purposes.

Examples abound concerning the political bickering and squabbling that result whenever the Congress attempts to exercise control over presidential arms control policy by means of the "certification" tactic. As part of the Defense Authorization Act, for instance, approved in October 1984 the Congress voted to prohibit the expenditure of funds for antisatellite (ASAT) testing against an object in space until the president had certified (a) that he was endeavoring in good faith to negotiate an ASAT agreement with the Soviet Union and (b) that, pending such agreement, ASAT testing was necessary for reasons of national security.[14] On August 20, 1985, President Reagan submitted certification to the Congress and proceeded with an ASAT test.[15] The president's excuse for testing was flimsy at best. An ASAT arms control agreement, he told the Congress, is not in the national interest, and therefore, he did not feel obliged to negotiate one. Annoyed legislators responded by placing on the president a far stricter "certification" requirement: in the future he could not conduct an ASAT test until he had certified to the Congress that the Soviet Union had already conducted such a test.

Congressional informational requirements do not fare much better. Annually, pursuant to Section 36 of the Arms Control and Disarmament Act, the President is required to furnish to the Congress a detailed statement on the arms control implications of his military budget for the year and the extent that planned weapons procurements are in line with existing U.S. arms control policy or international agreements. The information is provided by means of the Arms Control Impact Statement (ACIS), a document good in intentions but generally extremely poor in implementation.[16] The 1988 ACIS, for instance, arrived on Capitol Hill two full months *after* the administration's submission of its FY 1988 budget request to the Congress, the very process that the document was designed to support. In content, the 1988 ACIS was no best-seller either, with several of its sections, especially as they pertained to SALT II and the Antiballistic Missile (ABM) Treaty, being heavily biased in favor of administration policy.

The Arms Control and Disarmament Agency's (ACDA's) annual reports

to the Congress[17] similarly suffer from gross bias. The report for 1986 is a
good case in point. Despite a new sleek cover and expanded size, the ACDA
report raised serious doubts of the Reagan administration's sincerity for
containing the nuclear arms race. The United States was depicted in the
document as being more interested in winning a public relations contest
from the Soviet Union than in advancing the cause of arms control, which
after all is the mission of the agency. What else can explain the recurrent
characterizations in the report of the U.S. proposals as "historic" and "notable" but those of the Soviet Union as "disappointing," "devious," and
"designed for propaganda"?

Other Sources of Friction

Friction between Congress and the president is evident also whenever the
Congress, in the conduct of its other constitutional responsibilities, attempts
to influence unduly presidential arms control policy.

The Senate, for instance, regularly makes it a practice to demonstrate
concern for specific arms control issues while providing "advice and consent" on presidential appointments. It did so in 1983, when considering the
appointment of Ambassador Kenneth L. Adelman as ACDA director.[18] The
appointment was eventually approved by a vote of fifty-seven to forty-two
but not until some very critical comments had been made in committee and
on the senate floor concerning the candidate's arms control views and, by
implication, those of the president, who made the appointment. Similarly,
the nomination a few years earlier of Paul Warnke as director of the ACDA
and as chief SALT negotiator provoked considerable controversy. To many
members of the Senate, Warnke appeared to be too eager to sign a SALT
agreement with the Soviets. His nomination as director of the ACDA was
confirmed by a vote of seventy to twenty-nine but as chief SALT negotiator
by only fifty-eight to forty. Warnke's failure to receive a two-thirds majority
as negotiator was a clear signal to the president that any agreement Warnke
might conclude with the Soviet Union would have difficulty securing the
two-thirds vote necessary for advice and consent.

Increasingly, members of both houses are making use of "resolutions" to
nudge the administration in the direction of congressional arms control
policy.[19] The resolutions do not have the force of law, but by stimulating
debate on an issue they can alter administration policy significantly. In 1983,
for instance, the House of Representatives, after extensive hearings and
heated debate, approved a nuclear freeze resolution by a vote of 278 to
149. Even though the Senate later voted to table the resolution, subsequent
changes in Reagan administration arms control policy were undoubtedly
the direct result of the congressional nuclear freeze initiative.

Occassionally, congressional resolutions have a happy ending, as was the
case with Senate Resolution 329 of February 1, 1984, which called upon

the administration to negotiate with the Soviet Union the establishment of Nuclear Risk Reduction Centers in Washington and Moscow.[20] Although the Reagan White House initially resisted the idea of such centers, sustained pressure from the Congress, especially from two of the Senate's leading defense experts (Senators Sam Nunn [D-GA] and John Warner [R-VA]),eventually made realization of the centers possible. In pursuing its goal, the Congress used every weapon in its legislative arsenal: resolutions, hearings, floor debate, even appropriate language in the 1985 DOD Authorization Act.[21] Establishment of nuclear risk reduction centers, the Congress emphasized, could diffuse superpower confrontation brought about by misjudgment, miscalculation, or misunderstanding. In the end, the Congress prevailed.

THE DEFENSE BUDGET

The executive-legislative rivalry over constitutional prerogatives affects adversely the U.S. negotiating posture and the ability of this nation to confront the Soviet Union with a single and unified arms control policy. Equally detrimental to the cause of arms control is the annual battle of the defense budget,[22] an exercise noted more for petty partisanship and the practice of reelection politics than for a desire to stabilize or contain the nuclear arms race.

The congressional role for participating in the formulation of the defense budget should be obvious. It is, after all, the Congress that, under Section 8, Article I, of the Constitution, is responsible for raising and supporting armies and for providing and maintaining a navy. What makes this process cumbersome, however, is a sustained congressional effort (especially during the past two decades) to use the congressional review process of the defense budget as an instrument for influencing and even dictating U.S. arms control policy. Again and again, since the mid-1960s, the Congress used military funding decisions to influence the direction of the nation's arms control agenda:[23] the ABM and multiple, independently targeted reentry vehicle (MIRV) issues as they impacted on SALT I; the B-1 bomber and cruise missiles as they affected the SALT II negotiations; and, more recently, the MX, ASAT, Midgetman, and Strategic Defense Initiative votes to help define U.S. goals and objectives at the nuclear and space talks in Geneva.

The B-1B and B-2 Bombers

The B-1B is America's newest and theoretically finest bomber. It has been under development and procurement for more than twenty years, first as the B-70 bomber, later as the B-1A, and more recently as the B-1B.

Even though the plane has a history as long as nuclear arms control itself, its need has never been convincingly documented. Supporters of the B-1B have traditionally argued that the plane is needed to replace the aging B-52 and to provide U.S. negotiators with a bargaining chip in their talks with the Soviet Union. (This claim has been disproven by events.) Opponents of the plane continue to doubt its military worth, especially its ability to penetrate Soviet air defenses. Uncertainty over the plane's penetration capabilities was undoubtedly behind President Carter's decision in 1977 to cancel the B-1 program and to focus on the development of cruise missiles as more cost-effective deterrent systems.

The decision to build the B-1B was not made until October 1981, when President Reagan launched his strategic modernization program. A total of one hundred planes have since been built at a cost of $28.3 billion. Deployment[24] put an end to all of the idle talk about the plane serving as a bargaining chip (i.e., the plane is here to stay), with many of its funding decisions made to benefit pork barrel politics rather than sensitivity to and potential impact on arms control negotiations.

Pork barrel politics sounds like harsh term to describe a $28.3 billion plane. But that is exactly what did happen. The B-1B has experienced a lot of trouble with fuel leaks, causing the entire fleet to be grounded at least twice. Problems also haunt the plane's defensive electronics (to correct these deficiencies, the U.S. Air Force estimates that approximately $2 billion will be required) amid serious doubts that the plane can carry out its assigned mission in wartime.[25] These facts notwithstanding, powerful members of the Congress from districts that benefit from the plane have lobbied extensively to keep the plane's production lines open past the one hundredth bomber. A major argument in support of continued production was that 20,000 jobs would be at stake. The fact that additional bombers would have added significantly to the U.S. strategic arsenal and in the process complicated chances for an arms reduction agreement with the Soviet Union was hardly a consideration.

As expected, opposed to the production of additional B-1Bs were and are members of the Congress from districts where the Northrop Corporation maintains its principal manufacturing facilities. Their concern is understandable. Northrop is the builder of the Stealth bomber (or B-2),[26] the follow-on plane to the B-1B. The Stealth lobby wants the air force to stick to its original plan of 100 B-1Bs followed by 132 Stealths. The plane, it asserts, will be able to accomplish what the B-1B, despite its $28.3 billion price tag, reportedly cannot, that is, to penetrate Soviet air defenses and attack targets deep in the interior of the USSR.

The B-2's technical characteristics are still highly classified. The plane is said to be invisible to enemy radar, its surfaces and materials designed to hamper reflection.[27] Flight testing began in July 1989 despite an earlier Pentagon decision that called for a slowdown in B-2 development to redress certain yet unspecified "technical problems." Program costs are also highly classified with estimates for the 132 planes exceeding $70 billion, or more than $500 million per copy.

The MX and Its Follow-on Missile

The MX missile similarly has a history as long as arms control, and it, too, was originally justified as a bargaining chip for use in the negotiations with the Soviets. Not surprisingly, the MX chip was never played by the United States—it probably was never intended to serve that purpose.

Unlike the need for the B–1B, whose basic requirement was and remains obscure, the need for a new land-based missile to replace the aging Minuteman and enhance the U.S. deterrent in light of Soviet advances in missile weight and accuracy was never doubted in Washington. Its obvious need notwithstanding, opposition in the Congress to the missile has been deep and sustained, primarily due to two considerations: the missile's ever-changing basing scheme and its perception, especially among arms control activists, as a "destabilizing" weapon because of its size and extraordinary accuracy.

The unending search for a viable basing scheme made the MX the arms control and defense issue extraordinaire of the 1980s. The Carter administration—first to struggle with the basing problem—elected to go with 200 missiles deployed for survivability in a "race track" pattern of 4,600 shelters. The plan was junked by President Reagan in favor of 100 missiles deployed in closely spaced superhardened silos (the "dense pack"). That plan, too, was soon scrapped, this time by the Congress on the recommendation of the Scowcroft Commission, in favor of a force of only 50 missiles deployed in existing Minuteman silos.[28] Present research into MX basing options favors a rail-mobile configuration, with the missiles deployed on specially designed trains and rotated during a crisis to prevent Soviet detection.[29]

MX basing and funding debates on the Hill invariably have been linked to issues of arms control, with missile proponents arguing that the system is needed to convince the Soviets of the futility of an unrestrained arms race, and opponents arguing that the MX will destabilize the nuclear balance and intensify the arms race. In 1983, for instance, a bipartisan group of legislators used their influence on an MX funding decision to secure presidential endorsement for development of the Small ICBM (popularly known as the Midgetman) and for adoption of the "build-down" formula as the U.S. negotiating position at the Strategic Arms Reduction Talks (START). Under this formula the superpowers would pledge to destroy two nuclear warheads for each new warhead deployed. Later, when the Soviets walked out of the START negotiations following deployment of the Pershing II missiles in Europe, debate in the Congress turned to the possibility of using MX funding as a leverage to improve prospects for future negotiations. Various options were considered, from outright termination of the MX (would have re-warded the Soviets for walking out of the START talks) to placing restric-tions on future MX procurement to encourage both sides to pursue arms control. Eventually, procurement of a first increment of fifty MX missiles was approved by the Congress for deployment in existing Minuteman silos. All fifty are now deployed in the F. E. Warren Air Force Base, near Cheyenne, Wyoming.[30] Decision on a second increment of fifty MXs is not expected for at least another two years and not until after the Bush administration has had an opportunity to evaluate the MX rail-mobile configuration and its impact on U.S.–Soviet strategic stability.

The Bush administration finds itself in a quandary over the MX. It does not care for its present silo basing, which makes the force vulnerable to a Soviet surprise attack, but neither does it have a proven plan for enhancing MX survivability. Then there is the matter of the Small ICBM, a road-mobile missile for which there is very strong support on Capitol Hill and uncertainty in the White House. In an effort to promote bipartisanship and forestall a bruising fight with the Congress, President Bush agreed in the spring of 1989 to move ahead with both mobile missiles but with devel-opment of the rail-mobile MX assigned higher priority than development of the Small ICBM.[31]

The president's plan is encountering opposition from at least three quar-ters: (1) from members of Congress, who are concerned with the high cost of redeploying the MX from silos to train garages (expected to exceed $7 billion);[32] (2) from supporters of the Small ICBM, who suspect that the administration will probably drop the weapon once the MX rail-mobile has been procured;[33] and (3) from arms control advocates, who question the wisdom of proceeding with the development of two mobile systems when the U.S. position in the START talks in Geneva favors abolishing such systems.

Despite allocation of funds for its continued development, the future of the Small ICBM is far from insured. Formerly the darling of hawks and doves alike, the weapon now has formidable opposition, foretelling a de-velopment course even more uncertain than that which characterized the MX in the early 1980s.[34]

To understand the rationale behind the opposition as well as support for the Small ICBM, one must consider the events leading to its creation. The Small ICBM is essentially the product of the Scowcroft Commission, the same commission that was instrumental in convincing Congress of the need to deploy fifty MXs in Minuteman silos until an improved basing scheme for the missile could be developed. A small, mobile, single-warhead, less threatening ICBM (in addition to the MX) is essential, warned the com-mission, to enhance deterrence and advance the cause of arms control.

The Scowcroft Commission's call for a Small ICBM was an instant suc-cess. In an era of bigger, more powerful weapons, the suggestion for a small, mobile system enhancing stability was welcome news. Not surprisingly, President Reagan gave it his wholehearted support, and so did the Congress. Doves on the Hill especially liked the missile's small size, an obvious characteristic of a retaliatory rather than preemptive weapon. Hawks, on their part, were impressed with the missile's mobility and reputed capability to survive a surprise Soviet first strike.

Six years into the Scowcroft Commission's recommendation, however, enthusiasm for the Small ICBM is beginning to wane, especially among members of the Congress concerned more with pork barrel politics than with the missile's potential for enhancing international stability. For its part, the Reagan administration flip-flopped unsteadily on the issue, first authorizing the full-scale development of the weapon and then denying it funds for FY 1990 and also recommending to the Soviets in Geneva that all mobile systems (by implication also the Small ICBM) be banned.

The issue of the Small ICBM's high cost, estimated at $45 billion to $52 billion for 500 missiles, is being exploited vociferously by partisans of the rail-mobile MX. There is not enough money in the budget, they charge, for both the mobile MX and the Small ICBM. But the arguments of the MX supporters overlook a key consideration—the objective of the Small ICBM is not economy but survivability and stability.[35] Research to date supports the Small ICBM's survivability potential, whereas that of the rail-mobile MX must still be proven.[36] Knowledgeable persons suggest, for instance, that the Soviets would find targeting the MX easier in rail-mobile garrisons than in underground silos. The suspicion is that preference on the part of many members of the Congress for the rail-mobile MX over the Small ICBM is more directly related to jobs at their local constituencies than to the life and death issues of survivability and stability.

The Trident II

Cost considerations may eventually determine congressional disposition of the MX–Small ICBM issue. But the billions required to fund deployment of the navy's Trident II fleet are hardly causing a ripple on Capitol Hill or at the White House. Both houses of the Congress are solidly behind the Trident II, as evidenced by the overwhelming yes votes that regularly greet the navy's Trident II appropriations requests. Current plans call for the first Trident II submarine to reach initial operational capability in December 1989. Eventually, ten Trident II submarines will be built, along with eight Trident I's that will be upgraded to Trident II status. The General Accounting Office estimates that the life-cycle cost of the system will be $155 billion.

ASAT Weapons

The development of ASAT weapons is one issue over which Congress and the president have battled for years, the president favoring an aggressive

development and testing program (followed as soon as practicable by procurement and deployment) and the Congress remaining firmly opposed to
any ASAT testing activity likely to stimulate U.S.–Soviet weapons rivalry
in space.

The congressional effort to slow down the U.S. ASAT program has its
origins in the Reagan administration report on space arms control policy
dated March 31, 1984.[37] Negotiating an ASAT accord, the administration
explained, would encounter serious difficulties over crucial issues such as
verification and the definition of what constitutes an ASAT weapon; accordingly, until such time as solutions to these problems can be found, it
would not be productive to take part in formal international negotiations
on this issue. The administration's position angered many lawmakers and
triggered a move to challenge the president. Three related developments
added fuel to the congressional fire: (1) President Reagan's near-total preoccupation with SDI and his determination to pursue the program regardless
of financial and other cost; (2) his dismissal, outright, of Soviet proposals
for an ASAT test moratorium; and (3) a series of highly successful U.S.
ASAT tests, suggesting that the American weapon might be nearing readiness
for operational deployment.

Despite pleas by the Pentagon that ASATs were vitally needed to defend
against a Soviet surprise attack, for five consecutive years since 1983 the
Congress has enacted legislation banning the testing of U.S. ASAT weapons.
Under the legislation, the precise wording of which has varied from year to
year, the president was not allowed to test ASATs except in response to
specific Soviet "events." Since October 1985 the "event" that could trigger
U.S. action was the testing of a Soviet ASAT weapon.[38] By its prohibition,
the Congress hoped to induce the president, and also the Soviet Union, to
abandon weapons development in the ASAT area and in the process avert
a costly and destabilizing arms race in space. The effort has proven successful. For reasons known only to them, the Soviets have refrained from
conducting ASAT testing of their own for more than six years. Perhaps the
congressional message did reach Moscow. It certainly did reach the U.S.
Air Force, which in January 1988 abandoned its Miniature Home Vehicle
ASAT weapon program. Reportedly, the air force is now exploring the use
of SDI technology weapons for ASAT purposes.[39]

SDI Funding

Since inception of the SDI program, the annual debate over SDI funding
has provided the Congress with a unique opportunity to review and influence
the program almost at will. But the Congress has not taken up the challenge.
Although issues such as the basic objectives of the program (still uncertain
after six years) and its adverse effect on the ABM treaty have received
thorough airing on the Hill, Congress continues to allocate annually in-

creasing amounts of funds for SDI, in the process insuring that the program will move forward.[40] This has happened despite grave scientific doubts concerning SDI's likely success and widespread concern about the program's impact on the ABM treaty and on arms control in general.[41] Reluctance to vote against the defense budget and the likelihood of pork barrel contracts for SDI-related laboratories and facilities back home are major considerations that determine the manner in which many of our legislators cast their votes on issues of SDI funding.[42]

Although generally supportive of the need for SDI research, the Congress is sharply divided over the specific SDI tests and demonstrations that may be conducted under the program. The tests and demonstrations have a dual purpose: to support weapons development but also to impress the Congress and the American public that sufficient progress has been made under the program to justify an early, if only partial, deployment in the early 1990s. As expected, much of the congressional split focuses on the legality of the planned SDI tests and demonstrations, an area for which few clear-cut answers are available. The ABM treaty, which theoretically should provide answers to this predicament, is not at all clear, especially for tests and development of weapons based on advanced technologies.

Congressional response to specific SDI tests generally follows party lines, with Republicans favoring unimpeded SDI research and development, even at the expense of abrogating the ABM treaty, and Democrats opposed to weapons development that is likely to exceed the treaty's narrow or traditional interpretation.[43] In the eyes of the Democrats, abrogating the ABM treaty would signal the beginning of an open-ended, expensive, and destabilizing offense-defense arms race and would constitute a major U.S. blunder. Both sides are in agreement, though, that the development of advanced comprehensive missile defenses, of the type visualized by President Reagan in SDI, would be incompatible with the ABM treaty.

As of midsummer of 1989, the SDI issue on the Hill was a "draw," with the Congress continuing to fund the program at fairly high levels (though somewhat below those requested by the president) but with critics of the program gaining an upper hand on the specific SDI tests that may be conducted. The FY 1989 DOD bill, for instance, authorized $3.7 billion for SDI research, as against $4.5 billion sought by President Reagan. For FY 1990 President Bush requested $4.6 billion, as against $5.6 billion sought by his predecessor. Congress is not expected to appropriate more than $3.8 billion. The reduction is necessitated by budgetary considerations and does not reflect the new president's true feelings about SDI, which are still unclear.

Although troubled by many of the SDI tests planned by the administration, the Congress has consistently refused to rule on the legality of individual tests. Instead, it has elected to assert its views in a roundabout way by funding only tests done in a fixed, ground-based mode, that is, those permitted by the traditional interpretation of the ABM treaty.[44]

KEY ISSUES BEFORE THE CONGRESS

The nature and extent of congressional involvement in U.S. arms control policy at any time is a function of domestic politics. Generally, Congress tends to take a back seat whenever it and the executive branch belong to the same political party, as was the case during the Carter years, or when it perceives that the administration is trying in good faith to reach an accommodation with the Soviets for lessening the threat of nuclear war. Conversely, Congress becomes restless, and may even attempt to wrestle from the president the "lead" in arms control policy, if it senses foot dragging or reluctance on his part to pursue the cause of arms control. This is certainly what occurred intermittently during the first six years of the Reagan presidency.

As the Bush administration is beginning to establish itself in Washington, and with the Democrats in control of the House and the Senate, three arms control issues preoccupy the Congress: (1) SDI and its overall impact on the U.S.–Soviet arms control dialogue, (2) the Nuclear and Space Talks (NST) in Geneva, and (3) the issue of nuclear testing.

SDI and Its Impact on Arms Control

In its brief existence, SDI has had a profound impact on the East–West relationship. It has challenged the basic rationale employed by the superpowers to avert nuclear war, threatens the creation of a full-blown arms race in space, and is making conclusion of an arms reduction agreement in Geneva extremely difficult. No wonder the program is at the top of the congressional arms control agenda.

Despite the lapse of six years since President Reagan's *Star Wars* speech of March 1983,[45] Congress is still unsure of the ultimate objective of the program.[46] For a while Capitol Hill understood the program's objective to be a research effort designed to determine whether an advanced strategic defense was scientifically and technologically feasible. With each passing day, however, the objective of determining the feasibility of an SDI system and its capability of protecting the United States from a missile attack is gradually being lost. There is talk in Washington of early SDI deployment to protect U.S. missile silos, and key members of the Reagan and Bush administrations have succeeded in totally confusing everyone with conflicting stories on SDI and why it is being pursued.

At the Iceland Summit, for instance, President Reagan discussed SDI as if its feasibility decision had already been made. He argued against a trade of ballistic missiles for SDI and in favor of deploying the system even after all threatening Soviet ballistic missiles had been destroyed.[47] These missiles, incidentally, were the reason for launching the SDI program in the first place. When the Soviet leader inquired why SDI would be needed if there were no threatening ballistic missiles on his side, President Reagan report-edly answered that SDI was required as an insurance policy to protect against future arms control cheating and the possibility of a missile launched against U.S. territory by a mad foreign leader. Two years later, at the Washington and Moscow summits the deadlock over the future of SDI was as uncom-promising as ever. Both times, however, the superpowers in their eagerness to promote an aura of progress in the area of arms control agreed to conceal their differences by means of innocuous and totally ambiguous final com-muniqués.

Closely related to the uncertainties surrounding the very purpose of the SDI program are the various proposals for early and partial SDI deployment. The first of these proposals, advanced by the Reagan administration early in 1987,[48] was clearly politically motivated. Evidence the statement by for-mer Attorney General Edwin Meese that a partial SDI deployment was needed to prevent a future administration from tampering with the system. An immediate victim of the proposed early SDI would have been the ABM treaty, which the United States would have to abrogate.[49] Early SDI de-ployment, critics charged, no matter how partial, was an idea whose time definitely had not come. Deployment would not only be extremely costly (the original estimate of $115 billion was scaled down to $69 billion in 1988[50]) but also of doubtful military benefit in that it would have prompted the Soviets rapidly to increase their offensive strategic forces to overwhelm the increased U.S. defenses.

The Bush administration's plans for early SDI deployment have yet to be unveiled, but official reports suggest that "Brilliant Pebbles," a new concept, has the inside track. Brilliant Pebbles would involve swarms of tiny inter-ceptor missiles that would orbit the earth and attack enemy missiles on their way to the United States. The missiles would be able to detect the launching of enemy ICBMs from thousands of miles away and zoom toward them on command. The Strategic Defense Initiative Office, the DOD organization that manages SDI, states that the concept could be tested in two years and be ready for initial operational deployment in five years. Five to ten thousand such small missile interceptors, each three feet long and weighing perhaps one hundred pounds,[51] would be deployed at a cost of $25 billion.

The Reagan administration in its last three years in office promoted a new and revised interpretation of the ABM treaty, one designed to make possible the testing of lasers and other directed energy weapons for SDI purposes (see Chapter 4). Despite opposition on Capitol Hill, including the enactment of legislation that required compliance with the traditional or narrow interpretation in all SDI-related tests through the end of FY 1989, the United States is continuing to pursue the broad interpretation in its relations with the Soviet Union.[52] In the opinion of many members of the Congress, who still support the narrow or traditional interpretation, the administration's attempts to "sell" the broad interpretation to the other superpower without first obtaining congressional approval for this action represents a major breakdown in executive-congressional relations on a key foreign policy issue.

The Geneva Talks

To state that there is major congressional interest in the Geneva talks is to belabor the obvious. The talks are, after all, the most critical diplomatic negotiations ever undertaken by the U.S. government, with the future security of the United States and perhaps of all mankind depending on their outcome.

Traditionally, Congress stands behind the president whenever he is involved in delicate diplomatic negotiations with the other side. The talks in Geneva are no exception. Since initiation of START, later renamed NST, the Reagan and Bush administrations have enjoyed near-total support from the Congress in the form of laudatory resolutions by one or both houses and overwhelming approval of their negotiating positions. Both presidents have returned the goodwill by taking congressional leaders into their confidence, briefing them on developments in Geneva, and at times even incorporating into the U.S. negotiating position initiatives supported by them. The "build-down" concept, for instance, originally proposed by Senators Nunn and Cohen, became part of the U.S. START negotiating position as a gesture to the Congress.

The congressional–executive harmony, however, is being disrupted by two issues on which the views of the Congress and of the executive branch differ sharply. The foremost difference is SDI and U.S. insistence that the arms reduction agreement being negotiated in Geneva not restrict SDI weapons development and testing.[53] (How hard President Bush intends to push this position remains to be seen. His predecessor was totally unrelenting, preferring to forego a START agreement if its conclusion would have necessitated U.S. abandonment of SDI.) The second executive–congressional rift impacting on the talks in Geneva similarly has its roots in the Reagan presidency. The decision by President Reagan to abandon the numerical limits of SALT II still reverberates on Capitol Hill, causing charges and countercharges of political opportunism on both sides of the argument.

On the SDI issue, there is not a great deal that the Congress can do to influence the U.S. negotiating posture. Funding of the SDI program at a rate of $3 billion to $4 billion dollars annually makes the Congress at least a silent, albeit uncomfortable, partner in President Reagan's vision of a nuclear-free world. This vision consists of three phases: (1) a phase of radical reductions in the number and power of the strategic weapons on both sides (which is the goal of START), (2) followed by a transition away from reliance on nuclear weapons and toward the deployment of effective and survivable strategic defenses, and (3) the eventual elimination of all nuclear weapons. The vision by Soviet leader Gorbachev also provides for three phases: (1) a phase during which the superpowers will reduce their weapons by half and dismantle their INF weapons in Europe, (2) a phase during which all other nuclear powers dismantle their nuclear weapons and join the superpowers in a nuclear test ban, and (3) a phase to be accomplished by the year 2000, when all remaining nuclear weapons of the world will have been dismantled.[54] There is no provision in the Soviet plan for strategic defenses. In fact, the Gorbachev vision argues that halting SDI is a prerequisite to disarmament, because SDI would be inherently destabilizing by giving the United States a "first-strike" capability against the Soviet Union.

President Reagan's decision to abandon SALT II continues to agitate congressional opposition, with the Congress seeking repeatedly to keep the number of U.S. strategic vehicles within the limits established by the unratified treaty.[55] At issue is whether an imperfect agreement, which SALT II admittedly was, is better than no agreement. The congressional initiatives invariably encounter swift and unusually harsh opposition. The Congress is restricting the president's freedom of action in Geneva, complains the White House, and is complicating unduly the U.S. negotiating positions at the START talks. This is one area in which Congress could have successfully applied the power of the purse to dissuade the administration from an unwise policy. But the American people expect their Congress to line up behind the president whenever he is involved in highly sensitive negotiations with the other side. This is precisely what the Congress did when it yielded to the White House demands just before the Iceland[56] and Washington summits. (Would any member of the Congress dare to confront the president about to board the plane for Iceland for a meeting with Soviet leader Gorbachev?) For the record, the flexibility offered the president by the congressional compromises of 1986 and 1987—*surrenders* would be a more accurate term—apparently mattered little. No strategic arms agreement or even a breakthrough resulted from either summit.

The Issue of Nuclear Testing

Until the early 1980s, Congress pursued a generally "passive" posture on this issue despite genuine congressional concern over the long-term implications of continued nuclear testing and widespread support in both houses of the Congress for early conclusion of a Comprehensive Test Ban Treaty (CTBT). Actually, there was no need for Congress to take the initiative. Successive administrations since that of Dwight D. Eisenhower have shared the congressional concerns about the nuclear test issue and have favored resolution of the last verification obstacles delaying realization of the CTBT.[57]

Major policy decisions in Moscow and Washington in the mid-1980s led Congress to abandon its passive stance on the issue. One such decision was the Reagan administration's refusal to join the Soviet Union in a moratorium on nuclear testing, "because of the technological problems inherent in verifying a testing ban and the dubious record of Soviet compliance." Behind the refusal lay the Reagan administration's hardening stand on the CTBT. Nuclear testing, the administration maintained, was needed to maintain the reliability of the U.S. nuclear stockpile and to improve the safety of available weapons.[58] There was another far more urgent reason and one that the administration did not wish to admit publicly. Testing was needed to explore new sophisticated weapons for possible application in the SDI program.

In the House of Representatives, revolt against the nuclear test[59] policies of the Reagan administration surfaced first in 1986. On February 26 a nonbinding resolution was approved (268 for, 148 against) calling upon the president (a) to resume immediate negotiations with the Soviet Union for the purpose of concluding a CTBT and (b) to submit to the Senate for purposes of ratification two long dormant treaties: the Threshold Test Ban Treaty (TTBT) and the Peaceful Nuclear Explosions Treaty (PNET). Six months later, the House again was voting on the nuclear test issue, this time to impose a one-year moratorium and to refuse funding on all but the smallest U.S. tests (under one kiloton). The vote was 234 in favor and 155 opposed. There were, however, significant caveats in the House legislation: the moratorium would remain in effect only as long as the Soviet Union did not test above one kiloton and would be conditioned on Soviet willingness to accept mutual emplacement of in-country monitoring equipment and to confine tests to a single existing test site.

The House "revolt" was only minimally successful. Under administration pressure, justified in terms of the impending Iceland Summit ("don't tie the president's hands"), the House leadership agreed to withdraw its nuclear test funding restrictions in exchange for a presidential pledge to seek ratification of the TTBT and PNET treaties as the first order of business of the one hundredth Congress.[60] The treaties, it will be recalled, were signed in the early 1970s but had been gathering dust in the files of the Senate Foreign Relations Committee because of uncertainties over the adequacy of their verification provisions. As for the House resolution on the CTBT, the whole exercise was meaningless. It merely instructed the president to "resume negotiations," a far cry from "concluding an agreement," which was the objective. A president opposed to a CTBT could cite a million reasons for not finalizing an agreement, and there is nothing that the Congress could do about it. The point illustrates that there is no way that the Congress can coerce an administration to conclude a treaty or otherwise force one upon it by means of legislation.

A similar cycle of a House revolt squelched by a presidential power play occurred in 1987. The House vote, part of the defense authorization bill, required the president to observe a nuclear test ban as long as the Soviet Union also was abstaining from testing. This time the president enjoyed strong support from the Senate too. A vote in that body rejected by a vote of sixty-two to thirty-five a proposal by Senator Edward M. Kennedy (D-MA) to halt nuclear testing for two years on all but the smallest of nuclear weapons as long as the Soviet Union also suspended testing and agreed to on-site inspections and other verification requirements. In the ensuing House–Senate conference the House ban was defeated. Undoubtedly, the impending Washington Summit and the desire not to "tie the hands of the president" contributed to the demise of the House effort.

RATIFICATION BATTLES WON AND LOST

Since the advent of U.S.–Soviet arms control dialogue in the mid-1960s, the Senate has performed its constitutionally mandated role of advise and consent on five occasions. But despite extensive hearings and debate, the entire Senate was afforded the opportunity only twice to vote on a U.S.–Soviet bilateral arms control agreement: on September 30, 1972, when it overwhelmingly approved SALT I, and sixteen years later in May 1988, when the majority of U.S. senators present voted in favor of the INF treaty. On three other arms control accords (SALT II, the TTBT, and the PNET), the Senate held extensive hearings but was not allowed to pass final judgment.

SALT II

SALT II was the treaty that eluded the Senate's final verdict. The accord was signed by President Carter in Vienna on June 18, 1979.

President Carter, in submitting SALT II to the Senate, was well aware of the treaty's potential for difficulty. But he was optimistic that despite the instrument's complexity, occasional ambiguity in language, and provisions opposed by some members, the Senate would ultimately endorse his negotiating efforts. Along with many arms control activists of the 1970s, President Carter shared the view that a certain amount of risk taking was involved in all arms control undertakings. The risks associated with SALT II, he believed, were not inordinately high enough to justify Senate rejection.

Senate ratification debate on the SALT II treaty lasted nearly five months. A number of provisions aroused strong opposition. Most notable were those prohibiting the United States from matching the Soviet Union's 308 heavy ICBMs; the requirement that verification be by national technical means (NTM) exclusively, without the aid of on-site inspection;[61] the disproportionate advantage allowed the Soviets in missile throw-weight; and the failure to count the Backfire as a strategic bomber, even though the Soviet aircraft unquestionably has that capability. Before too long, congressional consideration of the treaty became embroiled in a number of additional issues, all the result of the deterioration in U.S.–Soviet relations and the

Iran hostage crisis. U.S. inability to free the hostages not only publicized America's impotence but also added another dimension of uncertainty over the treaty's future: the loss of the U.S. intelligence-gathering facilities in Iran suddenly made verification of key SALT II provisions a lot more unpredictable.

In retrospect it appears that had the Senate been given the opportunity to pass judgment on the SALT II treaty, it probably would have done so but on a very close vote. Throughout the treaty's debate, a fairly strong sentiment in favor of ratification was evident on the Hill but so was the opposition. These conflicting sentiments are reflected in the reports issued by two principal Senate committees that formally considered the treaty. The Committee on Foreign Relations, for instance, approved the treaty by a vote of nine to six, sending it to the Senate with the recommendation that it advise and consent to its ratification.[62] But the committee made its approval subject to twenty reservations, understandings, and declarations. The Committee on Armed Services, on the other hand, judged the SALT II Treaty to be "unequal and in favor of the Soviet Union." Major changes to the treaty were essential, according to the committee, if it was to serve U.S. national security.[63] The committee recommended also that a number of ambiguities in the treaty be clarified, before the rights and obligations of the parties could be fully understood and agreed to.

Eventually, the Soviet invasion of Afghanistan and a new administration in Washington settled the issue. On January 3, 1980, President Carter asked the Senate to suspend temporarily consideration of the SALT II treaty.[64] The suspension became permanent under President Reagan.

The TTBT and PNET Treaties

The TTBT and PNET treaties are companion agreements that were negotiated between the United States and the Soviet Union, during the 1970s in an attempt to place restrictions on underground nuclear testing. Such testing is permitted by the Limited Test Ban Treaty (LTBT). The TTBT limits underground nuclear weapons tests to yields no greater than 150 kilotons. The PNET extends the same 150 kiloton limit to peaceful underground nuclear explosions used for civilian development projects. Despite the lapse of time (the TTBT was signed in July 1974, the PNET in May 1976), neither treaty has as yet been ratified, although on two occasions testimony was taken on both treaties by the Senate Foreign Relations Committee.

Officially, at least, the lack of Senate action on the two treaties is due to certain inherent weaknesses in their verification provisions. This explanation is hard to concede, in light of the fairly generous verification terms already in both instruments. In the case of the PNET, there is even a protocol setting forth procedures for limited on-site inspection of test sites.

Although the TTBT and PNET were forwarded to the Senate for its advice and consent in July 1976, the first set of hearings on the treaties was not held until a year later. Much opposition surfaced, especially from two quarters: (1) from opponents of nuclear testing, who criticized the agreements' threshold of 150 kilotons as being too high; and (2) from supporters of testing, who claimed that continued development of weapons made testing above the 150 kiloton level essential. Not surprisingly, a confused Senate never advanced the two treaties past the hearings stage, electing instead to sit on them.

Ten years later, on February 19, 1987, the two treaties again made their appearance on Capitol Hill. Not much of any consequence had transpired in the intervening years, except possibly for the arrival in Washington of an administration (Reagan's) clearly committed to the need for continuous nuclear testing. Resistance by the administration to all suggestions for limiting nuclear testing eventually gave rise to widespread demands on the Senate for the ratification of the long-dormant TTBT and PNET treaties as well as resumption of negotiations toward a CTBT. A compromise agreement between Congress and the administration, just before the Iceland summit, eventually brought forth a pledge by the president to submit the two treaties for Senate ratification early in 1987[65] but with the reservation that the two treaties would not take effect "until their verification provisions had been strengthened."

The president's caveat (above) in effect caused the Senate soon to lose interest in both instruments. A brief debate ensued in committee, and the two treaties were again pushed to the back burner. (Why should the Senate provide advice and consent on agreements that the president admitted were incomplete?) By its action, the Senate was signaling to the White House that it would not consider any treaty unless the president certified that it was "ready" for congressional review.

Despite the twin setbacks, the TTBT and PNET treaties are far from dead, as SALT II certainly appears to be. As part of the Washington Summit, of December 1987, the United States and the Soviet Union have agreed to improve verification measures for the TTBT and PNET treaties by means of observing nuclear explosions at each other's sites during the summer of 1988.[66] The Joint Verification Experiment, as the tests became known, involved the use of seismic as well as hydrodynamic or CORRTEX equipment to measure the yield of nuclear devices. The use of seismic equipment for verification purposes is favored by the Soviet Union; CORRTEX is a U.S. device, believed by the United States to provide the best means for measuring accurately the yields of nuclear explosions.

The INF Treaty

Although the treaty banning intermediate and shorter range weapons in Europe enjoyed strong and bipartisan support in the Senate, its approval by that body was not entirely uneventful. A number of issues troubled the senators from the outset, causing much delay and political bickering and even a temporary shelving of the pact while Secretary of State George Shultz rushed to Geneva for last-minute discussions and clarifications with the other side on key verification provisions. In the end, the Senate gave its final approval to the accord as a symbolic but vitally important first step in weapons reductions, even though its principal issue of concern, that of the treaty's interpretation, had not been resolved to its full satisfaction. The final vote, ninety-three in favor of ratification and five against, was taken as President Reagan was about to embark on his last summit (his visit to the Soviet Union in May–June 1989).

The treaty encountered numerous snags on its route to approval, some serious and a few comical.[67] Among the latter was the objection raised by one senator who questioned Gorbachev's legal authority to sign the treaty on behalf of the Soviet Union. In the senator's judgment, Soviet President Andrei Gromyko, not the general secretary of the Communist party, should have signed. Additional objections by treaty opponents surfaced in the form of "killer" amendments.[68] Acceptance by the Senate of any of these amendments would have required reopening negotiations with Moscow, an option known to be unacceptable to the Soviet leadership. By lopsided votes, all "killer" amendments to the treaty were soundly defeated as were various other delaying tactics by senators generally opposed to the process of arms control.

Political rhetoric notwithstanding, two key issues preoccupied the Senate during its consideration of the INF treaty. The first dealt with futuristic weapons, that is, lasers, microwaves, or whatever else future science and technology might produce, and the extent that the treaty at hand outlawed their development and use.[69] The debate on futuristic weapons soon became reminiscent of congressional disputes over the weapons permitted (or prohibited) under the ABM treaty. The issue was eventually resolved by the treaty's negotiators themselves who, in a series of extraordinary meetings in Geneva just before the Senate was scheduled to vote on the issue, assured the Senate in writing that the INF prohibitions apply equally to present and future weapons in the intermediate and shorter ranges.

The issue of the INF treaty's interpretation was likewise resolved, but only briefly.[70] The dispute was over treaty powers and the extent that a president may interpret a treaty differently from the understanding provided to the Senate during the treaty's ratification process. The dispute had surfaced as a result of the Reagan administration's adoption of the broad or permissive interpretation of the ABM treaty, without prior consultation with the Senate. Opponents of the administration favored adoption of a provision in the resolution approving the INF treaty to the effect that the president cannot depart from a common understanding of a treaty unless the Senate gives its consent. Supporters of the president's position argued that such language would restrict the president's authority to interpret treaties and thus intrude on his responsibility for the conduct of foreign affairs. Compromise language was finally agreed upon banning future administrations from reinterpreting the INF pact without Senate consent. The issue is far from being over. Within days of the Senate's approval of the INF treaty, the White House asserted in a statement that the Senate condition would have no effect on the president's constitutional powers and responsibilities.[71]

NOTES

1. Congressional Research Service, Library of Congress, *Fundamentals of Nuclear Arms Control* (Washington, DC: U.S. Government Printing Office, 1986), pp. 420–24.

2. Article II, Section 2, of the Constitution.

3. Congressional Research Service, Library of Congress, *Fundamentals of Nuclear Arms Control*, pp. 386–87.

4. For instance, after the House of Representatives approved five arms control amendments to the DOD Authorization Bill for FY 1987, the president referred to the House bill as a "reckless assault upon the national defense of the U.S." (as reported by Congressman Dante B. Fascel in "Congress and Arms Control," *Foreign Affairs*, Fall 1986, pp. 731–49). See also Al Kamen "Bush Urges Lawmakers, Judges Not to Interfere in Foreign Policy," *Washington Post*, January 31, 1987.

5. The president's veto on August 3, 1988, of the FY 1989 Defense Authorization Act was justified as ignoring arms priorities and playing partisan politics. See also Lou Cannon and R. Jeffrey Smith, "President Blames SDI Delays on Hill's Irresponsible Cuts," *Washington Post*, March 15, 1988; and John Isaacs "Congress Tries Again on Arms Control," *Bulletin of Atomic Scientists*, June 1987.

6. Congressional Research Service, Library of Congress, *Fundamentals of Nuclear Arms Control*, pp. 387–88.

7. Ibid., p. 388.

8. Ibid., p. 391.

9. Ibid., p. 393.

10. U.S. Arms Control and Disarmament Agency, *Documents on Disarmament* (Washington, DC: U.S. Government Printing Office, 1982), pp. 479–81.

11. Ibid., pp. 698–703.

12. Congressional Research Service, Library of Congress, *Fundamentals of Nuclear Arms Control*, pp. 405–8.

13. U.S. Arms Control and Disarmament Agency, *Documents on Disarmament* (Washington, DC: U.S. Government Printing Office, 1985), pp. 744–56. See also Robert C. Gray, "Influencing Policy," *Arms Control Today*, March 1985, pp. 4–5.

14. Congressional Research Service, Library of Congress, *Fundamentals of Nuclear Arms Control*, p. 407.

15. White House, Statement by the Principal Deputy Press Secretary, August 20, 1985.

16. Betty G. Lall, "Arms Control Impact Statements: A New Approach to Slowing the Arms Race," in *Negotiating Security: An Arms Control Reader* (Washington, DC: Carnegie Endowment for International Peace, 1979), pp. 233–37.

17. The ACDA annual reports are mandated by Section 50 of the Arms Control and Disarmament Act. They are due to the Congress on January 31 of each year.

18. Congressional Research Service, Library of Congress, *Fundamentals of Nuclear Arms Control*, p. 415.

19. Ibid., pp. 416–17.

20. U.S. Arms Control and Disarmament Agency, *Documents on Disarmament* (Washington, DC: U.S. Government Printing Office, 1984), pp. 219, 379, and 750–51. The Nuclear Risk Reduction Centers in Moscow and Washington became operational in April 1988. The Washington Center is located on the seventh floor of the State Department building, next to the office of the Secretary of State.

21. Section 1108 of the DOD Authorization Act, 1985, urged the president to pursue negotiations toward the establishment of Nuclear Risk Reduction Centers (text in U.S. Arms Control and Disarmament Agency, *Documents on Disarmament*, 1984).

22. Congressional Research Service, Library of Congress, *Fundamentals of Nuclear Arms Control*, pp. 397–404. See also John Isaacs, "Committees Key to Arms Control Decisions," *Bulletin of Atomic Scientists*, January 1986; and idem, "Showdown on the Military Budget," *Bulletin of Atomic Scientists*, April 1986.

23. John Isaacs, "Congress and the Military Revisited," *Bulletin of Atomic Scientists*, February 1986; Stephen A. Cain and Gordon Adams, "Reagan's 1988 Military Budget," *Bulletin of Atomic Scientists*, March 1987.

24. Three B-1Bs have crashed. The remaining aircraft are being deployed in four sites: Dyess Air Force Base, Texas; Ellsworth Air Force Base, South Dakota; Grand Forks Air Force Base, North Dakota; and McConnell Air Force Base, Kansas.

25. David Evans, "The B-1: A Flying Edsel for America's Defense," *Washington Post*, January 4, 1987. See also four recent articles by Molly Moore in the *Washington Post*: "New Flaws Found in the B-1 Bomber," July 10, 1988; "Upgrading B-1 Could Cost $8 Billion, Hill Told," August 23, 1988; "Problems Ground Most B-1 Bombers," August 28, 1988; "B-1 Problems Persist, GAO Says," February 4, 1989.

26. Molly Moore, "Air Force to Unveil Stealth Bomber," *Washington Post*, August 5, 1988.

27. William A. Stanley, "A New Home for the B-2 Bomber," *The Military Engineer*, March/April 1989; Journal of the Federation of Atomic Scientists, *The Stealth Bomber: Even Less Than Meets the Eye*, October 1988.

28. Text of the President's Commission on Strategic Forces, April 6, 1983, is provided in U.S. Arms Control and Disarmament Agency *Documents on Disarmament* (Washington, DC: U.S. Government Printing Office, 1983), pp. 273–80.

29. According to DOD's Arms Control Impact Statement for FY 1988, during normal conditions the MX-carrying railroad cars would be stationed within U.S. Air Force bases but would be transferred in times of crises to existing railroad lines. The first operating base for the rail-mobile MX would be at the F. E. Warren Air Force Base, Wyoming. See also George C. Wilson, "Rail–Mobile MX is Pressed by Carlucci," *Washington Post*, May 19, 1988.

30. U.S. General Accounting Office, *ICBM Modernization: Availability Problems and Flight Test Delays in the Peacekeeper Program*, GAO/NSIASD–89–105 (Washington, DC, March 1989), p. 2.

31. The FY 1990 plan of the Bush administration calls for about $1 billion in

development costs for the MX rail–mobile missile but only $100 million for the development of the Small ICBM. The administration has promised, however, to shift almost $1 billion additional money to the Small ICBM for FYs 1992–1994.

32. U.S. General Accounting Office, *ICBM: Status of the Peacekeeper Rail-Garrison Missile System*, GAO/NSIASD–89–64 (Washington, DC, January 1989), p. 30.

33. Helen Dewar, "Missile Plan in Peril, Administration Warned," *Washington Post*, June 14, 1989; see also "Bush's Two Missile Proposal Jeopardized," *Washington Post*, June 19, 1989.

34. U.S. General Accounting Office, *ICBM Modernization: Selected Funding Options for the Small ICBM*, GAO/NSIASD–88–193 (Washington, DC, July 1988).

35. Senator Albert Gore, Jr., "Midgetman—Our Best Hope for Stability and Arms Control," *Arms Control Today*, November/December 1985.

36. Robert A. Zirkle, "MX: No Way to Run a Railroad," *Arms Control Today*, October 1987, pp. 17–21.

37. White House, *Report to the Congress: U.S. Policy on ASAT Arms Control* (Washington, DC, March 31, 1984).

38. Refer to Chapter 6 of National Academy of Sciences, *Nuclear Arms Control: Background and Issues* (Washington, DC: National Academy Press, 1985), for a detailed account of congressional efforts to force its ASAT policy on the administration.

39. Senator Tom Harkin, "Star Wars: A Trojan Horse for ASAT Weapons," *Arms Control Today*, March 1989, pp. 3–9.

40. Congressional Research Service, Library of Congress, *SDI: Budgetary Issues*, IB 86101 (Washington, DC, October 1987).

41. Ronald L. Tammen, James T. Bruce, and Bruce W. MacDonald, "Star Wars after Five Years: The Decisive Point," *Arms Control Today*, July/August 1988.

42. Thousands of SDI-related contracts have been let out since inception of the program. According to the Associated Press, nearly half of the $11 billion in SDI contracts have gone to companies and laboratories in California.

43. Thomas Halverson, "House Passes Defense Budget Bill, Endorsing Traditional Interpretation," *Arms Control Today*, June 1988, p. 16; Marcel A. Bryar, "Arms Control Legislation Stalls over SDI Testing and ABM Treaty," *Arms Control Today*, November 1987, p. 21; Matthew Bunn, "Star Wars Testing and the ABM Treaty," *Arms Control Today*, April 1988, pp. 11–19.

44. Refer to U.S. Department of Defense, Strategic Defense Initiative Organization, *Report to the Congress on the Strategic Defense Initiative* (Washington, DC: U.S. Government Printing Office, 1988), parag. C-3, for specific tests planned for FYs 1988 and 1989.

45. Complete text of the president's speech is in U.S. Department of State, Bureau of Public Affairs, *Security and Arms Control: The Search for a More Stable Peace* (Washington, DC: U.S. Government Printing Office, 1984), p. 37.

46. The Arms Control Association's *Star Wars Quotes: Statements by Reagan Administration Officials, Outside Experts, Members of the Congress, U.S. Allies, and Soviet Officials on the Strategic Defense Initiative* (Washington, DC, July 1986) illustrates the confusion prevailing in official circles on the goals of the SDI program. Throughout the years the program has been described as being designed to protect

the U.S. population, to eliminate nuclear weapons, to provide partial defenses, to protect the U.S. missile bases, and so on.

47. Refer to President Reagan's address to the Nation, October 13, 1986.

48. R. Jeffrey Smith, "Democrats Oppose Deploying SDI Soon: House Study Group Recommends More Long-Term Research," *Washington Post,* May 28, 1988; see also Matthew Bunn, "SDI Focus on Near-Term Deployment Continues," *Arms Control Today,* May 1988.

49. An excellent source on SDI/ABM treaty relationships is by Thomas K. Longstreth, John E. Pike, and John B. Rhinelander, *The Impact of U.S. and Soviet Ballistic Missile Defense Programs on the ABM Treaty* (Washington, DC: National Campaign to Save the ABM Treaty, 1985).

50. U.S. Department of Defense, Strategic Defense Initiative Organization, *Report to the Congress on the Strategic Defense Initiative* (Washington, DC: U.S. Government Printing Office, 1989).

51. Bruce Van Voorst, "Will Star Wars Ever Fly? Not at This Rate, Despite Six Years of Research and $17 Billion," *Time,* June 26, 1989.

52. Arms Control Association, *Defense and Space Talks: Background and Negotiating History,* Background Paper (Washington, DC, April 28, 1988), p. 7.

53. For a discussion of the Geneva Talks, their recent history, and the current positions of the two sides, see Congressional Research Service, Library of Congress, *Arms Control: The Geneva Talks,* IB 85157 (Washington, DC, April 1988). The publication is updated periodically.

54. For an analysis of the two visions, refer to Robert S. McNamara, *Blundering into Disaster: Surviving the First Century of the Nuclear Age* (New York: Pantheon Books, 1986), pp. 86–96.

55. Senators Dale Bumpers, John Chaffee, and Patrick Leahy, "Salvaging SALT II: The New Congressional Compromise," *Arms Control Today,* December 1987, pp. 3–6.

56. Congressional Research Service, Library of Congress, *Arms Control: Issues for Congress,* IB 87002 (Washington, DC, May 1988), pp. 9–11.

57. Chapter 7 of National Academy of Sciences, *Nuclear Arms Control: Background and Issues* (Washington, DC: National Academy Press, 1985), provides an excellent overview of the nuclear test policies of all U.S. administrations since that of President Eisenhower. See also U.S. Department of State, Bureau of Public Affairs, *Verifying Nuclear Testing Limitations* (Washington, DC, August 14, 1986).

58. U.S. Department of State, Bureau of Public Affairs, *Fundamentals of U.S. Foreign Policy* (Washington, DC: U.S. Government Printing Office, 1988), p. 19; see also idem, *U.S. Policy Regarding Limitations on Nuclear Testing,* Special Report no. 150 (Washington, DC, August 1986); and Paul Doty, "A Nuclear Test Ban," *Foreign Affairs,* Fall 1986.

59. Congressional Research Service, Library of Congress, *Arms Control,* p. 12.

60. Dante B. Fascel, "Congress and Arms Control," *Foreign Affairs,* Fall 1986, pp. 738–40.

61. Report by the Senate Select Committee on Intelligence, *Principal Findings on the Capabilities of the U.S. to Monitor SALT II,* October 1979. Text in U.S. Arms Control and Disarmament Agency, *Documents on Disarmament, 1979* (Washington, DC, June 1980).

62. Report by the Senate Committee on Foreign Relations, *Report on the SALT*

II Treaty, November 1979. Text in U.S. Arms Control and Disarmament Agency, *Documents on Disarmament, 1979,* pp. 671–82.

63. Report by the Senate Committee on Armed Services, *The Military Implications of SALT II Treaty,* December 4, 1979. Text in U.S. Arms Control and Disarmament Agency, *Documents on Disarmament, 1979,* pp. 534–52.

64. Text of the president's letter is in U.S. Arms Control and Disarmament Agency, *Documents on Disarmament, 1980* (Washington, DC, December 1983), pp. 1–2.

65. U.S. Department of State, Bureau of Public Affairs, *Senate Consideration of Unratified Treaties to Limit Nuclear Testing,* Special Report no. 161 (Washington, DC, January 1987).

66. The first test under the Joint Verification Experiment was conducted underneath the Nevada desert on August 17, 1988.

67. John Isaacs, "The Ratification Circus," *Bulletin of Atomic Scientists,* April 1988, pp. 3–4. See also R. Jeffrey Smith, "INF Treaty Is Mired in Controversy," *Washington Post,* May 1, 1988.

68. Helen Dewar, "Senate Nears Debate on INF Treaty, Geneva Agreement Eases Hill Concerns," *Washington Post,* May 14, 1988; idem, "Final Hitches Resolved, INF Treaty Debuts in Senate," *Washington Post,* May 18, 1988.

69. Helen Dewar, "INF Treaty Called Unclear on Futuristic Weapons," *Washington Post,* March 29, 1988. See also Michele A. Flournoy, "INF Ratification Back on Track after Shultz–Shevardnadze Meeting," *Arms Control Today,* June 1988, pp. 15–19.

70. Helen Dewar, "GOP Senators Side with President in Power Struggle," *Washington Post,* May 9, 1988; idem, "INF Treaty Debate Slows: Dole Warns Objectors, Cranston Seeks Compromise on Interpretation," *Washington Post,* May 20, 1988.

71. R. Jeffrey Smith, "President Disputes Hill on Treaties," *Washington Post,* June 11, 1988.

6

The Endless Negotiations

The superpowers have been negotiating reductions in their strategic arsenals for more than twenty years. They have been negotiating the cessation of nuclear testing even longer (since the mid-1950s). With success eluding them on both accounts, the question logically arises: are the issues involved in these negotiations really so complex as to require this inordinate amount of time to reach a successful conclusion? Or is it possible that the superpowers are merely going through the motions, that their heart is not really in it.

STRATEGIC REDUCTIONS

Strategic Arms Limitation Talks (SALT) I

For the origins of the SALT process (predecessor to the Strategic Arms Reduction Talks [START]) one must look to the days of the Johnson administration.[1] It was President Johnson who, on prodding by then Secretary of Defense Robert S. McNamara, first suggested to the Soviet Union in December 1966 the possibility of bilateral talks on strategic arms limitations. The Soviets seemed interested, but it was not until three years later that negotiations toward a treaty to restrain strategic arms (both offensive and defensive) actually got under way. Not surprisingly, in the intervening years it was business as usual in the weapons laboratories of the superpowers. In the United States, the process of MIRVing warheads was being perfected (MIRV stands for multiple, independently targeted reentry vehicle) and tested, and a decision was made to deploy a "thin" antiballistic missile (ABM) defense against the possibility of a Chinese missile attack. In the

Soviet Union, the acquisition of intercontinental ballistic missiles (ICBMs) and of submarine-launched ballistic missiles (SLBMs) proceeded with the same urgency that had characterized Moscow's weapons procurement program since the early 1960s. The Soviets fared especially well by the delay, agreeing to begin discussions only after they had achieved rough parity[2] in strategic intercontinental systems with the United States. To emphasize this point and demonstrate the implications of their newly found power, they even invaded Czechoslovakia in the summer of 1968, despite loud protests by the civilized world.

The negotiations phase of SALT I lasted about two and a half years (from November 1969 to May 1972). It addressed essentially two issues: offensive arms and strategic defenses. On the first issue, little could be accomplished. The asymmetry of the opposing forces,[3] and sharply differing views by the superpowers on what the negotiations were to accomplish, precluded a meaningful agreement, except possibly for the codification of the status quo. The resulting accord, the SALT I Interim Agreement, satisfied no one. It simply approved the strategic buildup of the superpowers and provided them with all kinds of excuses (under the euphemism of weapons modernization) for building additional and more powerful systems in the years ahead.[4] On the U.S. side, for instance, SALT I did not inhibit the acceleration of Trident I development, continuation of work on the B-1 bomber, or research and testing of sea-launched cruise missiles (SLCMs).

In contrast to the stalemate on the issue of offensive arms, superpower agreement on strategic defenses came relatively easy. Conclusion of the ABM treaty is evidence that by the early 1970s the superpowers were generally in accord on the need to prevent a costly and ultimately destabilizing race in strategic defenses. During the preceeding decade both sides had experimented with such systems and had found them wanting, both from the viewpoint of cost and also feasibility (strategic defenses can be overcome easily by increased offensive forces). Before too long, plans for areawide ballistic missile defenses were abandoned by both superpowers, with final proof of their declining interest for such defenses coming in 1974, when the number of ABM sites allowed each side under the terms of the ABM treaty was reduced from two to one.[5]

Strategic Arms Limitation Talks (SALT) II

With the ABM issue temporarily out of the way (it was reopened ten years later by President Reagan's *Star Wars* speech), the superpowers returned to the issue that had eluded them in SALT I, that of really limiting offensive nuclear arms. This time they negotiated for seven years, from November 1972 to June 1979, with three U.S. administrations participating in the process.

The effort proved even more difficult. The purely military issues that were responsible for the stalemate in SALT I were now being intensified by all sorts of additional considerations: Watergate and Vietnam at home, a rapidly changing international environment (the result of Soviet achievement of strategic parity with the United States), and constantly deteriorating U.S.– Soviet relations had a profound impact on the negotiating process. At the end, not a single strategic vehicle or warhead judged essential by either side was reduced because of the terms of SALT II; the agreement merely codified the strategic plans of the two parties. Whatever constraints were agreed upon were for weapons that neither side really wanted or that would have been eliminated by the superpowers anyway in the normal process of weapons upgrading or retirement.

Because of the inequities in the SALT I Interim Agreement and congressional demands that any future accord "not limit the United States to levels of intercontinental strategic forces inferior to the limits provided for the Soviet Union,"[6] the primary U.S. goal at SALT II was for a regime of equal strategic nuclear delivery forces. Once this issue had been settled, a process of reductions could be agreed upon, including the imposition of retraints on qualitative developments likely to threaten future stability. Underlying the U.S. goal were hopes for constraining the most threatening weapons in the Soviet inventory while keeping out of the scope of the negotiations the strategic weapons (bombers and cruise missiles) for which the United States had the upper hand.

Soviet SALT II plans were driven by an entirely different agenda. The Soviets favored a permanent treaty based on the ceilings agreed upon in SALT I as well as suspension of the Trident and B-1 efforts and removal from Europe of all U.S. forward-based systems. The latter would have included all nuclear battlefield weapons and tactical aircraft based on land or on aircraft carriers in Europe and capable of reaching Soviet territory. In line with superpower practice of confronting each other with grossly one-sided proposals, the kind that the other side is unlikely to accept, no restraints were suggested by the Soviets on any of their own far superior tactical forces in Europe.

The negotiations floundered hopelessly for two years. At a summit in Vladivostok, however, in November 1974, the two sides finally decided to set their squabbling aside. The resulting agreement was a real shocker. The superpowers agreed on *equal ceilings* for their strategic systems (a move favored by the United States) but did so with total disregard for the consequences of their action on the nuclear arms race. Under the terms of the agreement each side was allowed 2,400 ICBMs, SLBMs, and heavy bombers, with an aggregate limit of 1,320 on their ballistic missiles equipped with MIRV systems.[7] Even critics of the arms control process agreed that under the established ceilings an end to the arms race was nowhere in sight.

SALT II never did recover from the Vladivostok blunder. Despite the extremely high ceilings authorized by the agreement, critical differences on cruise missiles, MIRVing, the Soviet Backfire bomber, and a host of other issues soon made consideration of options for weapons reduction totally unreal. Before long, emphasis at the SALT talks shifted from the need to reduce strategic systems (theoretically, the next step in the process) to the sheltering and protection by the superpowers of their most prized weapons.

Weapons modernization and acquisition continued unabated in both camps during the entire seven-year period of SALT II negotiations—ostensibly, because of the possibility that the talks might fail; in practice, however, because of the momentum inherent in all weapons development. On the U.S. side, the 1970s witnessed the hardening and modernization of the Minuteman force (to increase its yield and accuracy); research and development on the MX missile, the stealth bomber, and cruise missiles; the construction of additional Trident boats equipped with longer range, more accurate SLBMs; and the upgrading of the B-52 fleet to enhance its survivability and penetrability.[8] In short, every element of the U.S. triad was improved and expanded while our diplomats in Geneva and elsewhere were negotiating with the other side the benefits of arms reductions and constraints.

The Soviets, too, did their share of arms buildup and modernization. During the period of the SALT II talks, they fielded three new ICBM types, deployed several new ballistic missile submarines armed with advanced SLBMs, developed cruise missiles and a new strategic bomber (the Blackjack), and began the introduction into Europe of elements of their SS-20 force. The deployments nearly doubled the inventory of Soviet warheads assigned strategic missions, hopelessly complicating the SALT negotiations process.

The SALT II agreement, when it finally did come, met none of the superpowers' professed expectations, except possibly the one favored by the United States: it established equal ceilings for most delivery vehicles then in the arsenals of the two nations and introduced modest constraints on ICBM modernization.[9] Cynics suggest that the superpowers were a lot more pleased with the treaty than their official statements appeared to indicate. After all, it did preserve for them intact their strategic arsenals and removed threats to their plans for weapons modernization. From the perspective of reversing the arms race, SALT II was a true disappointment. It did not eliminate a single delivery vehicle or warhead that the superpowers wished to retain, and neither did it impose the type of restraints needed to strengthen future international stability.

Strategic Arms Limitation Talks (SALT) III/Strategic Arms Reduction Talks (START)

In June 1982, after a three-year pause, the superpowers were at it again: same players, same weapons, same agenda, same one-sided proposals. There was a cosmetic difference, though. The latest series of talks became known as START to give credence to the superpowers' desire for effecting "reductions" in strategic arms, as opposed to mere "limitations," which the letter L in SALT implied.

This time, the superpowers talked for less than two years. On December 8, 1983, the Soviet Union suspended its participation in the START talks on news of the arrival on the European continent of the first elements of the U.S. Pershing II and Tomahawk missiles. (The deployment of these weapons in Europe had been authorized by the NATO dual track decision of December 12, 1979, as a response to the arrival in eastern Europe of units of the Soviet SS–20 force.) The Soviet walkout did not really set back the cause of arms control. Even if the Soviets had remained in Geneva, it is extremely doubtful that a substantive agreement would have resulted.

START was in trouble from the outset. At issue were the conflicting expectations of the superpowers on what the talks were to accomplish. To the U.S. side, disappointed with the "flawed" SALT II agreement, an entirely new approach was needed, one focusing first on the large Soviet MIRVed ICBMs, the single most serious threat confronting the U.S. mainland. A good START agreement, in the U.S. view, would have to cut deeply into the inventory of heavy Soviet ICBMs[10] while not constraining the United States from proceeding with the modernization of its strategic triad, especially the MX missile, advanced SLBMs for the Trident fleet, and the B-1, and the development of cruise missiles. The Soviet view of START was entirely different. The new talks, noted the Kremlin, were a mere continuation of the SALT process and as such should build on SALT, not abandon it. Reductions would have to be across the board and applicable to all SALT II systems: ICBMs, SLBMs, cruise missiles, and bombers.

As expected, the START proposals that the superpowers attempted to sell each other in Geneva were one sided, if not self-centered. Behind the noble words, the aim was always the same: to control or eliminate the systems threatening one's security while sheltering from possible cuts the systems for which one maintained the upper hand. The U.S. proposal, for instance, publicly announced by President Reagan on May 9, 1982,[11] called for a ceiling of 5,000 deployed ballistic missile warheads on each side, of which no more than 2,500 would be on ICBMs. Later, the president noted, similar reductions would be sought on other elements of the U.S. and Soviet strategic arsenals. The Soviet proposal was a lot more devious. It proposed an across-the-board reduction of 25 percent of the SALT II agreed-upon limits and sublimits. In effect, the Soviet proposal placed all strategic delivery vehicles in one category, whether fast and accurate as the Soviet MIRVed ICBMs are or slow and vulnerable as the U.S. bombers are. The SALT III/ START talks collapsed before the two sides even got close to reconciling the opposing viewpoints.

Nuclear and Space Talks (NST)/START

Sixteen months lapsed before the superpowers would agree to resume negotiations. But at the insistence of the Soviet Union, the talks about to open in Geneva on March 12, 1985, were to be "new," not a mere continuation of the SALT/START process. The issue was not just a matter of semantics. It reflected Soviet anxiety over the U.S. Strategic Defense Initiative (SDI) program and its implications on the East–West strategic balance.

The official communiqué announcing the opening of the talks was explicit in this regard. The two sides, it reported, "agree that the subject of the negotiations will be a complex of questions concerning *space and nuclear arms,* both strategic and intermediate range, with all the questions considered and resolved *in their interrelationship.*"[12] (Eventually, the United States would regret accepting this formula as the basis for the negotiations.) To further provide evidence that the talks would address space and nuclear arms issues *in their interrelationship,* each side was authorized only one delegation at the talks, divided into three groups, one each for intermediate-range forces, strategic arms, and defense and space issues. The talks were given the new designation of Nuclear and Space Talks (NST).

As 1989 is coming to a close, the NST talks are concluding their fifth year with agreement still far away on either the space or the strategic arms issues. It is not for lack of activity, however. Since launching the negotiations, in March 1985, the superpowers have held four summits (in Geneva, Reykjavik, Washington, and Moscow), eleven full rounds of talks in Geneva, and innumerable meetings of their foreign ministers and arms control experts. The proposals, counterproposals, and counter-counterproposals considered at these meetings could fill volumes.[13] What has been the result of this activity? Some modest gains have been made in the strategic arms area, but progress on space issues has been nil.

In the *strategic arms* area, the superpowers have reached agreement or basic understanding on seven key provisions of a future arms reduction accord.[14] Sharp differences, however, still separate them on many other issues. The areas of agreement include:

1. A 50 percent reduction in the number of the U.S. and Soviet strategic offensive nuclear forces, to ceilings of 1,600 delivery systems (ballistic missiles and heavy bombers) and 6,000 warheads on each side. The reductions are to take place over a five-year period, according to the Soviet plan, in seven years according to the United States. The 6,000-warhead ceiling may sound like an arms control breakthrough, but in fact it is not. It leaves the superpowers with enough weapons on hand to cause all sorts of trouble.

2. A sublimit of 4,900 on the aggregate number of ICBM and SLBM warheads, within the overall ceiling of 6,000 warheads. The United States favors a further sublimit of 3,300 warheads for ICBMs only, but the Soviet Union is opposed to this.[15]

3. A sublimit of 1,540 warheads on 154 heavy missiles.

4. A 50 percent reduction in the aggregate throw-weight of the Soviet ICBM and SLBM force, as a result of the above reductions, with both sides agreeing not to exceed this level. *Throw-weight* is the payload a missile can carry over a given range, an area in which the Soviets have an enormous advantage. The United States has fought hard to get Soviet agreement on this issue.

5. Agreement on counting rules for warheads on ballistic missiles. Specific procedures are still to be worked out but will be based on "declarations" made by the superpowers on the number of warheads deployed on each type of their ICBMs and SLBMs.

6. Agreement on counting each heavy bomber as one strategic delivery vehicle, with each heavy bomber equipped for gravity bombs and short-range attack missiles counting as one warhead in the 6,000 limit.

7. Agreement eventually to limit the nuclear-armed sea-launched cruise missiles (SLCMs) on each side. However, future SLCM limitations (still to be determined) will not be counted against the agreed-upon ceilings of 6,000 warheads and 1,600 strategic delivery systems.

The areas of disagreement include:[16]

1. The issue of the ABM treaty and SDI: This is by far the most serious obstacle to a START accord. The Soviets insist on making an agreement on strategic arms reductions contingent upon the resolution of the ABM treaty compliance/SDI issue. The United States wants the two issues separated (more on this later).

2. A sublimit for ICBMs only:[17] The United States wants a sublimit of 3,300 warheads; the Soviets are resisting this for fear that it will cut deeply into their ICBM force. They contend that the agreed-upon sublimit of 4,900 for ICBM and SLBM warheads sufficiently restricts both sides but also allows them flexibility to structure their strategic forces according to need. The U.S. view is that an ICBM sublimit will enhance stability by restricting the size of the ICBM forces of the superpowers and their capability to launch a first strike.

3. The issue of mobile missiles: The United States favors banning mobile missiles because of the difficulties that their verification would entail, particularly in a closed society such as the Soviet Union. The Soviets, having already deployed two ICBM systems in a mobile configuration (the SS-24 and SS-25), want the mobiles retained. It is unlikely that the United States will prevail on this one. There are sharp differences between the administration and the Congress on the issue of mobile missiles, the Bush administration favoring development of a rail-mobile version for the MX (in lieu of the present silo basing), the Congress leaning more in the direction of the mobile, single-warhead ICBM (the Small ICBM or Midgetman). Mobile missiles are considered "stabilizing" weapons. They cannot be wiped out in a surprise attack and are therefore available for purposes of retaliation. A U.S. agreement in Geneva retaining mobile missiles would be contingent on the adoption of an appropriate sublimit for these weapons, the banning of MIRVed mobile missiles and of acceptable verification provisions.

4. The issue of SLCMs:[18] The Soviet Union favors limits of 400 nuclear and 600 conventionally armed SLCMs. The United States maintains that limits on nuclear SLCMs would be unverifiable and that conventionally armed SLCMs should not be part of START. This is one weapons area in which the United States holds a definite advantage over the Soviet Union, one that it is obviously trying to protect. Both sides have agreed to restrict SLCMs eventually (see number 7 above). When they do, the SLCMs will *not* be included in the 6,000 warhead limit.

5. Counting of air-launched cruise missiles (ALCMs): At issue is how to count the ALCMs on strategic bombers, specifically how to distinguish bombers armed with cruise missiles from other planes. This is another area of U.S. technological advantage and one that it is trying to protect. Reportedly, the United States favors limiting the counting of ALCMs to ten per plane, although more than twenty can be carried on each bomber.

6. The Soviet Backfire Bomber: Even though the aircraft has intercontinental capabilities, and therefore meets the criteria of a strategic delivery vehicle, the Soviets refuse to include it under the treaty's 1,600 limit. The Soviet Union has about 300 Backfires but bases its position on SALT II, which did not impose any limits on the aircraft.

7. Verification: Both sides agree that a START accord must include an effective verification regime to enhance confidence in the arms reduction process. Reportedly, verification procedures generally will be modeled after those in the INF treaty and are to include base-line declarations; data exchanges; on-site inspections (OSI) before, during, and after weapons destructions; observations by national technical means (NTM) of verification; and prohibitions against concealment or other activities designed to impede verification. Four verification issues loom as especially difficult: the monitoring of mobile missiles,[19] distinction between nuclear and conventionally armed SLCM, assurance that neither side has an inventory of hidden (undeployed) ballistic missiles, and the adoption of counting rules of warheads on present and future MIRVed delivery systems. The U.S. intelligence community is providing major input into these deliberations to enhance its own capability to verify compliance adequately and also to limit Soviet opportunities for espionage under the OSI provisions of the treaty. On this, the U.S. intelligence community has the full support of the Senate. The START agreement, state key senators, will have to include air-tight verification provisions and enhance U.S. security or its ratification will be denied.

So much for superpower give and take on the route to START and on the issues still remaining before a reductions agreement can be consummated. To resolve the seven outstanding issues, warns the U.S. government, a great deal "of spade and shovel" work will be required,[20] and the Soviets will also have to correct the Krasnoyarsk radar violation (which apparently they are now prepared to do). Moscow is a lot more cavalier about future prospects. A START treaty can be signed, it claims, as soon as the United States pledges to adhere to the ABM treaty for ten years and promises to comply during that period with the treaty's traditional interpretation.

But assuming that the Soviets do decide to delink the ABM/SDI issue from START and an agreement does materialize in Geneva along the lines currently under consideration, what kind of accord would START be? Would its terms be cause for celebration?

Hardly!

If START had come into being in 1972, the year that SALT I was signed, perhaps there would have been cause for celebration. A 50 percent reduction package then would have contributed greatly to expectations of further reductions and would have enhanced international stability. But for the superpowers to engage each other in negotiations for nearly twenty years and then to come up with a "reductions" package that still leaves them with awesome nuclear power, many times that needed for their security, borders on fraud and raises serious doubts about the superpowers' commitment to the arms control process and their desire to enhance international stability.

Returning to basics, for instance, the purpose of the START talks, according to the Shultz–Gromyko agreement that launched them in January 1985, was "to work out effective agreements aimed at preventing an arms race in space and terminating it on earth, at limiting and reducing nuclear arms and at strengthening strategic stability." But how can 1,600 strategic vehicles and 6,000 warheads on each side (plus all sorts of additional nuclear armaments not included in the START package) terminate the arms race on earth and enhance international stability? Worse yet, the reductions package will not be fully implemented for another seven years.

In reality, the proposed reductions package will neither help avert nuclear war (which is the principal goal of arms control) nor lessen the superpowers' capability for fighting one. It will not affect the superpowers' capability to launch preemptive strikes or to carry out countercity or counterforce (second-strike) missions.[21] There is not a single nuclear mission that the superpowers are able to execute now with 10,000 warheads, that will be denied to them by the proposed reduction to 6,000. One could be generous with START and rationalize that half a loaf is better than none and that the treaty is "only the beginning."[22] But START's basic limitations are hard to dispute: The treaty does not withdraw a single warhead from the nuclear arsenals of the superpowers, which is judged by them to be essential for their security, eliminates only superfluous weapons, and in the process leaves the superpowers' capabilities for fighting nuclear war essentially intact.

Although the official text of the START agreement has not been released as yet, reports suggest that the superpowers are drafting an accord in Geneva full of loopholes and omissions. The Soviet Backfire bomber, for instance, although capable of reaching the continental United States, is not being counted in the treaty's total strategic delivery vehicles of 1,600. For that matter, neither are the U.S. "tactical" aircraft based in western Europe and in the Mediterranean, which are able to reach large sections of Soviet territory. Cruise missiles are similarly not counted in all cases. The United

States, for instance, eventually plans to build 4,000 SLCMs (how many of them will be nuclear armed is still classified information); yet only 400 SLCMs will be "controlled" by START. How long will it be before the Soviets similarly decide to build thousands of "conventionally armed" SLCMs? The count on ALCMs is likewise obscured, with ALCM ceilings in START being considerably lower than the theoretical capability of aircraft to carry them. The explanation given for this odd arrangement is that bombers normally carry fewer ALCMs than they are able to accommodate.

Despite its many drawbacks, START could have a beneficial effect on the East–West strategic balance in a roundabout way—by making it necessary for both superpowers to restructure their ICBM/SLBM forces for greater survivability.[23] The more survivable the strategic offensive systems of the United States and the Soviet Union are, the smaller the chance that either power will venture a surprise nuclear attack (preemptive, first strike, or otherwise). The need for restructuring results from the treaty provisions that limit both sides to a total of 1,600 delivery vehicles and 6,000 warheads, with a sublimit of 4,900 on the total number of ICBM and SLBM warheads.

In the United States, for instance, the distribution of the 4,900 ICBM and SLBM warheads among the various U.S. weapons will require tough decisions on the part of the Congress and the administration, especially on the issues of the Small ICBM, the rail-mobile configured MX, and the future composition and size of the Trident force.[24] At present, the Soviet Union targets 1,050 U.S. ICBMs (50 MXs, 500 Minuteman IIs, and 500 Minuteman IIIs). Under the limitations imposed by START, the United States would have to eliminate the inaccurate Minuteman II. But this would increase the vulnerability of the remainder of the U.S. ICBM force, because the Soviets would now need to target only 550 ICBMs. The greater the vulnerability of the U.S. ICBM force, the greater the U.S. anxiety over the possibility of a Soviet surprise attack. One solution to the U.S. predicament would be to acquire several hundred mobile Small ICBMs, each with a single warhead. The Soviets would have to sacrifice a major part of their missile throw-weight to target successfully such a force of mobile ICBMs, a price they would be unlikely to want to pay. Placing fewer warheads on more delivery vehicles would discourage a Soviet attack to the benefit of deterrence and stability.

The same rationale would guide a possible restructuring of the Trident force. As presently conceived, eighteen Trident boats would account for a total of 3,456 warheads (each boat with 24 missile tubes, each tube with 8 warheads). But that would be putting all of America's SLBM eggs in eighteen baskets. The vulnerability of the Trident force would decrease and stability would increase if the number of Trident boats would be increased to twenty-four or more while the number of Trident missiles on each boat would be reduced to eighteen or fewer. Dispersal and survivability would benefit, but at a very high monetary cost.

START and the Transition from Reagan to Bush

Although the last round of START negotiations conducted by the Reagan administration wound up its deliberations in November 1988, President Bush did not resume this effort until seven months later. A START hold, explained the new administration, was needed to allow President Bush and his advisors to conduct a comprehensive review of U.S. policy toward the Soviet Union. (One cannot help but wonder why old hands at the nuclear game such as George Bush and Brent Scowcroft needed to ponder nuclear arms control for seven months. In contrast, no hold was applied to non-nuclear arms control, the new administration embarking on chemical and conventional talks without delay on its assumption of power.)

During its first year in office, the Bush administration has been extremely secretive about its plans for START. Official secrecy notwithstanding, the issue of START verification appears to occupy center stage within the Bush White House. In a stunning reversal of Reagan policy, the United States now believes that START might not be verifiable, even with the inclusion in the proposed treaty of very generous OSI and other verification provisions. Reportedly, the president is seeking Soviet cooperation in a Joint Test Experiment, during which both sides will explore the mechanics of verification by conducting trial inspections of each others weaponry in factories, silos, and deployment areas. (If all goes well during the experiment, the Verification Protocol to the treaty will then be finalized.) The purpose of the experiment, the administration claims, is not to delay START but to accelerate it by developing measures that will prevent verification from becoming a killer issue when the treaty is presented to the Senate for ratification.[25]

NST/Defense and Space

The other half of the NST concerns the talks designed to find a solution to the defense and space issue. The Shultz–Gromyko agreement of January 1985, which launched the NST, identified space arms and the desire to prevent an arms race in space as coequal to the negotiations on reductions in strategic nuclear arms.

Defense and space became an issue in March 1983 when President Reagan announced plans for an antiballistic missile defense program (SDI), a situation aggravated two years later when the United States announced its support of the "broad" or "permissive" interpretation of the ABM treaty. The Soviet Union objected to both moves, arguing, as the United States did in the 1960s and 1970s, that development and deployment of nationwide strategic defenses would destabilize the strategic balance and inhibit the two sides from undertaking deep reductions in their strategic offensive systems. At the negotiations in Geneva the Soviets have called for a ban on the development, testing, and deployment of any space-based weapon able to strike objects in space or on earth, as well as on any system targeted against satellites (the Soviet designation for such weapons is "space strike" arms). They also have stressed the interrelationship between offensive and space strike arms, asserting that no reductions would be possible on the former without a ban on the latter.[26] The United States, for its part, countered the Soviet moves by suggesting that the two sides "manage jointly a stable transition to a deterrence regime that would increasingly rely on defensive systems" (whatever the statement means). To build confidence in the process, the American delegation in Geneva even has offered an open-laboratories initiative,[27] in which the two sides would regularly brief each other and visit each other's laboratories and associated facilities where strategic defense research is undertaken.

During the years that the NST talks have been in progress the positions of the superpowers on the defense and space issue have shifted only minimally.[28] One aspect, though, on which there has been absolutely no movement is the basic link between reductions in offensive systems and the future of strategic defenses. The Soviet Union continues to insist, as it did in 1985, that no major strategic reductions are possible as long as the United States is committed to an SDI program under the ABM treaty's broad or permissive interpretation. The United States, on the other hand, holds firm to the view that reductions in strategic arsenals should stand on their own merit and not be linked to limits of SDI research, development, and testing.

The opposing positions involve essentially three primary issues: (1) the length and time during which the two sides would agree not to withdraw from the ABM treaty in order to deploy defenses, (2) what happens during that period, and (3) what happens at the end of the nonwithdrawal[29] period. A very wide gap still separates the two sides on all three primary issues. The latest formal U.S. proposal, for instance, dated April 1987, calls for a mutual commitment not to withdraw from the ABM treaty through 1994; strict observance during this period with all ABM treaty provisions, but with research, development, and testing permitted (i.e., activities would be in accordance with the broad interpretation of the ABM treaty); and permission for either side to deploy advanced strategic defenses after 1994, if it so chooses. The Soviet position is based on a mutual pledge for a ten-year adherence to the treaty, with testing of ABM components and systems during that period limited by the treaty's traditional interpretation. At the end of the ten-year nonwithdrawal period, the ABM treaty would remain in force, but both sides would be free to withdraw on six months' notice if their supreme national interests would so dictate.

The defense and space issue took a special twist during the Washington Summit, when the superpowers, in their eagerness to avoid another stalemate of the type they encountered in Reykjavik, decided to handle the ABM/SDI issue with the greatest of care. As if by mutual understanding, neither side addressed the subject in earnest during the summit or worked hard at convincing the other of its point of view. In the words of the chief U.S. negotiator, the superpowers merely decided to "kick the can down the road."[30] The communiqué released at the end of the talks was a masterpiece of ambiguity. It reported:

Taking into account the preparation of the Treaty on Strategic Offensive Arms, the leaders of the two countries also instructed their delegations in Geneva to work out an agreement that would commit the sides to observe the ABM Treaty, as signed in 1972, while conducting their research, development, and testing as required, which are permitted by the ABM Treaty, and not to withdraw from the ABM Treaty for a specified period of time.

But just in case the communiqué was misunderstood by the Soviet Union as a softening of its ABM/SDI position, the United States, within days of the Washington Summit, tabled a draft treaty in Geneva. Its title said it all: "Treaty on Certain Measures to Facilitate the Cooperative Transition to the Deployment of Future Strategic Ballistic Missile Defenses." As expected, the Soviets protested the implication of ballistic defenses, especially the suggestion that a "transition" was required.[31] The United States ignored the protests, recommending next that an area in space be designated as the "Space Test Range" for use by the superpowers in their SDI weapons testing.

This, then, was the status of the defense and space talks as of midsummer 1989. Are there prospects for agreement? Is a compromise in the opposing positions likely? Without the benefit of inside information, one can only speculate. The likelihood of compromise will depend on the reasons that the superpowers are in Geneva.

There are several possible explanations, for instance, for the U.S. position at the Geneva talks.[32] The United States may only be seeking arms reduction concessions from the Soviet Union, not limitations in ballistic defense programs. By holding out the possibility of an agreement also on space and defense arms, which apparently the Soviets want, the United States is keeping them in the arms reduction negotiations. Or perhaps the United States intends to go ahead with SDI anyway, regardless of Soviet opposition. The space talks in Geneva, then, are a mere charade, designed to lay the groundwork for the eventual U.S. withdrawal from the ABM treaty. The extent that SDI might be a bargaining chip provides yet a third explanation. The United States might eventually be prepared to abandon SDI in return for major Soviet concessions in their most threatening strategic systems. But the Soviet concessions would have to be at an extremely high level before the United States will consent to giving up its SDI program.

On the Soviet side, there are similarly three alternative explanations for the defense and space position followed in Geneva. One is that the Soviet Union has no plans for making reductions in strategic offensive systems and is using the talks for propaganda purposes to promote a favorable image of the USSR as a global peacemaker. The SDI provides a convenient reason for deadlocking the talks and blaming the United States. Another possible explanation is that the Soviets continue to seek superiority over the United States and are exploiting the talks to stall for time while they are developing a nationwide ABM defense coupled with enhanced offensive capabilities. By promising reductions in strategic arms, they influence the Congress to slow down the strategic modernization and SDI programs. Finally, the Soviets might be genuinely interested in stopping the U.S. SDI program for fear that it will alter the strategic relationship in favor of the United States.

Considering the likely reasons why the superpowers are in Geneva, an agreement on defense and space issues appears extremely remote. Potential areas of compromise exist, but without strong political will and a genuine desire for agreement on both sides, the development of space arms and debate on how best to control them could continue well into the 1990s.

CESSATION OF NUCLEAR TESTING

For the record at least, American and Soviet negotiators have been pursuing a Comprehensive Test Ban Treaty (CTBT) since 1955.[33] This is a very long time to be working on a treaty (no matter how complex) that raises serious doubts about the commitment of the superpowers to the concept of a nuclear test-free world. The reasons for the U.S. and Soviet foot dragging on the issue are not particularly hard to discern. The CTBT is bound to affect their status as superpowers by limiting their capability to develop new weapons and by denying them the opportunity to test the combat readiness of their nuclear stockpiles. Without new weapons and confidence in the existing ones, the superpowers are minus their principal clout in the international arena and the assurance that is essential in a nuclear confrontation.

The Limited Test Ban Treaty (LTBT)

The idea of a nuclear test ban is probably as old as the bomb itself. But it was not until the United States and the Soviet Union exploded their first hydrogen devices in 1952 and 1953 that the concept gained momentum. Not surprisingly, the principal voices of protest came from nonnuclear nations, concerned over the constantly increasing size of the weapons being tested, the resulting radioactive fallout, and the possibility that cumulative contamination of the environment might result from continued testing. In March 1954 the issue received additional impetus, when a U.S. experimental thermonuclear device tested at the Bikini atoll turned out to be twice as powerful as originally planned. The unexpected high yield contaminated the surrounding area, causing radiation illness and death to members of the crew of a Japanese fishing boat.

The resulting public outcry eventually led the two superpowers (and also the other nuclear powers of the day—the United Kingdom, France, and Canada) to the negotiating table. Eight years of utter waste ensued during which the superpowers debated the real issues impacting on a CTBT (such as verification)[34] and dozens of nonissues, linked and delinked proposals to prevent an agreement from materializing, held firm on some positions only to reverse them later, compromised very little, and generally behaved as if impasse in the talks was preferable to progress.

Verification of underground nuclear tests proved the central and most persistent issue. The Western nations, claiming that existing technology for detecting nuclear explosions was inadequate, demanded a very extensive system of verification[35] controls with no less than seven on-site inspections annually. For its part, the Soviet Union would agree only to the most rudimentary of verification arrangements, augmented perhaps by three annual inspections. In January 1962 the talks reached a total impasse, and the superpowers agreed to abandon their further search for a CTBT.

Within two years, largely as a result of the Cuban Missile Crisis, which brought the superpowers to the brink of nuclear war, the two sides (including the United Kingdom) began talking again. A CTBT was still unattainable, so in its place they decided to seek agreement on a "limited" package, one that would outlaw nuclear tests in those environments where both sides agreed that existing verification systems could adequately police a ban. The three-power meetings began on July 15, 1963, and it took Averell Harriman for the United States, Lord Hailsham for the United Kingdom, and Andrei Gromyko for the Soviet Union merely ten days[36] to reach concensus. The speed with which agreement was reached proved once again that when their national interests are at stake, the superpowers have no difficulty addressing issues with urgency and genuine concern.

The resulting agreement, the LTBT, was hailed worldwide. True, supporters claimed, it only banned nuclear testing in the atmosphere, under water, and in outer space (underground testing was unaffected), but the treaty was a symbolic first, a forerunner of further agreements limiting nuclear testing. The Senate shared that view, and in September, after extensive hearings and almost three weeks of floor debate, it consented to the ratification of the treaty by a vote of eighty to nineteen. There were also a great many voices of concern. The LTBT, critics pointed out, did not really limit superpower nuclear testing, end the threat of nuclear war, halt the production of nuclear weapons, or reduce stockpiles. Under the terms of the treaty the superpowers could continue the development of new weapons as long as the associated nuclear testing was done underground. Hawks in the United States were especially critical. The Soviet Union, they charged, had made tremendous strides in weaponry as a result of its weapons tests concluded just before the signing of the LTBT, an advantage that it was trying to protect by acceding to the treaty.

Statistics on nuclear testing since 1963, the effective date of the LTBT, support the contention that the superpowers gave up very little by agreeing to the treaty. More than 1,200 nuclear tests have been conducted since that date, as opposed to 544 tests during the eighteen years before the treaty. If anything, nuclear testing has doubled since the LTBT, with the United States leading the Soviet Union in the number of tests carried out, 553 to 452.[37]

The Miniagreements (Phase One)

In the preamble to the LTBT the superpowers proclaimed their intent to work for an agreement to discontinue "all test explosions of nuclear weapons for all time." This pledge notwithstanding, during the ensuing fourteen years, the United States and the Soviet Union never really addressed the issue of a CTBT in earnest, choosing instead to work on minor, peripheral aspects of the problem, the kind on which an illusion of progress could be given. The superpowers had little incentive for real action. The LTBT had silenced their critics and had left them free to pursue their prize weapons development activities.

Under the circumstances, it took nearly a decade before the superpowers would return to the subject of underground testing. The sudden interest was motivated by considerations of world politics, not an overwhelming desire for a nuclear test-free world. With a summit scheduled for mid-1974, both sides suddenly became anxious for evidence of movement on the long dormant issue, provided that such movement did not interfere with their plans for continued nuclear testing. The safest and least controversial route to this goal, Moscow and Washington reasoned, was by means of a treaty that would outlaw the very large nuclear explosions, those that could be verified without complicated verification mechanisms. All other detonations would continue to be allowed. A 150 kiloton threshold appeared to meet these criteria and was quickly agreed upon. The resulting treaty, the Threshold Test Ban Treaty (TTBT), was signed in Moscow on July 3, 1974.[38]

There were few surprises in the treaty. In their rush to finalize it in time for the Moscow Summit, the superpowers decided in favor of a bilateral as opposed to a multilateral undertaking, omitting the customary provisions for other nuclear weapons nations to join. Thus, technically, the TTBT applies to only two of the six nations that presently acknowledge status as nuclear powers. To no one's surprise, the superpowers repeated in the preamble to the treaty their intention to "seek to achieve the discontinuance of all test explosions of nuclear weapons for all time, and to continue negotiations to this end." This is the same pledge they had made in connection with the LTBT and the Treaty on the Non-Proliferation of Nuclear Weapons. One can only speculate why the United States and the Soviet Union feel compelled to repeat this pledge when they obviously do not really mean it.

At home the TTBT received mixed reviews. At issue was not only the size of the threshold adopted but also the process of attempting to regulate nuclear testing by establishing thresholds. Critics charged that thresholds would perpetuate nuclear testing by continuing to allow tests below a certain level. Any hope for a CTBT would thus be doomed. As for the 150 kiloton TTBT threshold, some judged it to be low, others very high. As expected, supporters of unlimited testing protested that the 150 kiloton threshold would constrain essential weapons development; opponents argued that the threshold made the treaty inconsequential. Practically any test that the superpowers wished to undertake could be done so legally under the terms of the treaty.

Having established the precedent of a 150 kiloton threshold for underground nuclear tests, the superpowers moved next to adopt a similar threshold for peaceful nuclear explosions.[39] Presumably, such a limit was needed to prevent the superpowers from testing large military devices under the guise of conducting nuclear explosions for peaceful purposes. The Peaceful Nuclear Explosions Treaty (PNET), signed in May 1976, extended the 150 kiloton threshold to individual peaceful nuclear explosions. Group explosions could also be held for peaceful purposes but only if the individual explosions in the group did not have aggregate yields exceeding 150 kiloton. An arms control breakthrough? Hardly!

As of 1989, for a variety of political and technical reasons the United States has not formally ratified either the TTBT or the PNET. Both superpowers are on record, however, as honoring the treaties as long as the other side also does. In the United States, uncertainty over the verification provisions of the treaties has been cited as the principal reason for delaying their consideration by the Senate. (Refer to Chapter 5.) Considering, however, the very extensive verification protocols that accompany both treaties, the allegation is hard to accept.

A Glimmer of Hope

For a brief moment during the late 1970s, the superpowers came close to concluding a CTBT. After years of preoccupation with partial measures, the concept of a total nuclear ban suddenly was moved to the front burner in the fall of 1977. A new administration in Washington (President Carter's) and flexibility in Moscow seemed for a while to make progress possible.

But early in 1979 the CTBT negotiations began slowing down, primarily due to Washington's preoccupation with SALT II and the ensuing ratification uncertainties of the new treaty. In the Senate, opposition to SALT II

was already brewing. Confronting the senators with two controversial treaties, a CTBT in addition to SALT II, the Carter administration reasoned,
could doom them both. Not surprisingly, SALT II was given the green light
while work on the CTBT was temporarily shelved. A year later the negotiations themselves recessed, not to be resumed for nine years.

In retrospect, the progress that the superpowers made during the late
1970s toward a CTBT was respectable. It addressed most of the key issues
separating the two sides, and it even seemed to solve the perennial issue of
verification. There were no thresholds or other exceptions in the proposed
agreement; it outlawed all nuclear weapons testing—in all environments.
The treaty, however, would have had a life span of only three years. At the
end of this period the superpowers could either extend it or abandon it in
favor of resuming nuclear testing. The three-year life span also was meant
as a warning to France and China to either come on board or face the
consequences of an unlimited nuclear future.

The draft CTBT treaty, reportedly, made major inroads in the field of
verification. In addition to the NTM of each side, verification was to be
supported by twenty or so unmanned seismic stations positioned on the
territories of the superpowers and by provision for on-site inspections to
investigate suspicious events. The latter, however, would be by "challenge"
(i.e., when events justified them) and be unlimited in number.

The Miniagreements (Phase Two)

Nine years passed before the superpowers would agree to resume their
CTBT work. This delay occurred despite recurrent declarations of their
undying commitment to freeing the world of nuclear weapons, which presumably would also mean an end to all nuclear testing.

There are numerous official explanations for the nine-year "hold." Responsibility rests with the Soviets, claims the United States, for violating
existing arms control agreements and for stalling on the renegotiation of
the verification provisions of the TTBT and the PNET. Once the verification
aspects of these treaties have been rectified and the two instruments ratified,
the United States would be prepared to enter into negotiations on ways to
implement a step-by-step program to limit and ultimately end nuclear tests.
Not surprisingly, the Soviets blame the Americans for the impasse and for
demanding that treaties previously agreed upon and signed be renegotiated.
The mutual incriminations notwithstanding, there is far less enthusiasm for
a CTBT among U.S. and Soviet ruling circles today than ever before in
history. If anything, every passing day seems to be working against the
adoption of a CTBT.

The Soviet Union has been particularly deceptive in its opposition to the
CTBT, concealing it behind offers for a nuclear test moratorium (precon-
ditioned on the United States adopting a comparable stance) and by appeals

for the immediate conclusion of an agreement. The United States, for its part, has stopped pretending. A CTBT, it believes, is contrary to its security interests.[40] As long as the free world must depend on nuclear deterrence for security, nuclear weapons must be safe, reliable, and survivable. Such assurance is only possible through continuous nuclear testing. Despite declaring opposition to a CTBT, the United States does not preclude entirely the possibility of an agreement. A CTBT will eventually come to pass, it states, sometime in the far future, after the superpowers have reduced their strategic arsenals and ultimately eliminated their nuclear weapons.[41]

The search for improvements in the verification provisions of the TTBT and the PNET has been keeping the superpowers busy for more than three years. Through the summer of 1989, numerous sessions were held at the expert level as well as four formal rounds of negotiations. By all indications this is busy work *par excellence,* the only accomplishment to date being an agreement for a Joint Verification Experiment, which was conducted during 1988 in Nevada and at Semipalatinsk.[42] The experiment provided each side the opportunity to measure the yield of a nuclear explosion carried out by the other. The measuring of nuclear yields was made by the CORRTEX technique in the case of the United States (this involves the burying of a cable containing electronic sensors at the explosion site) and by means of a seismic measuring device, which measures tremors generated by the explosion, in the case of the Soviets. The choice of measuring devices was significant. Throughout the years, the United States has insisted that the CORRTEX cable be used for verification of all blasts expected to exceed 50 kilotons.[43] The Soviets are opposed to this idea for fear that it will result in a continuous U.S. presence at their nuclear test sites.

Is There Hope for a CTBT?

The superpowers today are in the midst of a massive arms buildup, one based primarily on a new generation of first-strike weapons. Extensive testing will be required before many of these "new" weapons are approved for operational deployment. Short of a miracle, only a CTBT can end the senseless weapons spiral and the development of future generations of weapons, which the superpowers are so eagerly embracing in their never-ending pursuit for nuclear advantage.

The chances for a CTBT are almost nil. Perhaps the prophets of gloom are correct in their assessment that the end of nuclear testing will not be realized until the superpowers have perfected the "ultimate weapon," and testing is no longer necessary.

NOTES

1. Chapter 4 of Albert Carnesale, ed., "Learning from Experience with Arms Control," a manuscript prepared for the U.S. Arms Control and Disarmament

Agency, Washington, DC, September 1986, provides an excellent description of the negotiations leading to SALT I and of the domestic politics surrounding the treaty's consideration on Capitol Hill.

2. U.S. Department of State, Bureau of Public Affairs, *Security and Arms Control: The Search for a More Stable Peace* (Washington, DC: U.S. Government Printing Office, 1984), pp. 26–30.

3. The asymetry of the U.S. and Soviet strategic forces has been and continues to be a major stumbling bloc in the negotiations. Refer to Walter Pincus, "Incompatible Arsenals and Strategies Hinder Arms Negotiations," *Washington Post,* November 17, 1985; see also Congressional Research Service, Library of Congress, *Fundamentals of Nuclear Arms Control* (9 parts) (Washington, DC: U.S. Government Printing Office, 1986), p. 29.

4. The text of SALT I, including its *Protocol* and the *Agreed Statements, Common Understandings, and Unilateral Statements* accompanying the document are given in U.S. Arms Control and Disarmament Agency, *Arms Control and Disarmament Agreements: Texts and Histories of Negotiations* (Washington, DC: U.S. Government Printing Office, 1982), pp. 150–57. A good commentary on the treaty is provided in Chapter 2 of National Academy of Sciences, *Nuclear Arms Control: Background and Issues* (Washington, DC: National Academy Press, 1985).

5. U.S. Arms Control and Disarmament Agency, *Arms Control and Disarmament Agreements,* pp. 161–63.

6. Congressional Research Service, Library of Congress, *Fundamentals of Nuclear Arms Control,* p. 388.

7. Chapter 5 of Albert Carnesale, ed., "Learning from Experience with Arms Control," provides a detailed description of the events leading to SALT II, the negotiations, and the outcome. For the text of the treaty, its *Protocol,* and the *Joint Statement of Principles and Basic Guidelines for Subsequent Negotiations,* refer to U.S. Arms Control and Disarmament Agency, *Arms Control and Disarmament Agreements,* pp. 239–77.

8. Albert Carnesale, ed., "Learning from Experience with Arms Control," pp. 31–32.

9. National Academy of Sciences, *Nuclear Arms Control,* pp. 58–80; and Congressional Research Service, Library of Congress, *Fundamentals of Nuclear Arms Control,* pp. 144–45.

10. Paul H. Nitze, "The Case for Cutting Strategic Arms," *Washington Post,* June 21, 1988.

11. U.S. Department of State, Bureau of Public Affairs, *Realism, Strength, Negotiation: Key Foreign Policy Statements of the Reagan Administration* (Washington, DC: U.S. Government Printing Office, 1984), contains the text of President Reagan's speech of May 9, 1982 (the Eureka College speech).

12. Text of the Joint Communiqué issued in Geneva, as reported by the Associated Press, March 12, 1985.

13. The Arms Control Association's Background Paper *Strategic Offensive Arms Negotiations* (updated periodically) is an excellent source on the START/NST negotiations. It includes a summary of activity at each negotiating round, key proposals made, and agreements (when appropriate).

14. The superpowers have used the Washington and Moscow summits to publicize the few agreements reached thus far in the START/NST negotiations. Refer

to *Selected Excerpts* for texts of the Final Communiqués of the Washington Summit (December 1987) and of the Moscow Summit (May–June 1988).

15. U.S. Arms Control and Disarmament Agency, *Annual Report to the Congress, 1988* (Washington, DC: U.S. ACDA, March 14, 1989), pp. 12–14. See also Congressional Research Service, Library of Congress, *Negotiations to Reduce Strategic Offensive Nuclear Weapons,* IB 86051 (Washington, DC, March 1988), pp. 4–5.

16. U.S. Arms Control and Disarmament Agency, *Annual Report to the Congress, 1987,* (Washington, DC: U.S. ACDA, February 24, 1988), pp. 36–39. See also Congressional Research Service, Library of Congress, *Negotiations to Reduce Strategic Offensive Nuclear Weapons,* pp. 6–7.

17. Michele A. Flournoy, "A Rocky START: Optimism and Obstacles on the Road to Reductions," *Arms Control Today,* October 1987, pp. 7–13. See also Strobe Talbott, "Inside Moves," *Time,* May 30, 1988, p. 36.

18. R. Jeffrey Smith, "Soviets Seek Cruise Data Verification," *Washington Post,* July 23, 1988. See also Michael Getler and Gary Lee, "U.S. Sea Cruise Missiles Seen as Summit Spoiler," *Washington Post,* April 6, 1988; James P. Rubin, "Limiting SLCMs: A Better Way to START," *Arms Control Today,* April 1989, pp. 10–16.

19. Kenneth L. Adelman, *Verification in an Age of Mobile Missiles,* Current Policy no. 987 (Washington, DC: U.S. Department of State, Bureau of Public Affairs, June 16, 1987). See also Michael Krepon, "START Can Be Verified Too," *Washington Post,* March 23, 1988. Rowland Evans and Robert Novak reported an opposing view on the very large number of railroad tunnels in the Soviet Union capable of hiding the Soviet SS-24 rail-mobile system. Refer to their article "Restarting START, Slowly," *Washington Post,* March 24, 1989.

20. Edward L. Rowny, *Hard Work Ahead in Arms Control,* Current Policy no. 1014 (Washington, DC: U.S. Department of State, Bureau of Public Affairs, October 16, 1987).

21. National Academy of Sciences, *Reykjavik and Beyond* (Washington, DC: National Academy Press, 1986), pp. 11–16. See also John D. Steinbruner, "The Effect of Strategic Force Reductions on Nuclear Strategy," *Arms Control Today,* May 1988, pp. 3–5.

22. Jack Mendelsohn, "START Is a Good Beginning," *Arms Control Today,* May 1988, pp. 10–13.

23. Michele A. Flournoy, "START Thinking about a New U.S. Force Structure," *Arms Control Today,* July/August 1988, pp. 8–14. See also Harold Brown, "We Are off to a Good START, But as We Cut Back Nuclear Forces, We'll Need Smaller, Mobile Weapons," *Washington Post,* December 13, 1987.

24. Henry Kissinger, "START: A Dangerous Rush for Agreement," *Washington Post,* April 24, 1988. See also American Association for the Advancement of Science, Program on Science, Arms Control, and National Security, *Strategic Modernization under Arms Control and Budget Constraints,* Background Paper (Washington, DC, June 1, 1989).

25. R. Jeffrey Smith, "U.S. to Seek Inspections to Ensure Strategic Arms Pact Is Verifiable," *Washington Post,* June 17, 1989; White House, "Statement by the President," June 19, 1989.

26. U.S. Arms Control and Disarmament Agency, *Annual Report to the Congress, 1987,* pp. 39–47.

27. Congressional Research Service, Library of Congress, *Arms Control: Negotiations to Limit Defense and Space Weapons,* IB 86073 (Washington, DC, March 1988), pp. 4–5.

28. The Arms Control Association's Background Paper *Defense and Space Talks: Background and Negotiating History* (Washington, DC, April 1988) is an excellent source on the negotiations. It includes a summary of activity at each negotiating round and of the contrasting viewpoints by the two sides.

29. Paul Nitze, "Beyond the Summit: Next Steps in Arms Control," Address before the National Press Club, Washington, DC, December 15, 1987.

30. Refer to U.S.–Soviet statement at the end of the Washington Summit (December 7 to 10, 1987) in *Arms Control Today,* January/February 1988, p. 16.

31. Don Oberdorfer and R. Jeffrey Smith, "Soviet Accuses U.S. of Reneging on Space Arms Understanding," *Washington Post,* January 30, 1988.

32. Arms Control Association, *Defense and Space Talks,* pp. 6–8.

33. An excellent history of nuclear test negotiations from Eisenhower to Reagan is provided in Chapter 7 of National Academy of Sciences, *Nuclear Arms Control.*

34. The events leading to the conclusion of the LTBT are summarized in U.S. Arms Control and Disarmament Agency, *Arms Control and Disarmament Agreements,* pp. 34–40; and in National Academy of Sciences, *Nuclear Arms Control,* Chapter 7.

35. U.S. Department of State, Bureau of Public Affairs, *Verifying Nuclear Test Limitations,* Special Report no. 152 (Washington, DC, August 14, 1986).

36. Chapter 2 of Albert Carnesale, "Learning from Experience with Arms Control," provides a detailed description of the events leading to the LTBT and of the debate over the treaty's major issues.

37. Arms Control Association, *Nuclear Tests: July 16, 1945 to October 23, 1987,* Fact Sheet (Washington, DC, October 26, 1987).

38. U.S. Arms Control and Disarmament Agency, *Arms Control and Disarmament Agreements,* pp. 164–89.

39. U.S. Department of State, Bureau of Public Affairs, *Security and Arms Control: The Search for a More Stable Peace* (Washington, DC: U.S. Government Printing Office, 1984), p. 68.

40. For a brief statement of U.S. nuclear test policy, refer to U.S. Department of State, Bureau of Public Affairs, *U.S. Policy Regarding Limitations on Nuclear Testing,* Special Report no. 150 (Washington, DC, August 1986); see also U.S. Arms Control and Disarmament Agency, Office of Public Affairs, *Chronology of Reagan Administration Initiatives on Nuclear Testing,* Issue Brief (Washington, DC, July 19, 1988).

41. White House Statement, "Nuclear Testing Talks Conclude Round Three," December 15, 1988.

42. Jesse James, "Nuclear Test Agreement Signed at Summit," *Arms Control Today,* January/February 1988, p. 25. See also U.S. Arms Control and Disarmament Agency, *Annual Report to the Congress, 1988,* pp. 33–35.

43. R. Jeffrey Smith, "Soviet Team to Monitor H-Bomb Test," *Washington Post,* August 16, 1988; see also "CORRTEX—Backbone of U.S. Testing Policy," *Arms Control Today,* June 1988, p. 22; and American Association for the Advancement of Science, Program on Science, Arms Control and National Security, *Verifying Limits on Nuclear Testing,* Issue Paper (Washington, DC, 1988).

Appendixes

A. TECHNOLOGY MILESTONES
Note that each technological innovation by one side was quickly matched by the other.

	U.S.	Soviet
Atomic Bomb	1945	1949
Hydrogen Bomb	1952	1953
Intercontinental		
Bomber	1948	1955
ICBM	1958	1957
SLBM	1960	1964
ABM	1974	1966
ASAT	1963	1968
MIRV	1970	1975

Source: Based on Appendix II in Robert S. McNamara, *Blundering into Disaster: Surviving the First Century of the Nuclear Age* (New York: Pantheon Books, 1986), p. 151.

B. NUCLEAR TESTING, 1945–1988
The Limited Test Ban Treaty (LTBT), which outlaws all but underground nuclear tests, was signed in 1963. The treaty, however, has not slowed down nuclear testing. Twice as many nuclear tests have been conducted since the LTBT came into effect than in the years before the treaty.

	1945-1963	1964-1988	Total
United States	346	553	899
Soviet Union	166	452	618
United Kingdom	23	18	41
France	9	153	162
China	0	33	33
India	0	1	1
Totals	544	1,210	1,754

Source: Based on annual test statistics in the *Bulletin of Atomic Scientists*, March 1988, p. 56.

C. THE RACE FOR BETTER AND MORE POWERFUL STRATEGIC WEAPONS, 1974–1988

	U.S.	Soviet
ICBMs	Minuteman III (MK 12)	SS-17
	Silo-based MX	SS-18
	Small ICBM*	SS-19
	Rail-mobile MX*	SS-24
		SS-25
		SS-X-26*
SSBNs	Trident (Ohio Class)	Delta II, III, IV
		Typhoon
SLBMs	Trident I C-4	SS-N-17
	Trident II D-5*	SS-N-18
		SS-N-20
		SS-N-23
Bombers	B-1B	Bear II
	B-2 (Stealth)	Backfire
		Blackjack
Cruises	ALCM	ALCM AS-15
	SLCM	ALCM AS-X-19*

(*) under development

Sources: U.S. Department of Defense, *United States Military Posture, FY 1989* (Washington, DC: U.S. Government Printing Office, 1988); and U.S. Department of State, *Atlas of the Soviet Union* (Washington, DC, September 1987).

D. THE STRATEGIC DELIVERY VEHICLES OF THE SUPERPOWERS, 1988

		U.S.		Soviet
ICBMs	Minuteman II	500	SS-11	420
	Minuteman III	500	SS-13	60
	MX	50	SS-17	138
			SS-18	308
			SS-19	350
			SS-24	10
			SS-25	100
		-----		------
		1,050		1,386
SLBMs	Poseidon C-3	256	SS-N-5	36
	Trident I C-4	384	SS-N-6	256
			SS-N-8	286
			SS-N-17	12
			SS-N-18	224
			SS-N-20	100
			SS-N-23	64
		-----		-------
		640		978
Bombers	B-52 G	167	Bear	160
	B-52 H	96	Backfire	321
	FB-111	61		
	B-1B	97		-------

		421		481

Sources: U.S. Department of Defense, *Soviet Military Power: An Assessment of the Threat 1988* (Washington, DC: U.S. Government Printing Office, 1988); and U.S. Department of Defense, *United States Military Posture, FY 1989* (Washington, DC: U.S. Government Printing Office, 1988); updated from later press reports and congressional testimony.

E. STRATEGIC WEAPON INVENTORIES, 1988

	Delivery Vehicles		Warheads	
	U.S.	Soviet	U.S.	Soviet
ICBMs	1,050	1,386	2,500	6,846
SLBMs	640	978	5,632	3,232
Bombers	421	481	5,170	1,170
Totals	2,111	2,845	13,302	11,248

Sources: U.S. Department of Defense, *Soviet Military Power: An Assessment of the Threat, 1988* (Washington, DC: U.S. Government Printing Office, 1988); and U.S. Department of Defense, *United States Military Posture, FY 1989* (Washington, DC: U.S. Government Printing Office, 1988); updated from later press reports and congressional testimony.

F. IMPACT OF START AGREEMENT

	Delivery Vehicles		Warheads	
	U.S.	Soviet	U.S.	Soviet
1988	2,111	2,845	13.302	11,248
With START	1,600	1,600	6,000	6,000
Without START *	2,300	3,050	15,300	15,000

* Mid to Late 1990s

G. STRATEGIC WEAPON LEVELS, MID TO LATE 1990s (ASSUMING CONCLUSION OF A START AGREEMENT)

	Delivery Vehicles		Warheads	
	U.S.	Soviet	U.S.	Soviet
Heavy ICBMs	100	154	1,000	1,540
Other ICBMs)	)	)	)	)
)	1,250	)	) 4,000	) 4,460
SLBMs)		) 1,446	)	)
)		)	)	)
Bombers	250	)	1,000	)
START limits	1,600	1,600	6,000	6,000

How the superpowers will elect to structure their strategic forces in the post-START era is a matter of speculation. On the U.S. side, 100 MX ICBMs (silo and rail-mobile) will probably be deployed, along with a mix of 1,250 light ICBMs and SLBMs. The U.S. force will include also 250 intercontinental bombers (B–1Bs, B–52s, and B–2s [Stealth]). The Soviet mix of strategic delivery vehicles will undoubtedly include 154 "heavy" ICBMs (the SS–18 or its follow-on system) allowed by the treaty.

H. STRATEGIC OFFENSIVE WEAPONS DURING THE DECADE OF THE 1990s

During the 1990s the superpowers are expected to add several new strategic weapons to their nuclear arsenals. Their deployment will not be affected by the START agreement, which reportedly will permit the "modernization" of existing systems within the agreed-upon limits for delivery vehicles and warheads.

United States

MX: A force of one hundred launchers is probable, with fifty silobased and the remainder in a rail-mobile configuration.

Small ICBMs: The decision on the number of launchers is still pending. The START limit of 1,600 delivery vehicles may force scaled-down procurement, perhaps to no more than 200 launchers.

Trident SSBNs: A fleet of fifteen to twenty boats appears likely, with about half equipped with Trident II D-5 SLBMs.

B-1B: One hundred aircraft have been procured (three planes have crashed).

B-2 (Stealth): A fleet of 132 aircraft is planned as a replacement for the B–52.

ALCMs; SLCMs: The acquisition of several thousand conventional or nuclear cruise missiles is under way.

Soviet Union

Follow-on ICBM/SLBMs: Replacements for the SS-17, SS-18, SS-N-20, SS-24, and SS-25 are currently under development and expected to enter the Soviet force during the 1990s.

Typhoon SSBNs: A fleet of a dozen boats is likely; equipped with the SS-N-20 or its follow-on system.

Blackjack Bomber: This is an add-on weapon to the Bear and Backfire fleets.

SLCMs: SS-N-21 and SS-NX-24 SLCMs are to be carried by several naval platforms.

Warheads: Assuming continuation of the Soviet Union's modernization tempo, 15,000 strategic warheads could be deployed during the 1990s (compared with 11,248 in 1988).

Source: Projections on U.S. strategic weapons are based on press reports and congressional testimony. Estimates on likely Soviet actions are based on the U.S. Department of Defense, *Soviet Military Power: An Assessment of the Threat 1988* (Washington, DC: U.S. Government Printing Office, 1988).

I. STRATEGIC DEFENSES DURING THE DECADE OF THE 1990s
In the absense of an agreement limiting SDI programs, a great variety of sensors and weapons against satellites and ballistic missiles are likely to enter the nuclear arsenals of the superpowers during the decade of the 1990s.

United States

—Advanced technology weapons capable of disabling satellites

—Advanced technology sensors capable of detecting and tracking missiles in flight and of discriminating decoys from warheads

—Space-based platforms capable of launching interceptors at incoming missiles and ground-based interceptors capable of attacking missile warheads just before their reentry into the atmosphere (SDI Phase I deployment)

—Independently orbiting interceptors capable of attacking missile boosters before burnout (Project Brilliant Pebbles)

Soviet Union

—Greatly enhanced nationwide civil defense preparations, with increased emphasis on the construction of underground installations

—Enhancements to the Moscow ABM system and to its associated networks for surveillance and tracking of ballistic missiles

—Advanced technology sensors capable of disabling satellites

—Advanced weapons able to intercept ballistic missiles in flight

Source: Projections on U.S. strategic defenses are based on press reports and congressional testimony. Estimates on likely Soviet actions are based on the U.S. Department of Defense *Soviet Military Power: An Assessment of the Threat, 1988* (Washington, DC: U.S. Government Printing Office, 1988).

J. INF AND SHORTER RANGE WEAPONS, 1988

Listed are the weapons affected by the INF treaty. Note that delivery vehicles only will be destroyed; nuclear warheads will be preserved by the superpowers for possible use elsewhere.

	Delivery Vehicles		Warheads	
	U.S.	Soviet	U.S.	Soviet
Pershing IIs	235		235	
Tomahawk GLCMs	442		442	
Pershing IAs	169		169	
SS-4		150		150
SS-5		5		5
SS-12		745		745
SS-20		654		1,962
SS-23		212		212
SSC-X-4		80		80
Totals	846	1,846	846	3,154

Source: Arms Control and Disarmament Agency, *INF Numbers Based on Updated Data*, Fact Sheet, (Washington, DC, October 6, 1988); and various press reports.

K. TACTICAL AND BATTLEFIELD WEAPONS, 1988

The following weapons, although deployed on the European continent, are not affected by the INF treaty. All figures are approximate.

	U.S.	Soviet	NATO
Battlefield Range			
Missile Launchers	108	1,100	99
Nuclear Capable			
Aircraft	500	2,000	1,300
Nuclear Artillery			
Launchers	1,000	3,600	2,000
Warheads (est)	3,500	3,000 to 7,000 *	1,700

* Soviet warhead figures are extremely soft.

Source: Committee on International Security and Arms Control, National Academy of Sciences, *Reykjavik and Beyond* (Washington, DC: National Academy Press, 1988), p. 40.

L. THE LESSER NUCLEAR POWERS: THE PRC, FRANCE, and THE UNITED KINGDOM

FRANCE

5 SSBNs (1 additional SSBN is planned)

33 Mirage Bombers

15 IRBMs

U.K.

4 Polaris SSBNs

    (planned for replacement with Trident SSBNs)

55 Bulkan Bombers

PRC

Strategic	INF and Short-Range
20 ICBMs	About 100 IRBMs
24 SLBMs	15-30 aircraft
100 Bombers	

Sources: Data on U.K. and French nuclear forces are based on U.S. press reports. Data on the PRC are approximate, drawn mostly from the June 1989 issue of the *Bulletin of Atomic Scientists*.

Selected Excerpts

FINAL COMMUNIQUÉS OF SUMMITS

Geneva Summit (November 1985)

The sides have agreed that a nuclear war cannot be won and must never be fought. Recognizing that any conflict between the U.S.S.R. and the U.S. could have catastrophic consequences, they emphasized the importance of preventing any war between them, whether nuclear or conventional. They will not seek to achieve military superiority....

They agreed to accelerate the work at the Nuclear and Space Talks with a view to accomplishing the tasks set down in the Joint U.S.–Soviet Agreement of January 8, 1985, namely to prevent an arms race in space and to terminate it on Earth, to limit and reduce nuclear arms and enhance strategic stability.

Noting the proposals recently tabled by the U.S. and the Soviet Union, they called for early progress, in particular in areas where there is common ground, including the principle of 50% reductions in the nuclear arms of the U.S. and the U.S.S.R., appropriately applied, as well as the idea of an interim INF (intermediate-range nuclear forces) agreement....

The sides agreed to study the question at the expert level of centers to reduce nuclear risk, taking into account the issues and developments in the Geneva negotiations. They took satisfaction in such recent steps in this direction as the modernization of the Soviet–U.S. hotline.

General Secretary Gorbachev and President Reagan reaffirmed the commitment of the U.S.S.R. and the U.S. to the Treaty on the Nonproliferation of Nuclear Weapons and their interest in strengthening together with other countries the nonproliferation regime, and in further enhancing the effectiveness of the treaty, *interalia* by enlarging its membership....

The U.S.S.R. and the U.S. reaffirm their commitment, assumed by them under the Treaty on the Nonproliferation of Nuclear Weapons, to pursue negotiations in good faith on matters of nuclear arms limitation and disarmament in accordance with Article VI of the treaty....

Reykjavik Summit (October 1986)

An official communiqué was not issued at the conclusion of talks, but both leaders soon thereafter addressed the principal substantive differences that caused the summit to break down.

News Conference by General Secretary Mikhail Gorbachev (October 12, 1986)

The Soviet leadership remains loyal to the commitments it assumed in Geneva. We extended our moratorium on any nuclear explosions. The Soviet Union put forward a program for the elimination of nuclear weapons by the end of the current century....

We brought here (in Iceland) a whole package of major proposals which could, if accepted, lead within a truly short period of time to progress in all directions of the struggle for disarmament, for the limitation of nuclear weapons, avert the threat of nuclear war....

We put forward a proposal for cutting strategic armaments by 50%, and not less, so that these most deadly weapons be abolished by the turn of the century.... We all, living in the socialist world, in the capitalist world and in the developing world, have a unique chance for starting real work to end the arms race, ban nuclear weapons, eliminate them, and divert the nuclear threat from mankind ... we put forward the following proposal to the President—to start full-scale talks on banning nuclear explosions immediately after our meeting in Reykjavik....

We were on the verge of taking major, history-making decisions. Since the American administration, as we understand now, is out to make a breakthrough via SDI to military superiority, it even went so far as to bury the accords on which we already reached agreement....

In the final analysis, it was an interesting meeting, important and promising meeting. Thus far, it has ended that way, but let us not despair.... We were drawing closer, but when we diverged on the ABM, the discussion was broken, the search was disrupted, and we ended our discussion. We, the Americans and world public opinion should now give thought to the main question, that of war and peace, the question of nuclear threat.

The President's Address to the Nation, Washington, D.C. (October 13, 1986)

The implications of these talks are enormous and only just beginning to be understood. We proposed the most sweeping and generous arms control proposal in history. We offered the complete elimination of all ballistic missiles—Soviet and American—from the face of the Earth by 1996. While we parted company with this American offer still on the table, we are closer than ever before to agreements that could lead to a safer world without nuclear weapons....

Both sides ... willing to find a way to reduce to zero the strategic ballistic missiles we have aimed at each other. This then brought up the subject of SDI.

I offered a proposal that we continue our present research and, if and when we reached the stage of testing, we would sign now a treaty that would permit Soviet observation of such tests. And if the program was practical, we would both eliminate our offensive missiles, and then we would share the benefits of advanced defenses. I explained that even though we would have done away with our offensive ballistic missiles, having the defense would protect against cheating or the possibility of a madman sometime deciding to create nuclear missiles. . . .

The General Secretary wanted wording that, in effect, would have kept us from developing the SDI for the entire 10 years. In effect, he was killing SDI. And unless I agreed, all that work toward eliminating nuclear weapons would go down the drain—cancelled.

I told him that I had pledged to the American people that I would not trade away SDI—there was no way I could tell our people their government would not protect them against nuclear destruction. . . .

SDI is America's insurance policy that the Soviet Union would keep the commitments made at Reykjavik. SDI is America's security guarantee—if the Soviets should—as they have done too often in the past—fail to comply with their solemn commitments. . . .

What Mr. Gorbachev was demanding at Reykjavik was that the United States agree to a new version of a 14-year old ABM Treaty that the Soviet Union has already violated. . . .

Washington Summit (December 1987)

The two leaders signed the INF Treaty . . . historic both for its objective—the complete elimination of an entire class of U.S. and Soviet nuclear arms—and for the innovative character and scope of its verification provisions. . . .

The President and the General Secretary discussed the negotiations on reductions in strategic offensive arms. They noted the considerable progress which has been made toward conclusion of a treaty implementing the principle of 50% reductions . . . they agreed to instruct their negotiators to accelerate resolution of issues within the Joint Draft Treaty including early agreement on provisions for effective verification . . . including agreement on ceilings of no more than 1,600 strategic offensive delivery systems, 6,000 warheads, 1,540 warheads on 154 heavy missiles . . . and an agreement that as a result of the reductions the aggregate throw-weight of the Soviet Union's ICBMs and SLBMs will be reduced to a level approximately 50% below the existing level. . . .

The leaders of the two countries also instructed their delegations in Geneva to work out an agreement that would commit the sides to observe the ABM Treaty, as signed in 1972, while conducting their research, development, and testing as required, which are permitted by the ABM Treaty, and not to withdraw from the ABM Treaty, for a specified period of time. . . .

Moscow Summit (May 1988)

The President and the General Secretary . . . reaffirmed their solemn conviction that a nuclear war cannot be won and must never be fought, their determination to prevent any war between the United States and Soviet Union, whether nuclear or conventional, and their disavowal of any intention to achieve military superiority. . . .

The President and the General Secretary signed the protocol on the exchange of instruments of ratification of the Treaty . . . on the Elimination of Intermediate-Range and Shorter-Range Missiles. The two leaders welcomed the entry into force of this historic agreement, which for the first time will eliminate an entire class of U.S. and Soviet nuclear arms. . . .

The two leaders noted that a Joint Draft of a Treaty on Reduction and Limitation of Strategic Offensive Arms has been elaborated . . . important additional work is required before this Treaty is ready for signature . . .

The sides have continued negotiations to achieve a separate agreement concerning the ABM Treaty building on the language of the Washington Summit Joint Statement dated December 10, 1987. . . .

The Joint Draft Treaty on Reduction and Limitation of Strategic Offensive Arms reflects the earlier understanding on establishing ceilings of no more than 1,600 strategic offensive delivery systems and 6,000 warheads, as well as agreement on subceilings of 4,900 on the aggregate of ICBM and SLBM warheads and 1540 warheads on 154 heavy missiles.

The draft Treaty also records the sides' agrement that as a result of the reductions the aggregate throw-weight of the Soviet Union's ICBMs and SLBMs will be reduced to a level approximately 50% below the existing level and this level will not be exceeded . . . the sides agreed on a counting rule for heavy bomber armaments according to which heavy bombers equipped only for nuclear gravity bombs and SRAMs will count as one delivery vehicle against the 1,600 limit and one warhead against the 6,000 limit . . . the exchanges on START resulted in the achievement of substantial additional common ground, particularly in the areas of ALCMs and the attempts to develop and agree, if possible, on a solution to the problem of verification of mobile ICBMs. . . . The two sides also discussed the question of limiting long-range, nuclear-armed SLCMs. . . .

The agreement on notifications of launches of ICBMs and SLBMs . . . is a practical new step reflecting the desire of the sides to reduce the risk of outbreak of nuclear war, in particular as a result of misinterpretation, miscalculation or accident. . . .

The leaders reaffirmed the commitment of the two sides to conduct in a single forum full-scale, stage-by-stage negotiations on the issues relating to nuclear testing. In these negotiations the sides as a first step will agree upon effective verification measures which will make it possible to ratify the U.S.–U.S.S.R. Threshold Test Ban Treaty of 1974 and Peaceful Nuclear Explosions Treaty of 1976, and proceed to negotiating further intermediate limitations on nuclear testing leading to the ultimate objective of the complete cessation of nuclear testing as part of an effective disarmament process. . . . In implementing the first objective of these negotiations . . . the sides agreed to design and conduct a Joint Verification Experiment at each other's sites. . . .

The two leaders noted that this year marks the 20th anniversary of the Nuclear Non-Proliferation Treaty, one of the most important international arms control agreements with over 130 adherents. They reaffirmed their conviction that universal adherence to the NPT is important to international peace and security. . . .

CONCLUDING DOCUMENTS OF U.N. SPECIAL SESSIONS ON DISARMAMENT

First Special Session of the U.N. General Assembly on Disarmament, 1978

Mankind today is confronted with an unprecedented threat of self-extinction arising from the massive and competitive accumulation of the most destructive weapons ever produced. Existing arsenals of nuclear weapons alone are more than sufficient to destroy all life on earth. Failure of efforts to halt and reverse the arms race, in particular the nuclear arms race, increases the danger of the proliferation of nuclear weapons. Yet the arms race continues.... The vast nuclear stockpiles ... pose incalculable threats to peace....

The arms race ... runs counter to efforts to achieve further relaxation of international tensions ... is incompatible to the principles of the Charter of the United Nations.... Indeed the massive accumulation of armaments ... presents a challenging and increasingly dangerous obstacle to a world community faced with the urgent need to disarm.... Enduring international peace and security cannot be built on the accumulation of weaponry nor be sustained by a precarious balance of deterrence or doctrines of strategic superiority....

Removing the threat of a world war—a nuclear war—is the most acute and urgent task of the present day. Mankind is confronted with a choice: we must halt the arms race and proceed to disarmament or face annihilation.... The prevention of nuclear war has the highest priority. To this end, it is imperative to remove the threat of nuclear weapons, to halt and reverse the nuclear arms race until the total elimination of nuclear weapons and their delivery systems has been achieved, and to prevent the proliferation of nuclear weapons....

The achievement of nuclear disarmament will require urgent negotiation of agreements ... for the cessation of the qualitative improvement and development of nuclear-weapon systems; for the cessation of the production of all types of nuclear weapons and their means of delivery, and of the production of fissionable material for weapons purposes; and a comprehensive, phased program ... for progressive and balanced reduction of stockpiles of nuclear weapons and their means of delivery, leading to their ultimate and complete elimination at the earliest possible time.... The cessation of nuclear weapon testing by all States ... would be in the interest of mankind....

Second Special Session of the U.N. General Assembly on Disarmament, 1982

The first special session devoted to disarmament, held in 1978, was an event of historic significance. The special session was convened in response to a growing concern among the peoples of the world that the arms race, especially the nuclear arms race, represented ever-increasing threat to human well-being and even to the survival of mankind. At that session the international community of nations achieved ... an international disarmament strategy, the immediate goal of which was the elimination of the danger of nuclear war and implementation of measures to halt and reverse the arms race....

Developments since 1978 have not lived up to the hopes engendered by the (first) special session...the objectives, priorities and principles laid down in the Final Document of the first session have not been generally observed.... The arms race, in particular the nuclear arms race, has assumed more dangerous proportions and global military expenditures have increased sharply. In short, since the adoption of the Final Document in 1978, there has been no significant progress in the field of arms limitation and disarmament and the seriousness of the situation has increased. ...

The General Assembly expresses its profound preoccupation over the danger of war, in particular nuclear war, the prevention of which remains the most acute and urgent task of the present day. The Assembly urges all members to consider relevant proposals designed to secure the avoidance of war, in particular nuclear war, thus ensuring that the survival of mankind is not endangered....

FIVE CONTINENT PEACE INITIATIVE

Five Continent Peace Initiative (Mexico City Declaration), 1986

Exactly 41 years ago, death and horror descended upon Hiroshima. The most dreadful war in history came to an end, and the world's nuclear nightmare began. Since then we have lived on borrowed time. All that is precious and beautiful, all that human civilization has reached for and achieved, could, in short time, be reduced to radioactive dust.

For four decades the nuclear weapon states have had almost sole responsibility to end the nuclear arms race, while the rest of the world has been forced to stand anxiously on the sidelines. The nuclear arms race has continued and become more intense. In the face of the consequent danger of common annihilation, the distinction between the powerful and the weak has become meaningless. We are therefore determined that countries such as ours which possess no nuclear arsenals will be actively involved in all aspects of disarmament. The protection of this planet is a matter for all people who live on it; we cannot accept that a few countries should alone decide the fate of the world alone....

When an accident at a peaceful nuclear plant (Chernobyl) has such great international repercussions, everyone can see very clearly the terrible consequences which would result from the use of even a small fraction of the nuclear armaments which now exist in the world.... We call for a binding international agreement which outlaws every use of nuclear weapons....

In January 1985...we called for an immediate halt to nuclear testing...for a cessation in the production and development of all nuclear weapons and delivery systems as well as for a prohibition on the testing, production and deployment of space weapons. We also expressed our hope that the United States and the Soviet Union would make rapid progress in their bilateral negotiations toward the abolition of all nuclear weapons.... We are deeply concerned about the lack of evident progress so far in these negotiations.... Security is not improved by increasing the capacity for destruction through the accumulation of weapons; on the contrary, true security is better ensured through the reduction of armaments....

We remain convinced that no issue is more urgent and crucial today than bringing to an end all nuclear tests. Both the qualitative and the quantitative development of nuclear weapons exacerbate the arms race, and both would be inhibited by the complete abolition of nuclear weapons testing.... To facilitate an immediate cessation of nuclear testing we are presenting in a separate document a concrete offer of assistance to achieve adequate verification arrangements.... These could greatly enhance confidence in a U.S.–Soviet moratorium and constitute important steps towards the establishment of an adequate verification system for a comprehensive test-ban treaty....

We reiterate our demand that an arms race in outer space be prevented. Space belongs to all humanity, and as participants in this common heritage of mankind, we object to the outer space of our earth being misused for destructive purposes. It is particularly urgent to halt the development of anti-satellite weapons, which would threaten the peaceful space activities of many nations. We urge the leaders of the U.S. and the Soviet Union to agree on a halt to further tests of anti-satellite weapons, in order to facilitate the conclusion of an international treaty on their prohibition.
...

The spirit of Geneva must be revived and strengthened. And we stress again our determination to try to facilitate agreement between the nuclear-weapon states, and to work with them as well as with all other nations, for the common security of humankind and for peace....

Five Continent Peace Initiative (Stockholm Declaration), 1988

During the last few decades, a handful of nations have acquired the capability of destroying not only one another but all others as well. Their war machines could terminate civilization and all life on Earth.

No nation has the right to use such instruments of war. And what is thus morally wrong should also be explicitly prohibited by international law through a binding international agreement....

Crucial decisions to prevent the ultimate catastrophe lie with those who possess nuclear weapons. It is their responsibility to live up to the objective of eliminating all of them.

But the rest of us, the non-nuclear weapon states, have a legitimate interest in the abolition of these awesome weapons. We demand it. We owe it not only to ourselves, but also to future generations. The fate of weapons systems which can spread death and destruction regardless of national borders must not be left in the hands of only a few states....

The signing in Washington on December 8 of the INF Treaty can be seen as a historic event.... Even after the implementation of the INF Treaty, thousands of tactical nuclear weapons will still remain in Europe and elsewhere. In fact, these weapons could actually be the ones to trigger a nuclear holocaust. We urge that also these tactical nuclear weapons be completely abolished without delay....

Military competition must not be introduced into new fields. Space belongs to us all, and the number of countries growing more and more dependent on the benefits of the peaceful utilization of outer space is increasing. It must not be used for destructive purposes.

There is still time to prevent an arms race in space. We call on the parties to the

Anti-Ballistic Missile Treaty to strictly abide by that Treaty. We also reiterate our call for a complete banning of anti-satellite weapons....

Agreements to reduce existing nuclear arsenals must be backed up by decisive measures to check the unbridled development of new generations of ever more dreadful and sophisticated nuclear weapons.... The single most effective measure would be to end all nuclear-weapon tests by all states....

The total abolition of nuclear weapons, and the rapid movement towards that end is a fundamental and moral imperative for humankind without qualification by reference to any struggle for justice and development in the world....

The nuclear threat remains real. Our world order is still built on the edge of the nuclear abyss. As we move into the last decade of the twentieth century, the goal must remain not to avert the holocaust, but ultimately to eliminate all nuclear weapons.

Each and everyone can and must play a part in safeguarding our survivial, strengthening our security and creating the conditions for a life in dignity.

We urge the nuclear weapons states to fulfill their obligation to pursue the process of nuclear disarmament....

SELECTED MAJOR CHURCH STATEMENTS

Pastoral Letter on War and Peace by the National Conference of Catholic Bishops, 1983

The crisis of the moment is embodied in the threat which nuclear weapons pose for the world...the arms race poses a threat to human life and human civilization which is without precedent....

The arms race is one of the greatest curses on the human race; it is to be condemned as a danger, an act of aggression against the poor, and a folly which does not provide the security it promises....

Under no circumstances may nuclear weapons or other instruments of mass slaughter be used for the purpose of destroying population centers or other predominantly civilian targets. Retaliatory action which would indiscriminately and disproportionately take many wholly innocent lives...must also be condemned.

We do not perceive any situation in which the deliberate initiation of nuclear war, on however restricted a scale, can be morally justified.... First imperative is to prevent any use of nuclear weapons....

We support immediate, bilateral verifiable agreements to halt the testing, production and deployment of new nuclear weapons systems...we support efforts to achieve deep cuts in the arsenals of both superpowers...we support early and successful conclusion of negotiations of a comprehensive test ban treaty...we urge new efforts to prevent the spread of nuclear weapons in the world....

The nuclear era is an era of moral as well as physical danger. We are the first generation since Genesis with the power to threaten the created order. We cannot remain silent in the face of such danger....

The whole world must summon the moral courage and technical means to say no to nuclear conflict; no to weapons of mass destruction; no to an arms race which robs the poor and the vulnerable; and no to the moral danger of a nuclear age which places before humankind indefensible choices of constant terror or surrender....

In Defense of Creation, the Nuclear Crisis, and a Just Peace: Pastoral Letter by the United Methodist Council of Bishops, 1986

We have prayerfully and penitently reflected on the continuing buildup of nuclear arsenals by some nations. We have become increasingly aware of the devastation that such weapons can inflict on planet earth. . . .

We write in defense of creation. We do so because the creation itself is under attack. Air and water, trees and fruits and flowers, birds and fish and cattle, all children and youth, women and men live under the darkening shadows of a threatening nuclear winter. . . . It is a crisis that threatens to assault not only the whole human family but planet earth itself. . . .

Therefore, we say a clear and unconditioned No to nuclear war and to any use of nuclear weapons. We conclude that nuclear deterrence is a position that cannot receive the church's blessing. We state our complete lack of confidence in proposed "defenses" against nuclear attack and are convinced that the enormous cost of developing such defenses is one more witness to the obvious fact that the arms race is a social justice issue, not only a war and peace issue. . . .

Our document sets forth a number of policies for a just peace, including such disarmament proposals as a comprehensive test ban, a multilateral and mutually verifiable nuclear weapons freeze and the ultimate dismantling of all such weapons, and bans on all space weapons. . . . We encourage independent U.S. and Soviet initiatives to foster a political climate conducive to negotiations. . . .

Selected Bibliography

ARMS RACE

Aldridge, Robert C. *First Strike: The Pentagon's Strategy for Nuclear War.* Boston: South End Press, 1983.

Arkin, William M. and Fieldhouse, Richard M. *Nuclear Battlefields: Global Links in the Arms Race.* Cambridge, MA: Ballinger, 1986.

Barash, David P. *The Arms Race and Nuclear War.* Belmont, CA: Wadsworth, 1986.

Betts, Richard K. *Nuclear Blackmail and Nuclear Balance.* Washington, DC: Brookings, 1987.

Blair, Bruce G. *Strategic Command and Control.* Washington, DC: Brookings, 1985.

Boffey, Philip M. et al. *Claiming the Heavens.* New York: Random House, 1988.

Bowman, Robert M. *Star Wars: A Defense Expert's Case against the Strategic Defense Initiative.* Chesapeake Beach, MD: Institute for Space and Security Studies, 1986.

Bracken, Paul. *The Command and Control of Nuclear Forces.* New Haven: Yale University Press, 1983.

Brandt, Willy. *Arms and Hunger.* New York: Pantheon, 1986.

Bundy, McGeorge. *Danger and Survival: Choices about the Bomb in the First Fifty Years.* New York: Random House, 1988.

Caldicott, Helen. *Missile Envy: The Arms Race and Nuclear War.* New York: Bantam Books, 1986.

Carlton, David and Schaerf, Carlo, eds. *The Arms Race in the 1980s.* New York: St. Martin's Press, 1982.

Carter, Ashton B. and Schwartz, David N. *Ballistic Missile Defense.* Washington, DC: Brookings, 1984.

Carter, Ashton B. et al. *Managing Nuclear Operations.* Washington, DC: Brookings, 1987.

Cartright, John and Critchley, Julian. *Cruise, Pershing, and SS-20*. London: Brassey's, 1985.

Cochran, Thomas et al. *Nuclear Weapons Databook. Vol. 1, U.S. Nuclear Forces and Capabilities*. Cambridge, MA: Ballinger, 1984.

Cockburn, Andrew. *The Threat: Inside the Soviet Military Machine*. New York: Vintage Books, 1984.

Collins, John M. *U.S. Soviet Military Balance, 1980–85*. Pergammon-Brassey's, 1985.

Congressional Research Service, Library of Congress. *Nuclear Proliferation Handbook*. Washington, DC: U.S. Government Printing Office, 1985.

———. *Strategic Forces: MX ICBM*. IB 84046. Washington, DC, March 1987.

———. *Strategic Forces: Small ICBM–Midgetman Missile*. IB 84044. Washington, DC, March 1987.

Cox, Arthur Macy. *The Dynamics of Detente: How to End the Arms Race*. New York: Norton, 1976.

Defense Science Board. *Small Intercontinental Ballistic Missile Modernization*. Washington, DC, 1986.

Dunn, Lewis A. *Controlling the Bomb: Nuclear Proliferation in the 1980s*. New Haven: Yale University Press, 1982.

Dyson, Freeman. *Weapons and Hope*. New York: Harper and Row, 1984.

Green, William C. *Soviet Nuclear Weapons Policy: A Research and Bibliographic Guide*. Boulder, CO: Westview Press, 1987.

Halloran, Richard. *To Arm a Nation: Rebuilding America's Endangered Defenses*. New York: Macmillan, 1986.

Halperin, Morton H. *Nuclear Fallacy: Dispelling the Myth of Nuclear Strategy*. Cambridge, MA: Ballinger, 1987.

Harvard Nuclear Study Group. *Living with Nuclear Weapons*. Cambridge, MA: Harvard University Press, 1983.

Holdren, John and Rotblat, Joseph, eds. *Strategic Defenses and the Future of the Arms Race*. New York: St. Martin's Press, 1987.

Kaku, Michio and Axelrod, Daniel. *To Win a Nuclear War: The Pentagon's Secret War Plans*. Boston: South End Press, 1987.

Longstreth, Thomas K., Pike, John E., and Rhinelander, John B. *The Impact of U.S. and Soviet Ballistic Missile Defense Programs on the ABM Treaty*. Washington, DC: National Campaign to Save the ABM Treaty, 1985.

McNamara, Robert S. *Blundering into Disaster: Surviving the First Century of the Nuclear Age*. New York: Pantheon Books, 1986.

Morris, Charles R. *Iron Destinies, Lost Opportunities: The Arms Race between the U.S.A. and the U.S.S.R., 1945–1987*. New York: Harper and Row, 1988.

Mosley, Hugh G. *The Arms Race: Economic and Social Consequences*. Lexington, MA: Lexington Books, 1985.

Office of Technology Assessment. U.S. Congress. *Ballistic Missile Defense Technologies*. Washington, DC: U.S. Government Printing Office, 1985.

Paul, Joseph and Rosenblaum, Simon, eds. *Search for Sanity: The Politics of Nuclear Weapons and Disarmament*. Boston: South End Press, 1984.

Powaski, Ronald E. *March to Armageddon*. New York: Oxford University Press, 1986.

Reiss, Mitchell, *Without the Bomb: The Politics of Nuclear Proliferation*. New York: Columbia University Press, 1988.

Riverside Church Disarmament Program. Fourth Annual Conference. *The Arms Race and Us*. New York, 1982.

Schneider, Barry R. et al., eds. *Missiles for the Nineties: ICBMs and Strategic Policy*. Boulder, CO: Westview Press, 1984.

Scott, Robert T., ed. *The Race for Security: Arms and Arms Control in the Reagan Years*. Lexington, MA: Lexington Books, 1986.

Solomon, Frederic and Marston, Robert O., eds. *The Medical Implications of Nuclear War*. Washington, DC: National Academy Press, 1986.

Spector, Leonard S. *Going Nuclear*. Cambridge, MA: Ballinger, 1987.

———. *The New Nuclear Nations*. New York: Random House; Vintage Books, 1985.

———. *The Undeclared Bomb: The Spread of Nuclear Weapons, 1987–8*. Cambridge, MA: Ballinger, 1988.

Stares, Paul B. *The Militarization of Space: U.S. Policy, 1945–1984*. Ithaca, NY: Cornell University Press, 1985.

———. *Space and National Security*. Washington, DC: Brookings, 1987.

Stockholm International Peace Research Institute. (SIPRI). *The Arms Race and Arms Control, 1983*. Stockholm, 1984.

———. *World Armaments and Disarmament. SIPRI Yearbook*. Stockholm, 1987.

Tirman, John, ed. *Empty Promise: The Growing Case against Star Wars*. The Union of Concerned Scientists. Boston: Beacon Press, 1986.

Turner, John and SIPRI. *Arms in the 80s: New Developments in the Global Arms Race*. Stockholm, 1985.

Union of Concerned Scientists. *The Fallacy of Star Wars*. New York: Vintage Books, 1984.

U.S. Arms Control and Disarmament Agency. *Fiscal Year 1988: Arms Control Impact Statements*. Washington, DC: U.S. Government Printing Office, 1987.

U.S. Department of Defense. *Soviet Military Power: An Assessment of the Threat, 1988*. Washington, DC: U.S. Government Printing Office, 1988.

———. *Soviet Military Power: Prospects for Change*. Washington, DC: U.S. Government Printing Office, 1989.

———. *The Soviet Space Challenge*. Washington, DC: U.S. Government Printing Office, 1987.

———. Strategic Defense Initiative Organization. *Report to the Congress on the Strategic Defense Initiative*. Washington, DC: U.S. Government Printing Office, 1989.

———. *United States Military Posture, FY 1989*. Washington, DC: U.S. Government Printing Office, 1988.

U.S. Department of Defense and U.S. Department of State. *Soviet Strategic Defense Programs*. Washington, DC: U.S. Government Printing Office, 1985.

U.S. General Accounting Office. *ICBM Modernization: Availability Problems and Flight Test Delays in Peacekeeper Program*. GAO/NSIAD–89–105. Washington, DC, March 1989.

———. *ICBM Modernization, Status, Survivable Basing Issues, and Need to Es-*

tablish a National Consensus. GAO/NSIAD–86–200. Washington, DC, September 1986.

———. *Navy Strategic Forces: Trident II Proceeding toward Deployment.* GAO/ NSIAD–89–40. Washington, DC, November 1988.

———. *Nuclear Winter: Uncertainties Surround the Long-Term Effects of Nuclear Winter.* GAO/NSIAD–86–62. Washington, DC, March 1986.

Wilson, John L. and Xue Litai. *China Builds the Bomb.* Stanford, CA: Stanford University Press, 1988.

York, Herbert F. *Making Weapons, Talking Peace: A Physicist's Odyssey from Hiroshima to Geneva.* New York: Basic Books, 1987.

ARMS CONTROL POLICY AND ISSUES

ACCESS Information Service. *The Strategic Defense Initiative: Where Do You Stand?* Washington, DC, December 1987.

American Association for the Advancement of Science. Program on Science, Arms Control, and National Security. *The INF Agreement: Implications for NATO Security.* Washington, DC, December 1987.

———. *SDI and the ABM Treaty.* Washington, DC, September 1987.

———. *Strategic Modernization under Arms Control and Budget Constraints.* Washington, DC, June 1, 1989.

Arms Control Association. *Arms Control and National Security. An Introduction.* Washington, DC: Arms Control Association, 1989.

———. *Star Wars Quotes: Statements by Reagan Administration Officials, Outside Experts, Members of the Congress, U.S. Allies, and Soviet Officials on the Strategic Defense Initiative.* Washington, DC, July 1986.

Arms Control Association and the Ploughshares Fund. *Countdown on SALT II: The Case for Preserving SALT II Limits on U.S. and Soviet Strategic Forces.* Washington, DC: Arms Control Association, 1985.

Berkowitz, Bruce D. *Calculated Risks: A Century of Arms Control.* New York: Simon and Schuster, 1987.

Carnesale, Albert, ed. "Learning from Experience with Arms Control." Unpublished text prepared for the U.S. Arms Control and Disarmament Agency, Washington, DC, 1986.

Carnesale, Albert and Haass, Richard, eds. *Superpower Arms Control: Setting the Record Straight.* Cambridge, MA: Ballinger, 1987.

Cimbala, Stephen J. *Nuclear War and Nuclear Strategy: Unfinished Business.* Westport CT: Greenwood Press, 1987.

———, ed. *Challenges to Deterrence: Resources Technology, Policy.* New York: Praeger, 1987.

———, ed. *Ending a Nuclear War: Are the Superpowers Prepared?* Washington, DC: Pergamon-Brassey's, 1988.

Committee on International Security and Arms Control. National Academy of Sciences. *Nuclear Arms Control: Background and Issues.* Washington, DC: National Academy Press, 1985.

Conference on Disarmament. *Report of the Conference on Disarmament to the General Assembly of the United Nations.* Geneva, September 20, 1988.

Congressional Research Service. Library of Congress. *Arms Control: Issues for Congress.* IB 87002. Washington, DC, May 1988.

———. *Fundamentals of Nuclear Arms Control* (9 parts). Washington, DC: U.S. Government Printing Office, 1986.

———. *The Treaty on the Non-Proliferation of Nuclear Weapons: The 1985 Review Conference and Matters of Congressional Interest.* Washington, DC, April 22, 1985.

Episcopal Diocese of Washington. *The Nuclear Dilemma: A Christian Search for Understanding.* Cincinnati: Forward Movement Publications, 1987.

Garfinkle, Adam M. *The Politics of the Nuclear Freeze.* Philadelphia: Foreign Policy Research Institute, 1984.

Garthoft, Raymond. *Policy vs. the Law: Reinterpretation of the ABM Treaty.* Washington, DC: Brookings, 1987.

Joint Commission on Peace. *To Make Peace.* Cincinnati: Forward Movement Publications, 1982.

Kampelman, Max et al. *The INF Treaty: Negotiations and Ratification.* Current Policy no. 1039. Washington, DC: U.S. Department of State, Bureau of Public Affairs, January 26, 1988.

Krepon, Michael, *Strategic Stalemate: Nuclear Weapons and Arms Control in American Politics.* New York: St. Martin's Press, 1984.

Mayers, Teena Karsa. *Understanding Nuclear Weapons and Arms Control: A Guide to the Issues.* Washington, DC: Pergammon-Brassey's, 1986.

Menos, Dennis. *Arms Control Fact Book.* Jefferson, NC: McFarland, 1985.

———. *World at Risk: The Debate Over Arms Control.* Jefferson, NC: McFarland, 1986.

Myrdal, Alva. *The Game of Disarmament.* New York: Pantheon Books, 1976.

National Conference of Catholic Bishops. *The Challenge of Peace: God's Promise and Our Response.* A Pastoral Letter on War and Peace. Washington, DC: United States Catholic Conference, 1983.

Newhouse, John. *War and Peace in the Nuclear Age.* New York: Knopf, 1988.

Nixon, Richard. *1999: Victory without War.* New York: Simon and Schuster, 1988.

Nye, Joseph S. et al. *Fateful Visions: Avoiding Nuclear Catastrophe.* Cambridge, MA: Ballinger, 1988.

Scheer, Robert. *With Enough Shovels: Reagan, Bush, and Nuclear War.* New York: Random House, 1982.

Schell, Jonathan. *Fate of the Earth.* New York: Avon Books, 1982.

Talbott, Strobe. *Deadly Gambits.* New York: Knopf, 1984.

———*The Master of the Game: Paul Nitze and the Nuclear Peace.* New York: Knopf, 1988.

United Nations. Department for Disarmament Affairs. *The United Nations and Disarmament, 1945–1985.* New York: United Nations, 1985.

———. *The United Nations and Disarmament: A Short History.* New York: United Nations, 1988.

———. *The United Nations Disarmament Yearbook. Vol. 12, 1987.* New York: United Nations, 1987.

———. *The United Nations General Assembly and Disarmament, 1987.* New York: United Nations, 1988.

United Methodist Council of Bishops. *In Defense of Creation: The Nuclear Crisis and a Just Peace*. Nashville: Graded Press, 1986.

U.S. Arms Control and Disarmament Agency, *Annual Report to the Congress, 1988*. Washington, DC: U.S. ACDA, 1989.

———. *Arms Control and Disarmament Agreements: Texts and Histories of Negotiations*. Washington, DC: U.S. Government Printing Office, 1982.

———. *Documents on Disarmament, 1985*. Washington, DC: U.S. Government Printing Office, 1988.

———. *Treaty between the United States of America and the Union of Soviet Socialist Republics on the Elimination of Their Intermediate-Range and Shorter-Range Missiles*. Washington, DC: U.S. Government Printing Office, 1987.

U.S. Department of State. Bureau of Public Affairs. *Fundamentals of U.S. Foreign Policy*. Washington, DC: U.S. Government Printing Office, 1988.

———. *Realism, Strength, Negotiation: Key Foreign Policy Statements of the Reagan Administration*. Washington, DC: U.S. Government Printing Office, 1984.

———. *Security and Arms Control: The Search for a More Stable Peace*. Washington, DC: U.S. Government Printing Office, 1984.

———. *A Short Guide to U.S. Arms Control Policy*. Washington, DC: U.S. Government Printing Office, 1984.

Waller, Douglas C. *Congress and the Nuclear Freeze: An Inside Look at the Politics of a Mass Movement*. Amherst: University of Massachusetts Press, 1987.

Windass, Stan, ed. *Avoiding Nuclear War: Common Security as a Strategy for the Defense of the West*. London: Brassey's, 1985.

NEGOTIATIONS

American Association for the Advancement of Science. Program on Science, Arms Control, and National Security. *The New Force Reductions Negotiations in Europe: Problems and Prospects*. Washington, DC, February 1988.

———. *The START Negotiations in Moscow: Implications for National Security*. Washington, DC, June 1988.

Arms Control Association. *Defense and Space Talks: Background and Negotiating History*. Background Paper. Washington, DC, April 1988.

———. *Strategic Offensive Arms Negotiations*. Background Paper. Washington, DC, May 1988.

Committee on International Security and Arms Control. National Academy of Sciences. *Reykjavik and Beyond*. Washington, DC: National Academy Press, 1988.

Congressional Research Service. Library of Congress. *Arms Control: The Geneva Talks*. IB 85157. Washington, DC, April 1988.

———. *Arms Control: Negotiations to Limit Defense and Space Weapons*. IB 86073. Washington, DC, March 1988.

———. *Arms Control: Negotiations to Reduce Strategic Offensive Nuclear Weapons*. IB 86051. Washington, DC, March 1988.

Fetter, Steve. *Toward a Comprehensive Test Ban*. Cambridge, MA: Ballinger, 1988.

May, Michael et al. *Strategic Arms Reductions*. Washington, DC: Brookings, 1988.

Nitze, Paul H. "Beyond the Summit: Next Steps in Arms Control." Address before the National Press Club, Washington, DC, December 15, 1987.

VERIFICATION AND ARMS TREATY COMPLIANCE

Adelman, Kenneth L. *Verification in an Age of Mobile Missiles*. Curent Policy no. 987. Washington, DC: U.S. Department of State, Bureau of Public Affairs, June 16, 1987.

Burrows, William E. *Deep Black: Space Espionage and National Security*. New York: Random House, 1986.

Congressional Research Service. Library of Congress. *Verification: Soviet Compliance with Arms Control Agreements*. IB 84131. Washington, DC, October 1987.

Duffy, Gloria et al. *Compliance and the Future of Arms Control*. Cambridge, MA: Ballinger, 1988.

Jasani, Bhupendra and Toshibomi, Sakata. *Satellites for Arms Control Monitoring*. New York: Oxford University Press, 1987.

Krass, Allan S. *Verification: How Much Is Enough?* Lexington, MA: Lexington Books, 1986.

Krepon, Michael. *Arms Control Verification and Compliance*. New York: Foreign Policy Association, 1984.

Potter, William C., ed. *Verification and Arms Control*. Lexington, MA: Lexington Books, 1985.

Tsipis, Kosta et al., eds. *Arms Control Verification: Technologies That Make It Possible*. Washington, DC: Pergammon Brassey's, 1986.

U.S. Arms Control and Disarmament Agency. *Soviet Noncompliance*. Washington, DC: U.S. Government Printing Office, February 1986.

U.S. Department of State. Bureau of Public Affairs. *Soviet Noncompliance with Arms Control Agreements*. The President's Report to the Congress. Special Report no. 163. Washington, DC, March 1987.

———. *Soviet Noncompliance with Arms Control Agreements*. The President's Report to the Congress. Special Report no. 175. Washington,DC, December 2, 1987.

White House. *The President's Unclassified Report on Soviet Noncompliance with Arms Control Agreements*. Washington, DC, March 10, 1987.

Index

Adelman, Kenneth L., 100

Advancing national interests, 31–38, 45, 49, 50

Afghanistan, Soviet invasion of, 19, 20, 27, 80, 114

Agreement Governing the Activities of States on the Moon and Other Celestial Bodies, 52, 59

Air-launched cruise missiles (ALCMs). *See* Cruise missiles

Ambiguous language (in treaties), 73–74, 79

Antarctic Treaty, 52

Anti-ballistic missile weapons and systems. *See* SDI, Soviet; Strategic Defense Initiative (SDI), U.S.

Anti-Ballistic Missiles (ABM) Treaty, 75, 84–90; ABM/SDI interaction, 84, 85, 107, 109, 129; Congressional views on, 86–88, 101; development of, 14, 89, 124; impact on space weapons negotiations, 89, 133, 134, 135; impact on Strategic Arms Reduction Talks (START), 36, 37, 39, 41; provisions of, 15, 76, 77, 79, 85–88, 89, 107, 124; Reagan administration views on, 86, 99; reinterpretation of, 38, 84, 85–88, 107, 108, 113, 116; Soviet proposals for future compliance, 29, 89, 130, 134, 157; U.S. charges of Soviet violation, 76–77; U.S. proposals for future compliance, 89, 134, 157

Antisatellite (ASAT) weapons: congressionally imposed prohibitions, 99, 106; Soviet weapons, 4, 14, 44, 99, 106; U.S. refusal to negotiate, 42, 44; U.S. weapons, 44, 99, 101, 106

Antisubmarine (ASW) forces, 4, 9, 12

Arms control: agreements and treaties (*see* specific agreements and treaties); compliance issues (*see* Arms treaty compliance); constitutional aspects, 95–98, 100, 101, 113, 115; negotiating tactics, 38–43; negotiations (*see* Nuclear testing; Space weapons control; Strategic Arms Reduction Talks [START]); purpose of, 25–26, 45; reporting requirements, 98–100; Soviet objectives and policy, 18, 25, 26–27, 28, 33, 71, 136; U.S. objectives and policy, 25, 26, 27–28, 33, 71, 135

Arms Control and Disarmament Act, 96, 99

Arms Control and Disarmament Agency (ACDA), 99–100

Arms Control Impact Statement
   (ACIS), 99
Arms race, 1–2, 26, 30, 59–60; escala-
   tion, 61, 62, 141, 146, 147, 160,
   161; impact on arms control, 27, 45,
   53, 126; reasons for, 1, 2; risks, 61–
   63
Arms treaty compliance, 71, 72–84
—Congressional views on, 73, 79
—Soviet charges of U.S. violations, 75,
   79
—U.S. charges of Soviet violations, 72,
   73, 74, 75; of ABM Treaty, 15, 76–
   77; on nuclear testing, 77–78; of
   SALT II Treaty, 78–79
AS–15, 147
AS-X–19, 147

B–1A aircraft, 101, 102, 124
B–1B bomber, 81, 125, 127; cost, 102;
   mission, 9, 10, 101, 103, 147, 148,
   149, 150; technical problems, 102
B–2 aircraft (the Stealth bomber), 9,
   36, 81, 102–3, 126, 147, 149, 150
B–52 bomber, 82, 84, 102, 126, 148,
   149
Backfire (Soviet bomber), 113, 126,
   130, 131, 147, 148, 150
Baker, James (Secretary of State), 40
Ballistic missile defenses. See SDI, So-
   viet; Strategic Defense Initiative
   (SDI), U.S.
Bear H (Soviet bomber), 147, 148, 150
Biological and Toxin Weapons Con-
   vention, 73, 75
Blackjack (Soviet bomber), 10, 126,
   147, 150
Brilliant Pebbles. See Strategic Defense
   Initiative (SDI), U.S.
Build-down formula, 103, 110
Bush, George, 30, 40, 43
Bush administration
—negotiating positions on: CFE, 18,
   37, 43; START, 133
—weapons policies, 104

Campaign for Nuclear Disarmament,
   65

Canada, 30, 50, 54, 137
Carter administration: and the MX,
   103, cancellation of the B–1A air-
   craft, 101, 102, 124; nuclear testing
   policies, 57, 139–40; SALT II
   Treaty, 27, 80, 113, 114, 140
Chemical non-proliferation, 34–35
China nuclear policies, 54, 56, 61,
   140, 153
Church statements regarding nuclear
   arms: Catholic, 66, 67, 162; Episco-
   pal, 66; Methodist, 66, 67, 163
Cohen, William, 110
Commission on Strategic Forces. See
   Scowcroft Commission
Comprehensive Program on Disarma-
   ment. See United Nations, General
   Assembly
Comprehensive Test Ban Treaty
   (CTBT), 35, 40, 42, 58, 111, 112,
   115, 136, 138, 139–41
Conference on Disarmament, 50, 60;
   comprehensive program, 53; nuclear
   testing, 57, 58, 59; prevention of
   arms race in outer space, 60
Confidence and Security-Building
   Measures and Disarmament in Eu-
   rope, 33
Conventional Forces in Europe (CFE)
   talks, 18, 37, 42, 43
CORRTEX verification technique, 115,
   141
Countercity strategy, 7
Counterforce strategy, 7, 8, 11
Cruise missiles: air-launched (ALCMs),
   84, 130, 132, 147; ground-launched
   (GLCMs), 32, 65, 127, 152; sea-
   launched (SLCMs), 42, 124, 129,
   130, 132, 147; U.S. capabilities, 3,
   36, 42, 84, 101, 102, 124, 126, 127,
   132; verification aspects in START,
   41, 42, 129, 130
Cuban missile crisis, 6, 137
Czechoslovakia, Soviet invasion of, 27,
   124

D–5, 3, 4, 9, 36, 81, 83, 127, 147,
   150

Defense budget, 101–7
Delta (Soviet submarine), 147
Deliberate concealment, 74, 78, 82
Deterrence, 2, 6, 56, 141
Dimona nuclear plant (Israel), 21
Disarmament Commission (U.N. body), 50, 55

Effects of nuclear war, 4, 5, 31
Eisenhower, Dwight D., 41, 111
Encryption of telemetry, 74, 78, 82
European peace movement, 65–66

FB–111, 148
First Disarmament Decade, 50
Federal Republic of Germany (nuclear policies), 18, 32, 37, 65
First strike, 2, 5–13, 21; definition of, 10; delivering a first strike, 10–12; Soviet capability, 8, 9–10, 11, 131; U.S. capability, 8–9, 11, 131; weapons (see entries for individual weapons)
First use of nuclear weapons, 56
Five Continent Peace Initiative, 60–63, 160–62
France: nuclear forces, 17, 32, 153; nuclear policies of, 54, 56, 58, 61, 65, 137, 140
FROG–7, 18
Fylingdales radar, 79

General Advisory Committee on Arms Control and Disarmament, 75
General and complete disarmament. See United Nations, General Assembly
General Assembly. See United Nations, General Assembly
Geneva Protocol, 75
Gomel ABM components, 76
Gorbachev, Mikhail
—arms control proposals, 27, 28, 29, 38, 39, 40, 43, 111
—nuclear testing moratorium, 29, 35, 62, 63, 112, 140
—policy statements regarding arms control, 30–31, 156

—views on: SDI, 43–44, 134, 156; START, 36, 44, 128–30
—vision for future, 21, 31, 39, 111
Gromyko, Andrei, 116, 131, 133, 137
Ground-launched cruise missiles (GLCMs). See Cruise missiles

Helsinki Final Act, 76
Hiroshima, 1, 5, 21, 26, 63, 160

India, nuclear policies and programs of, 19–20, 54, 55, 56
Interchurch Peace Council, 65
Intercontinental Ballistic Missiles (ICBMs): restructuring as a result of START, 132; SALT I provisions, 80, 81; SALT II provisions, 81, 125; START provisions, 127, 128, 129, 132. See also entries for individual ICBMs
Intermediate-range Nuclear Forces (INF) Treaty, 16–17, 32, 75; development of, 29, 32, 39; linkages, 39, 40, 41; ratification of, 95, 115–17, 158; significance of, 16–17, 152, 157, 161
International Atomic Energy Agency (IAEA), 20, 34
International Convention on the Prohibition of the Use of Nuclear Weapons, 55
Israeli nuclear programs, 20–21

Johnson administration, 123
Joint Verification Experiment, 36, 57, 115, 141, 158

Kahuta (nuclear plant), 20
Kennedy, Edward M., 113
Kennedy, John F., 6
Krasnoyarsk radar, 15, 38, 76, 89, 130

Lance, 18
Latin American Nuclear Free Zone Treaty, 52
Levin, Carl, 87

Limited Test Ban Treaty (LTBT), 52, 57, 75, 77, 114, 136–38, 146
Linkage as a delaying tactic, 40–41

McCloy/Zorin Agreement, 52, 53
McNamara, Robert S., 6, 123
Midgetman. See Small ICBM
Military superiority. See Strategic superiority
Minuteman II and III, 3, 103, 126, 132, 147, 148
Mobile missiles
—Soviet, 10, 42, 78, 79, 82, 129, 147, 148, 150
—U.S.: rail-mobile MX, 103–5, 129, 132, 147, 149; Small ICBM, 79, 81, 101, 103–5, 129, 132, 147, 150
—verification issues in START, 41, 42, 129, 130
Moscow ABM Complex. See SDI, Soviet
Multiple, independently targeted reentry vehicles (MIRV), 6, 50, 81, 101, 123, 125, 129
Mutual and balanced forces reduction (MBFR) talks, 38, 43
Mutual assured destruction (MAD), 5–6
MX, 79, 81, 103–5, 126, 147, 148, 149, 150; basing schemes, 103, 104, 149; Bush administration policy on, 104; mission of, 8–9; rail-mobile configuration, 103–5, 129, 132, 147, 149; Reagan administration policy on, 103, 127

Nagasaki, 5
National Technical Means (NTM), 83, 113, 114, 130, 140
Nehru, Jawaharlal, 57
Nitze, Paul, 87
Nonproliferation Treaty (NPT), 19, 27, 34, 52, 76, 155, 158; Article VI, 35, 45, 139
North Atlantic Treaty Organization (NATO): conventional forces, 39, 43; nuclear capabilities of, 7, 10, 17, 18, 37, 38, 44, 66, 127

Nuclear and Space Talks (NST). See Space weapons control; Strategic Arms Reduction Talks (START)
Nuclear deterrence. See Strategy of nuclear deterrence
Nuclear freeze, 42, 62, 64–65, 100
Nuclear proliferation, 18–21
Nuclear Risk Reduction Centers, 32–33, 96, 101
Nuclear superiority. See Strategic superiority
Nuclear testing, 35–36, 137–41, 158, 160; Carter administration policies on, 57, 139–40; Comprehensive Test Ban Treaty (CTBT), 35, 40, 42, 58, 111, 112, 115, 136, 138, 139–41; Congressional views on, 108, 112, 113; CORRTEX Verification Technique, 115, 141; Joint Verification Experiment, 36, 57, 115, 141, 158; Limited Test Ban Treaty (LTBT), 52, 57, 75, 77, 114, 136–38, 146; moratorium on (Soviet), 29, 35, 62, 63, 112, 140; negotiations, 36, 58, 141; Peaceful Nuclear Explosions Treaty (PNET), 58, 59, 112, 114, 115, 139, 140, 141, 158; Soviet policy on, 35, 59, 140, 141; statistics on, 138, 146; Threshold Test Ban Treaty (TTBT), 58, 59, 76, 77, 112, 114, 115, 138, 139, 140, 141, 158; TTBT/PNET ratification, 58, 112, 114–15, 139, 158; U.N. debate on, 56–59, 60; U.S. charges of Soviet violation, 77–78; U.S. policy on, 35, 56, 59, 112, 115, 140, 141; verification, 36, 40, 42, 57, 58, 59, 62, 114, 137, 138
Nuclear war: casualties from, 8, 10, 61; effects of, 4, 5, 31; prevention of, 6, 30, 32, 33, 96, 101, 155; threat of, 32, 33, 61, 62, 157, 160–62; "winning," 2, 29
Nuclear weapons. See entries for individual weapons
Nuclear winter, 5, 61
Nunn, Sam, 87, 88, 101, 110

On-site inspection, 57, 58, 63, 112, 113, 130, 140

Open skies regime, 40
Outer Space Treaty, 52, 59, 76

Pakistani nuclear programs, 19–20
Peaceful Nuclear Explosions Treaty
  (PNET), 58, 59, 112, 114, 115, 139,
  140, 141, 158
Peacekeeper. See MX
Peace movements (U.S. and European),
  64–66
Pershing II, 17, 32, 61, 65, 103, 127,
  152
Poseidon SSBN, 84, 148
Presidential certification requirements,
  96–97
Prevention of Dangerous Military Ac-
  tivities Agreement, 33
Prohibition of fissionable materials
  production, 54

Quayle, Dan, 40

Reagan administration
—and ABM Treaty, 86, 89
—and ABM Treaty reinterpretation,
  38, 84, 85–88, 107, 108, 113, 116
—ASAT testing, 99, 106
—and INF weapons control, 29
—negotiating positions on: nuclear
  testing, 35, 36, 59, 112, 115, 140,
  141; space weapons control, 134;
  Strategic Arms Reduction Talks
  (START), 127
—and SALT II, 80, 99, 114, 127
—and SDI, 29, 41, 107, 108, 109,
  156–57
—weapons policies: B–1B, 102; MX,
  103, 127; Small ICBM, 79, 105
Reagan, Ronald: policy statements regarding arms control, 29–30, 39, 45,
  99, 127; vision for future, 110, 156–
  57

Scowcroft Commission, 103, 104, 105
SDI, Soviet, 3, 4, 14–15, 84, 151;
  Moscow ABM system, 14, 15, 76,
  88
Seabed Treaty, 52, 76

Sea-launched cruise missiles (SLCMs).
  See Cruise missiles
Second-strike missions and weapons, 9,
  131
Senate Armed Services Committee, 114
Senate Foreign Relations Committee,
  97, 98, 112, 114
Shultz, George, 131, 133
Shevardnadze, Edward, 33
Small ICBM, 79, 103–5, 132, 149, 150
Space weapons control, 133–36, 157;
  and the ABM Treaty, 89, 133, 134,
  135; link with START, 36, 37, 39,
  41; Reagan administration negotiat-
  ing position, 134; Soviet proposals
  on, 29, 89, 130, 134, 157; U.S. pro-
  posals on, 89, 134, 157; Washington
  summit, 135, 157
Special Sessions on Disarmament,
  United Nations General Assembly,
  51, 159–60
SS–4, 152
SS–5, 152
SS–11, 148
SS–12, 152
SS–13, 79, 148
SS–17, 10, 147, 148, 150
SS–18, 9, 37, 83, 147, 148, 149, 150
SS–19, 10, 147, 148
SS–20, 32, 65, 126, 127, 152
SS–21, 18
SS–23, 152
SS–24, 10, 42, 79, 129, 147, 148
SS–25, 10, 42, 78, 79, 82, 129, 147,
  148, 150
SS–N–5, 148
SS–N–6, 148
SS–N–8, 148
SS–N–17, 147, 148
SS–N–18, 147, 148
SS–N–20, 4, 10, 147, 148, 150
SS–N–21, 150
SS–N–23, 147, 148
SS–NX–24, 150
SS–X–26, 147
SSC–X–4, 152
Standing Consultative Commission
  (SCC), 73

Star Wars. *See* Strategic Defense Initiative (SDI), U.S.
Stealth bomber. *See* B–2 aircraft (the Stealth bomber)
Strategic Arms Limitation Talks (SALT)
—Reagan administration views on, 90, 99, 114, 127
—SALT I Interim Agreement, 73, 75, 80, 123–24: and the Congress, 81, 97, 113
—SALT II Treaty, 75, 81, 124–26; and the Carter administration, 27, 80, 113, 114, 140; and the Congress, 83, 84, 97, 98, 110, 111, 113, 125; effects of cancellation, 82, 83; Interim Restraint Policy, 38, 71, 72, 78, 80, 81–82, 110, 111; provisions of, 78, 113, 125; ratification of, 27, 83, 84, 97, 113, 114, 140; U.S. charges of Soviet violation, 78–79
Strategic Arms Reduction Talks (START): 36–37, 42, 126–33, 155, 157, 158: Bush administration negotiating position on, 133; and the Congress, 103, 108, 110; Reagan administration negotiating position on, 127; relationship to ABM Treaty, 36, 37, 39, 41; restructuring of U.S. strategic forces, because of, 132, 133; SDI link, 39, 40, 41, 108, 110, 128, 134; Soviet negotiating positions on, 36, 44, 128–30; U.S. negotiating positions on, 37, 76, 104, 105, 110, 127; verification issues, 42, 129, 130, 133, 158
Strategic aviation: SALT II provisions, 82, 125; START provisions, 127, 129, 130, 132. *See also* entries for individual aircraft
Strategic balance, 2–5, 124
Strategic Defense Initiative (SDI), U.S.: ABM/SDI interaction, 84, 85, 107, 109, 129; Bush administration views on, 107, 109, 110; Congressional views on SDI testing, 88, 107; early SDI deployment, 16, 88, 107, 109, 151; funding of, 13, 16, 86, 87, 88,

106–7, 109, 110; impact on strategic arms reduction talks (START), 39, 40, 41, 108, 110, 128, 134; Reagan views on, 29, 41, 107, 108, 109, 156–57; SDI/nuclear testing interaction, 35, 112; shielding the strategic triads, 12–13, 21; Soviet views on U.S. SDI, 34, 44, 134, 156
Strategic forces. *See* Antisatellite (ASAT) weapons; cruise missiles; Intercontinental Ballistic Missiles (ICBMs); SDI, Soviet; Strategic aviation; Submarine-launched ballistic missiles (SLBMs)
Strategic modernization program, U.S., 2, 4, 28, 42, 64, 102
Strategic superiority, 3, 64
Strategy of nuclear deterrence, 2, 6, 56, 141
Submarine-launched ballistic missiles (SLBMs): restructuring as a result of START, 132, 133; SALT I provisions, 80, 81; SALT II provisions, 81, 125; START provisions, 128, 132, 149. *See also* entries for individual SLBMs
Summits (Gorbachev-Reagan), 36, 37, 71, 128; Geneva, 33, 37, 40, 62, 155; Iceland, 37, 41, 43, 84, 89, 95, 108, 111, 112, 115, 156–57; Moscow, 37, 109, 116, 157–58; Washington, 37, 39, 40, 90, 95, 109, 111, 113, 115, 135, 157

Tactical weapons in Europe, 17, 18, 29, 32, 37, 40, 65, 125, 131, 152, 161
Telemetry, 74
Threshold Test Ban Treaty (TTBT), 58, 59, 76, 77, 112, 114, 115, 138, 139, 140, 141, 158
Thinking "the unthinkable," 3
Third zero, 37–38
Tomahawk GLCM. *See* Cruise missiles
Trident I (C–4), 124, 147, 148
Trident II (D–5), 3, 4, 9, 36, 81, 83, 127, 147, 150

Trident (Ohio Class) SSBN, 4, 9, 36, 105, 125, 126, 132, 147, 150
Typhoon SSBN, 4, 10, 147, 150

United Kingdom: nuclear forces, 17, 32, 61, 153; nuclear test policies, 54, 56, 58, 59, 137; peace movement, 65
United Nations, General Assembly: cessation of nuclear testing, 56–59, 60; comprehensive program on disarmament, 53; general and complete disarmament, 50, 52; nonuse of nuclear weapons, 55–56; nuclear disarmament, 53–55; prevention of arms race in outer space, 59–60; Soviet proposals before the U.N., 49, 52; Soviet reaction to U.N. initiatives, 49, 54, 55, 56, 58, 59; U.S. proposals before the U.N., 49, 52; U.S. reaction to U.N. initiatives, 49, 54, 55, 56, 58, 59
U.S. Congress, 108–17; and ABM Treaty, 86–88, 101; and arms treaty compliance issue, 73, 79; and ASAT testing, 99, 106; and nuclear testing, 108, 112, 113; role in arms control, 95–98, 100, 101, 113, 115; on SALT I Interim Agreement, 81, 97, 113; on SALT II, 83, 84, 97, 98, 110, 111, 113, 125; on SDI testing, 88, 107; on START negotiations, 103, 108, 110

Verification
—as a negotiating tactic, 41–42
—of nuclear testing, 36, 40, 42, 57, 58, 59, 62, 114, 137, 138
—in START, 42, 129, 130, 133, 158; cruise missiles, 41, 42, 129, 130; mobile missiles, 41, 42, 129, 130
—U.S. policy on, 41–42
Vladivostok summit, 125

Warheads, 4, 65; INF reductions, 17, 152; Soviet, 12, 126, 149; START ceilings, 127, 128, 131, 132, 149, 158; U.S., 7, 12, 149
Warner, John, 101
Warnke, Paul, 100
Warsaw Pact, 37, 39
Window of vulnerability, 2, 28
World disarmament, 26, 27
World Disarmament Campaign (U.N. initiative), 51

Year 2000 Disarmament Plan, 29, 31, 39, 111

Zero option, 29

About the Author

DENNIS MENOS is a research and management consultant and writer on national security affairs. He formerly served at the Department of Defense in senior analyst and executive positions.